SUPPORTING STUDENTS WITH COMMUNICATION DISORDERS

A Collaborative Approach

A Resource for Speech-Language Pathologists,
Parents and Educators

MARY E. EANNACE, M.A., CCC/SLP, M.A. ED
Speech-Language Pathologist & Autism and Educational Consultant

Supporting Students with Communication Disorders. A Collaborative Approach

A Resource for Speech-Language Pathologists, Parents and Educators

print ISBN: 978-1-66783-120-6

ebook ISBN: 978-1-66783-121-3

CONTENTS

CHARTS

APPENDICES

DEDICATION

This book is dedicated to my grandchildren, Ellie and Evan, and to all children everywhere. I am thankful for all the wonderful experiences I have had with so many beautiful children. They are my inspiration! Children have brought so much joy and peace into my life. They have taught me to always seek the spirit of everyone! May all children play, laugh, wonder, reach and grow within trusting, loving environments. May God grant them happiness, courage, resilience, tolerance, kindness, joy and unconditional love!

ABOUT THE AUTHOR

Mary E. Eannace is a highly respected licensed speech-language pathologist, autism and educational consultant with extensive and diverse experience. Ms. Eannace practiced for thirty-five years within dynamic school settings, serving students with diverse communication disorders. She is currently engaged in private practice as a communication, autism and educational consultant. She has presented numerous seminars, training programs and consultations to school districts, special education cooperatives, professional organizations and parent groups on various topics. Ms. Eannace previously served as an adjunct professor at St. Xavier University in Chicago, Illinois and Lewis University in Romeoville, Illinois.

In addition to a Master's Degree in Speech-Language Pathology, Ms. Eannace has a Master's Degree in Educational Administration and Supervision. She holds the Certificate of Clinical Competence in Speech-Language Pathology from the American Speech, Language and Hearing Association and the following Illinois Teaching Certificates: Speech-Language Pathology (preschool through secondary teaching), Type 75 Administrative Certificate and Director of Special Education.

PREFACE

A friend and colleague gave me an inspirational children's book, *What Do You Do with an Idea?* by Kobi Yamada. This award-winning children's book is an inspiring story about a young child with an idea, yet not sure what to do with it. He keeps his idea a secret for a long time, as he was afraid of what people would think about his idea. Perhaps people would laugh and think his idea was silly or weird. Perhaps people would tell him his idea was a waste of time. The young child soon learned that when he had enough courage to take the chance and give his idea attention and care, his idea grew and became a source of happiness. He learned that his one single idea could actually change the world!

My idea for this book stirred in me for many years. Each time I met students, parents, speech-language pathologists and educators who inspired me with their stories, I would again decide that we needed to share their stories with other students, parents, speech-language pathologists and educators. My idea of writing a book would surface, soon to be put aside by fear, lack of confidence and concern over what people may think. Then one day I decided to take a chance and allow my idea to materialize. What if one student, parent or educator finds benefit in what they read and then they pass that on to one more and so on and so on and so on…? Perhaps we can change our students' and parents' worlds!

Students, parents, speech-language pathologists and educators, as well as my own two children, have been my inspiration for this book. All of the wonderful experiences interacting and working with them in schools, homes and out in the community gave me the courage to take chances and to cultivate the ideas within this book. The experiences with students, parents, speech-language pathologists and educators, along with the experiences raising my own two beautiful children, have truly made me The Lucky One! The parents, the teachers, the speech-language pathologists, the educators, the friends, family members, but most of all the children have brought so much joy to my life and have taught me so much. It is the children that have taught me to always seek the spirit, the soul of the whole person. It is the children who have taught me to listen to what they are saying and to look beyond their present reality into their spirit, their soul; that is where you will see beautiful people who have so much to offer to all of us! The children have taught me to always reach upward toward all their possibilities.

I have listened to parents discuss what works and what does not work for their children. I have heard and experienced parents' anxieties, their anger, their feelings of guilt, their feelings of hope, their joy, their feelings of frustration with the schools and their appreciation of the schools. I have observed and listened to our students' successes and frustrations. I have observed, spoken to and supervised speech-language pathologists who struggle to support their diverse caseloads within the dynamic school environment. I have heard educators say, "This cannot be done here." But I have also heard, "Where do we start?" It is the positive can-do attitudes that make positive differences in the lives of our students and their families.

In writing this text, I wanted to share all the wonderful experiences I have had. It has been my goal to write a book that not only teaches the DYNAMIC COMMUNICATION PROCESS, but also gives parents, students and educators the tools to successfully and efficiently navigate the dynamic school system, working together within a positive collaborative problem-solving model.

KNOWLEDGE IS POWER FOR OUR STUDENTS' SUCCESS!

The goal of this book is to provide shared vocabulary that allows us to engage in productive, collaborative problem-solving discussions. The way to successfully support our students is through a collaborative, reflective look at our current processes, practices and systems through an understanding of the dynamic communication process at all levels.

We all have titles behind our names: parent, teacher, occupational therapist, physical therapist, speech-language pathologist, autism consultant, assistive technology consultant, para- professional, social worker, administrator, etc., etc., etc. In fact, many of us have several titles and we proceed through our days with the knowledge that we are who we are. However, our students do not care what our titles define us to be. What matters to them is

- Are we someone they can **trust**?

- Are we someone who cares enough to take the time to **listen** to and **understand** their **perspective**, even if it does not make sense to us?

- Are we someone who is **culturally sensitive** to all the issues that are present within the classroom or someone who is annoyed by the workload that may be present with such diversity?

- Are we someone who will understand their behaviors (communications), or someone who will label them as "manipulative", "disrespectful", "odd"?

- Are we someone who will judge them and place them in some unknown grouping of "those kids who..."?

- Are we someone who will understand their fears, anxiety and anger and who will create a safe, nurturing environment in which they can actively participate and engage with their peers even if they make communication mistakes?

- Are we someone who will declare our classrooms and school environments as **"safe zones"**, in which students can take chances and not be afraid to make mistakes, not be afraid that they will be judged?

- Are we someone who will allow our students ample time to learn and integrate newly learned skills, and allow them to make mistakes and learn from those mistakes along the way?

- Are we someone who will put aside all the system barriers that keep us from working in a true collaborative effort, or someone that will continue to outline the reasons why we can't?

- Are we someone who will do all we can to help them become successful within an inclusive environment, or who will push them into a new classroom outside of their home school because they just don't fit into what we do?

In order to look at a true collaborative model, we need to take a reflective look at the school system we are working in. If we have the courage to work objectively, honestly and collaboratively through the problem-solving process, the world will be an oyster for our students, allowing them every advantage necessary to achieve success and all that life has to offer. This will mean something different for each student, just as it means something different for each one of us.

This book is not intended to be a cookbook for a fix, allowing you to say, "I want my child to be like everyone else!" "I want my child to be the doctor or firefighter, lawyer that I have always thought my child should be." "I want my child to go to the same university that I went to." Our children do not need to be fixed, rather to be simply UNDERSTOOD! Every one of us is unique with specific strengths, challenges, interests, likes, dislikes and of most importance, learning styles.

This book is not intended for educators who want a student to fit into a curriculum or into a no-tolerance rule system. I for one am glad I do not live my day-to-day life within such a system. Yes, we all need to learn the social rules and customs of our society, but don't we do that in individual ways. Think about that!

We will be asking some thought-provoking questions throughout this book. We will take a hard look at our current practices and our current system and toward all the possibilities for our students.

As we work toward our students' active engagement within the learning process, I challenge all of us to be ACTIVE PARTICIPANTS within our own teaching practice and parenting styles. Be reflective, teach with an open mind and heart and work within a Collaborative Problem-Solving Model. Think and work outside of your comfort zone.

CHAPTER 1:

INTRODUCTION

"The purpose of life is to live it, to taste experience to the utmost, to reach out eagerly and without fear for newer and richer experience." **Eleanor Roosevelt**

"Nothing ever becomes real till it is experienced." **John Keats**

"Give the pupil something to do, not something to learn, and the doing is of such a nature as to demand thinking; learning naturally results." **John Dewey**

The Importance of Experience

John Dewey (1938), wrote that it is in the experience that we create learning. True knowledge is gained through experience; experiences build upon one another. True knowledge is the understanding of experiences or the ability to interpret experiences, analyze these experiences and associate them to what we already know in order to apply and expand to present or future experiences. We have different perspectives due to the experiences we have had or not had. It is through experiences, both good as well as challenging, that we create knowledge and come to a set of beliefs and values. Our knowledge, as well as our beliefs and values, are altered or transformed throughout our lives as we encounter new experiences, new knowledge. Positive as well as challenging experiences will result in learning and positive growth.

Case Study: Eric

Introduction

Eric was an extremely bright junior high student with a diagnosis of Asperger's syndrome. Eric struggled with social interactions within communication contexts and was initially labeled as a student with behavior issues. His challenges, overt nonverbal and verbal behaviors (communications), were a direct result of a significant communication deficit.

Communication Interventions

Through the intervention process, Eric developed skills to become an effective social communicator. His communication therapy program focused on visual processing, visual problem-solving, thinking like a scientist and making conversations visual. (These interventions are discussed in Chapter 11.) The most significant and successful components of his communication therapy program was actively listening to what he was saying from his perspective. By applying active listening, we could (including his parents) implement effective visual processing interventions. It was when we supported and helped Eric work through difficult and often aggressive communication situations and interactions that he learned the most. In fact, he was then able to reflect and discuss communication options and was later able to integrate effective communication interactions within similar situations. This intervention process took time, and he made many mistakes along the way. It was by allowing him to make mistakes and work through the experiences of his mistakes that he was able to learn and grow. This, along with the positive communication experiences that were provided through his therapy and educational programs, supported this student in becoming an effective social communicator.

ALL CHILDREN, all people, are individuals who are at different stages in life and life's journey. All children, no matter where they are intellectually, spiritually, emotionally or physically, can and will learn and can enjoy and gain all of what life has to offer. John Dewey outlined a philosophy of education and knowledge that stated knowledge cannot be isolated from experience, that knowledge is not given to us as passive learners. We gain knowledge by doing, by creating. Children learn through active participation, discovery, problem solving, and inquiry. It is within the everyday life experiences, the everyday events and adventures, that true happiness and joy can be found. Students' active involvement and participation within the learning process and within their daily lives create learning and knowledge. Without the ability to communicate efficiently and effectively, students are not able to fully engage and participate within academic, social or vocational environments.

This is true for all students. Unfortunately, there are students in which there are obstacles to their access of the academic curriculum, social interactions, as well as learning environments for numerous reasons. Educators and parents have opportunities to provide our students (of all ages) with positive learning experiences that allow access to academic success and positive social interactions. Universal Design of Instruction along with modifications, adaptations, and differentiation allow all students access to academic and social curricula as well as positive social interactions.

We all experience life in individual ways. Do educators have a right to determine what experiences, what parts of the school curriculum (academic or social), what adventures, what episodes a child should have or not have based on their abilities, challenges or disabilities? It is our challenge to work collaboratively within the problem-solving model to remove or at least minimize possible barriers that inhibit our students' abilities at engaging and participating within academic and social experiences.

I am the second youngest of six children. My older sister was born profoundly deaf. We really never talked about her being deaf. She was just one of us. She attended an oral private Catholic school for the deaf (which was one of the only programs available to her; this was prior to PL 94-142; refer to Appendix 1). The focus of her program was on development of verbal speech and use of residual hearing. She was taught to talk and lip read. She was profoundly deaf; she had no residual hearing! We communicated with her; however, there were great gaps in our communication. We developed creative ways to communicate with each other. My sister learned sign language at the age of 19, which opened a whole new world for her. My parents did not embrace this new communication system and did not feel the need for her to sign; after all she could talk! They did not have the crucial knowledge regarding speech, language and communication that perhaps would have supported their decision in learning sign language. (Speech, language and communication are discussed in Chapter 4.)

I recall sitting in my first education class as a college student, learning about each different disability. We came to the chapter on hearing impairments, deafness. Yep, right there (I think it was Chapter 3) was deafness. Wait, are they saying being deaf was a disability? I remember thinking, "Oh wow, my sister has a disability!" I know that sounds odd, but I never thought of her as a deaf person or a person with a disability. She was my older sister who had different needs, because she could not hear. I can still see the expression on my professor's face when I said, "Being deaf is a disability?" As we moved from chapter to chapter discussing each different disability and all the "they can't", I decided that I needed to keep my focus on how to support students in bringing out their potentials and gifts. I never expected any child to be like the one sitting next to him/her. Every child is unique in his or her own way. Our role as educators and parents is to help students achieve and to live up to their potential by providing as many positive learning experiences as possible while engaging them in creating and learning.

I do not think I ever thought about my sister's deafness prior to that day. She was just who she was. I guess I was too busy looking at all the things she could do. She could beat me in any game we played. The one thing I remember most of all is that she could give me great comfort when I was sad or hurt. She is the most compassionate person I have ever met. She is smart, intelligent, funny, caring, and oh yes, she cannot hear. I do remember her using the fact that she could not hear to her advantage during our arguments. Yes, my siblings and I did argue! Lol. When I would say something, she did not like or want to hear, she would close her eyes and yell, "I can't hear you!"

Music was always a part of my life and yet I cannot sing a note or play a tune. I worked for many years in a hearing impaired program. I learned that our students did not attend music class. We learn the melody of language and of life through rhyme and rhythm. Should these children be denied these experiences? Life is a melody, a beat. How can we deny any child the experience of feeling this melody?

I recall the time I walked into a deaf club party with my sister. The music was so loud I could feel every beat of my heart. The vibrations could be felt as I walked across the floor. I recall the laughter and dancing. Oh yes, all the participants were hard of hearing or deaf! They were communicating through sign language, and although I knew some sign language, I had no way of keeping up with their dynamic conversations. Perhaps this is what our students with communication disorders experience within their daily lives.

My colleagues did not have the same experiences I had with my sister. Through collaboration, I was able to share the importance (creating a shared knowledge) of music and melody to our language and communication development. I took these experiences back to my own program. We worked out a schedule in which I and several of our para-professionals would have a music time weekly with our students. We adapted our music class, used multiple means of communication (sign language, gesture, speech, visuals). We used touch, vibration and amplification. The children laughed, danced and sang! We played musical instruments, danced to the Macarena and the Chicken Dance. We marched and wiggled. They didn't care that I could not carry a tune. Oh, what fun the children had! Oh, what fun I had! We then used these same rhythms and beats in our speech-language therapy sessions. These sessions became much more interactive and engaging, with great positive student outcomes! This is one example of how everyday experiences can be adapted and modified to actively engage students.

Engagement is One of the Strongest Indicators of Positive Student Outcomes

We know that engagement is one of the strongest predictors of positive student outcomes. Our students need to be actively engaged in the learning process. Throughout this book, we will attempt to answer the following questions by providing current best practice and educational research with application within the dynamic school environment:

- How do we ensure that students are engaged in learning through active participation, discovery, problem-solving and inquiry?

- How do we assist students in fully experiencing and engaging in the school academic and social learning environments?

- How do we ensure that our students are active participants within the learning process?

- How do we integrate assessment and interventions within the dynamic, ever-changing school system in order to create positive student outcomes?

- How do we develop and sustain a true collaborative focus, even when it is hard to do so?

- How do we maintain our child-centered focus, even when it is hard to do so?

- How do we ensure that our students with disabilities are given the same opportunities and experiences as our students without disabilities working toward independent, fulfilling, active lives?

- How do we collaboratively implement Universal Design of Instruction?

- Why, when and how do we collaboratively implement adaptations and modifications for individual students?

The answers to these questions can be found in a true collaborative problem-solving model in which educational teams (including parents) work toward active student engagement.

John Dewey outlined a philosophy of education and knowledge that stated knowledge cannot be isolated from experience; knowledge is not given to us as passive learners. We gain knowledge by doing. Children learn through active participation. Dewey's educational philosophy is as relevant today as it was when he wrote it in 1938. Educators still embrace his ideals when designing educational curriculum and learning experiences for students! Students need to be actively engaged within the learning process. He outlined the following when looking at all students' learning:

- Actively involve students in the learning process and learning experiences.
- Relate educational experiences to real life; make them as meaningful as possible.
- Teach children through real life experiences.
- Facilitate children's active participation within the learning process, not simply be passive observers.
- Provide children with materials that are relevant and meaningful.
- Consider children's interests when teaching.
- Consider children's prior knowledge and experiences.
- Help children become self-motivated learners.
- Create strong home-school and school-community relationships.

Knowledge is Power

Knowledge is power! Knowledge is not something permanent or unchangeable. What we know to be true today may be very different from what we will know tomorrow. (I grew up knowing that Pluto was our ninth planet—go figure!). Educators and parents have a great responsibility to ask thought-provoking questions and engage in problem-solving discussions in order to support our students. One of the most important questions to ask is, "Does this make sense?" (Speech-language pathologists are included within the title "educator" within this text.)

My first year as a licensed speech-language pathologist was most humbling. I was hired by a special education cooperative and assigned to a special education school in which children with the most significant needs were educated. I was feeling confident and prepared to begin my first assignment; after all, I did have a Master's Degree with High Honors in Speech-Language Pathology and a Certificate of Clinical Competence from The American Speech-Language-Hearing Association stating that I was highly qualified. I soon met my students. My first question was, "Do the universities really understand the dynamics of the school system and the multiple needs of the students?" Something was missing. I soon met Freddy. Freddy was a young child with autism. He was nonverbal and his only means of communication was through overt behavior. Thank goodness he had that! I met Freddy's mother on the first day of school. She drove Freddy to school every day, picked him up at the end of the day and brought him lunch. When she dropped him off at school, she would attempt to kiss him goodbye. Freddy would not allow this physical, sensory experience. Freddy's mother would look at us and say, "Well, maybe tomorrow." She came back at lunch. Every day she brought Freddy White Castle hamburgers, because this was the only food Freddy would eat. She would attempt to fool him by placing a vegetable on the hamburger. Freddy would immediately take out the vegetable and eat the burger. This was one of the few times I would see Freddy smile. Mom again would say, "Well, maybe tomorrow." This pattern continued through the Fall. I observed the love this mother had for her son and how she desperately wanted him to be successful.

It was now November and the infamous parent-teacher conferences were approaching. My confidence on the first day soon gave way to, "What am I doing?" "How do we support these students functionally?" What we were attempting to do DID NOT MAKE SENSE! I had many more questions than answers for most of my involved students and yet I was about to meet with each of their parents. I was a member of a multi-disciplinary team. The team's practice was that each professional met with the parents individually. THAT DOES NOT MAKE SENSE! (Educational teams are discussed in Chapter 3.)

My first conference was with Freddy's mother and father. I was not sure what I was going to tell these parents. I learned that day that sometimes it is best to be quiet, observe and listen. We really do not need to fill in every silent gap. She looked at me and with tears in her eyes said, "What did I do to cause this to my son?" At that time, some people held on to the early research that suggested autism was caused by the "refrigerator mother" theory. This theory attributed autism to an uncaring mother who lacked maternal warmth (Kanner, 1943). Current research [new knowledge] has replaced the concept of the refrigerator mother to one that defines or explains autism as a diverse neurological disorder. This is what she was told! THAT DOES NOT MAKE ANY SENSE! What pain, hurt and damage this theory caused these parents and many others, I am sure. This mother carried with her severe guilt thinking she caused autism in her child. Freddy and his mother taught me that the most important thing we can provide our parents is objective data (knowledge) regarding their child's disability and how to support them and their child. Freddy's mother's words gave me the courage and strength to say, "You did not cause your son to have autism. I have watched the love you have for him every day. I promise you, we will find answers to how we can successfully support your son."

I knew that I could not gain the knowledge I needed to support all of my students by myself. In order to support my students and facilitate their communication skills, I knew that I needed support. I looked to the people that I had been observing since the first day on the job, the physical therapist, the occupational therapist, the social worker, the school psychologist, the teachers, the adapted P.E. teacher, the bus drivers and of course the parents. I learned so much by simply observing them, watching and asking questions. However, just observing was not enough. I knew that we needed a more structured way to collaborate, share knowledge and grow as a team in order to support our students. What was the one thing I could do to become more collaborative with my educational team members? I knew that I was not in this alone! This began my motivation to research, develop and implement collaborative processes. This was the beginning of my collaborative team philosophy! This, along with a career of professional development, has taught me that we cannot isolate communication from any other domain, whether it be academic, sensory, motor, social-emotional, health or cognitive processes. **Our students' communication success is dependent on all of us working toward a common goal.**

I have spent my career working with parents, asking questions and looking for solutions based on sound data and evidence-based research that made sense to our students and their families. I encourage all educators and professionals to actively listen to parents and families and work with them in supporting their children. They know their children better than we ever will. What makes sense for one child may not make sense for another.

> Think outside your box of knowledge to all the possibilities: new research, new experiences, new knowledge, your potential, students' potential! Remember, our knowledge is based on our experiences, and our expectations are based on our knowledge. What may be true today, may not be true tomorrow!

No Room for Judgments

The children have taught me that we all have great potential and we all can be much more than what others judge of us. Unfortunately, we can quickly come to negative judgments of children, parents and each other basing this judgment not on solid data, but on perceptions. I too have made judgment calls on too many occasions. When I began to reflect on my own practices, I realized that my judgments were often not based on sound data but on perceptions. We do know that our perceptions drive our actions and our communications. Embracing the collaborative problem- solving model, in which interventions and communications are driven by objective data, shifts the focus from adult driven decision making to child centered decision making. This further shifts decision making based on negative perceptions to positive actions and outcomes.

Effective student outcomes increase when educators change judgment statements to assessment and intervention questions, in which data can be gathered and interventions implemented. Educators often make the following comments in regard to students' communications (behaviors).

- He only does what he wants to do!
- He is so manipulative!
- He is really just a bully.
- He is so disrespectful.
- He is just lazy. He has completed this before and just does not want to do it now.
- She can do it if she wants to.
- She will only work with whom she wants to.
- He really prefers to be alone and really does not want friends.
- He refuses to show his math work.
- She will do her work but refuses to turn it in.

As we work through the collaborative educational team process (engagement, assessment and interventions), we will take a hard honest look at these judgement statements. We will discuss the concept that all behaviors are true communications. We will use powerful data obtained from dynamic assessments to apply interventions across communication contexts. We will discuss, review and apply best practices as outlined in current research and apply this within the dynamic school system. We will listen to the voices of students, parents and each other!

CHAPTER 2

EFFECTIVE COMMUNICATION WITHIN THE INSTRUCTIONAL PROCESS

Teaching, Learning and Communication

Teaching and learning mirrors the dynamic process of communication. There are many different characteristics, skills and knowledge that go into being an effective educator. Effective communication is one of the most crucial skills within the instructional relationship. The dynamics of the student-teacher relationship is as complex as any relationship. Teaching and learning mirrors the dynamic process of communication in that it involves ongoing, two-way verbal and nonverbal interactions among sender, receiver, message and the content. It is when this ongoing communication (both verbal and nonverbal) process is efficiently orchestrated that teaching and learning are successful!

The ability to effectively communicate so that your message is interpreted by students, parents and other professionals the way you meant it to be (shared communication intents) is not only an important skill, but a challenging one. The ability to receive messages effectively is also important and can be just as challenging. There can be many sources of misunderstandings and/or miscommunications. It is the skilled educator who can avoid, or at least minimize, misunderstandings/miscommunications through the use of effective communication strategies such as

- ask relevant objective questions

- active listening

- "I statement"

- perception checks

- paraphrasing

- creating congruency between verbal and non-verbal messages

- avoiding judgment statements.

- understanding perspectives (even when they do not make sense to us)

- perceptual flexibility

- objective data-driven explanations and descriptions

- asking for objective feedback

It is important for educators to understand the process of communication and the effect that their communication style has on the student-teacher relationship, the parent-teacher relationship as well as on the effectiveness of the teaching-learning process. The foundation to all relationships is that of trust. Educators can build trusting relationships and environments through effective, open communications with students, parents and other educators. Educators can build on these relationships by sharing ideas, feelings and reactions to situations in a nonjudgmental, objective manner and by giving and receiving feedback objectively and constructively. Educators are often presented with situations in which they listen to concerns, problems, situations, opinions and perspective from students, parents and other educators. Active listening is an effective tool in these situations! We do not need to fill every silent gap with chatter or educational jargon.

Ongoing research and attainment of knowledge is an integral part of who we are and what we do. We have a great responsibility to decode, analyze, synthesize and associate the information present within educational and communication research to determine what is best practice and what is applicable to our programs and students. It is not a one-size-fits-all model.

Best practice is situational. What may work in one educational setting may not work in another. We can discuss best practice as it relates to our own school, classroom and students within a collaborative problem-solving model by open and honest discussions working toward mutual understanding and goals.

We can be active in our own practice by being REFLECTIVE AND HONEST! Honest reflections based on solid data vs. judgment statements. We can remain child centered by basing our practices within a collaborative problem-solving model. A true collaborative model allows educational teams opportunities to turn their focus from individual team members to student outcomes, by basing decisions on objective data, creating shared knowledge and shared common goals.

How can we make sure our students are the reason we make the decisions we make in our schools? How can we ensure our discussions and decisions are student centered? Discussions regarding student-centered education often stops at the schoolhouse door. Our decisions regarding students are often based on program, educational team or school policies and practices, rather than individual students' needs.

Following are examples of comments made by educators within formal team meetings as well as in informal conversations with school team members:

- "She has a one to one para-educator. You need to talk to her and provide her with training. I really do not have time in my schedule to meet with para-educators."
- "I was just given this caseload and do not have time."
- "All of my students receive 40 minutes of speech-language therapy weekly."
- "I do not have time to meet with my team members and am not at the school when they meet."

- "There is so much wasted time in team meetings."

- "I have too many students on my caseload. He needs to be in that group."

- "I only have one social language group and it does not work within his schedule."

- "I do not have any other time to meet with groups in my schedule."

- "I do not work with students individually."

- "We are a fully inclusive district; that is not an option for our students."

- "I cannot make teachers implement the student's behavior or communication plan."

- "I use this speech-language test battery for all my students."

- "I do not have time to observe students."

- "This is the reading program we use in our district; there is not another option."

The collaborative team problem-solving model supports effective implementation of Universal Design of Instruction principles for all students and adaptations and modifications for individual students. Embrace the collaborative problem-solving model and work within your current school system to implement best practice for all students. It may be necessary to prioritize. When doing so you should ask, "What is the one thing we can do today that will make a difference in the lives of our students?" We can begin this process by asking several questions.

- How do we work collaboratively in implementing Universal Design of Instruction for all students?

- How do we facilitate access for a particular student? (One size does not fit all.) What accommodations and/or modifications can be put in place?

- How do we make the curriculum relevant for our students?

- ○ Social/emotional environment

- ○ Academic environment

- ○ Work environment

- ○ Leisure environment

- How do we provide meaningful experiences and positive learning environments?

- How do we prioritize learning experiences?

Our students want to engage and learn. Students have a natural curiosity, along with enthusiasm, for learning and want to engage in the learning process. Educators have opportunities to provide students with life and learning experiences which are meaningful, in which they can themselves be active participants and through which they can create self-motivated learners. When we acknowledge individual students' learning styles, we can provide learning experiences and adventures in which all students can become actively involved and in which students will construct knowledge. Learning cannot be accomplished outside of the student.

H. Gardner's (1999) groundbreaking work introduced the concept of multiple intelligences. He discussed the idea that people possess a range of capacities and potentials, multiple intelligences. Gardner valued the individuality of each person, each student. He identified seven separate human intelligences (linguistic intelligence, logical-mathematical intelligence, musical intelligence, bodily-kinesthetic intelligence, spatial intelligence, interpersonal intelligence, and intrapersonal intelligence). Gardner later identified three additional intelligences, (naturalist intelligence, spiritual intelligence, existential intelligence). Shouldn't the learning experiences we provide for our students reflect this? Through Universal Design of Instruction, we can provide learning experiences that consider multiple intelligences as well as multiple learning styles.

> Embrace the concept of Universal Design of Instruction!
> There is no one-size-fits-all to learning!

Each child comes to the educational process (in and out of school) at different points in the learning process. Children are at different stages in their social, emotional, physical and intellectual development. Educators, who are aware of where each child is in their development, are able to present experiences appropriate for the child. When educators provide experiences that address the "whole child" (spiritual, emotional, intellectual and physical), we provide opportunities in which our children can develop, learn and grow! Your students will flourish within your classrooms and schools.

To All the Wonderful Parents

I had a discussion with a wonderful speech-language pathologist who is a young mother of a child diagnosed with apraxia of speech. Our discussion did not focus on the technicality of apraxia and treatment. Rather, it was a heart to heart talk between two mothers who have experienced the anxiety, guilt and stress that comes with knowing your child is struggling with a disorder that we simply cannot kiss away. She expressed to me how she feels every frustration her young toddler is experiencing when he tries to talk. How when she sees his sadness, her whole soul is overcome with grief. If only she could kiss it away.

I recall these same feelings when I was told my young seven-month-old son (Johnny) had a Wilms' tumor on his kidney and he would need surgery and treatment. The pain in my heart was stronger and deeper than any pain I had ever felt before. If only I could bear his pain and take this awful sentence away from him. But I knew I could not. All I could do was be there, love him and take care of him. I remember picking him up and he smiled at me with that beautiful smile he still has to this day. He is now 35 years old, a husband, a father and a commercial airline pilot. I needed to look beyond this disease and into the spirit of the child I knew and loved.

My son made it through surgery and his treatments and was on his way to the rest of his life.

In those months, Johnny learned to talk and walk and continued to be the most wonderful gift God has ever given my husband and I. However, I do recall spending so much time worrying that I had to remind myself to enjoy. I needed to remind myself that Johnny was healthy and happy and that he would be a baby just so long. When I had my second child, a beautiful baby girl, Michelle, all bright eyed and smiles, I remember worrying, "Will she too develop this illness or maybe something worse?" I would watch her, feel her and ask the doctor if she was ok. Again, I had to tell myself, stop worrying! My daughter never did develop this illness and she continued to grow and develop into a beautiful woman who dances like an angel, is a practicing attorney, wife and mother. How much time and energy I spent on worrying about the what ifs!

The experiences I have had with my own children and all the experiences I have had with mothers and fathers (just like the young speech pathologist) have taught me that we all share a bond. If only we could take away all the pain, learning difficulties, suffering, illness, challenges that our children may have to endure. If we could make it all go away! The fact is we cannot kiss away apraxia, language disorders, hearing impairments, cerebral palsy, autism or any other challenge or disorder. What we can do is to let our children know that we will be there and support them no matter what and that we accept and love them unconditionally. What we can do is allow our children opportunities to experience all the joys life has to offer by removing or minimizing any obstacles that we can and by creating successful experiences. We can allow them opportunities to work through (with our support) difficult and challenging times. We can look beyond and into the spirit of our children and allow that spirit to grow and flourish. We can be positive advocates for our children. We can work within the collaborative problem-solving model with our children's educational and medical teams to provide the supports and interventions that will enable our children to experience, flourish and live amazing lives.

What we can do for ourselves is to put our worries on the shelf, if only for short periods at a time, and enjoy all that our children have to offer. Watch them as they play, laugh, wonder, reach, touch and grow. I know I could not kiss Johnny's illness away, but I also knew he could kiss my worries away. Today, both my children can kiss and love all my worries away; I just have to open my heart and soul and allow it. I have learned more from them and have received more from them than I could ever give back.

Challenge to All Parents...

Whether you have a child with a disability or not, look beyond the challenges that may be present, hold onto the laughter, grab all the hugs and kisses you can and experience joy with your children. Allow them to experience joy and love! Let them experience challenges and difficulties and allow them to make mistakes, knowing that we will always be there to support them. Let your worries sit in a cup on the shelf, if only for a short while at a time.

Work with your child's educational team within the collaborative problem-solving model in creating a program that is individualized for your child and that will allow your child the opportunity to live a fulfilling, productive life. Work collaboratively with your child's educational team in developing an educational program that will allow your child active participation within the learning process! You are a full member of the collaborative team; engage and participate within each and every process along the way. Do not be afraid to ask the hard questions. Ask as many questions as you can and make sure you get answers based on sound data within dynamic environments. Parents, ask your questions; pause, stop talking and actively listen to what the educational team tells you. Write down exactly what they say. If you do not understand or are confused, ask them to clarify what they said. Don't be afraid or embarrassed to ask them to avoid using "educational jargon" and to use terms you can understand. Ask educators to paraphrase or rephrase information to make sure you have a full understanding. Make sure you write it down! Ask for the objective data to support educational decisions. Do not allow anyone, any educator and/or medical personnel to make you feel as if you are a burden. Do not ever leave a meeting without all of your questions answered. Ask, "What does that mean for my child?" Keep asking, *"WHY?"* or *"WHY NOT?"* Do not be afraid to be an advocate, a voice for your child. Don't be afraid to say, "That does not make sense!"

It is as important for parents to be effective communicators as it is for educators. Being an effective communicator will enhance the problem-solving process and create positive outcomes for your child. It is often difficult to express ourselves effectively when emotions are high. Fear, stress and anxiety can disrupt our abilities at expressing ourselves. (This is also true for our students.) Did you ever leave a meeting and on the way home you find the words you wanted to say in the meeting but couldn't? Have there been times you just did not have the vocabulary or the courage to express what you wanted? Throughout this book we are going to address how to increase your positive communications even when it is hard to do so. We are going to discuss shared vocabulary and knowledge, which you can bring into your child's educational team meetings. KNOWLEDGE IS POWER FOR OUR CHILDREN'S SUCCESS!

CHAPTER 3:

THE COLLABORATIVE PROBLEM-SOLVING MODEL

Throughout the chapters of this book, we will be discussing the importance of the Educational Team Collaborative Problem-Solving Model. Students' effective communication, positive outcomes and progress, as well parents' and educators' understanding of students' communication disorders, substantially increase when transdisciplinary teams (including parents) engage in collaborative problem-solving. Educational team members benefit through increased knowledge, shared understanding, increased efficiency and effectiveness in providing services. It is important that we (educators and parents) have a clear understanding (shared knowledge) of what the collaborative problem-solving model process entails.

Parents (Caregivers) as Full Members of Educational Collaborative Teams

The importance of parents (caregivers) involvement and participation as full members of educational collaborative teams throughout all educational processes cannot be overstated! Knowledge is power for our parents to advocate for and support their children throughout the educational process. Engaging parents within the collaborative problem-solving process allows a shared knowledge base. It allows parents the opportunity to engage in discussions that provide detailed information regarding their child. It is important that educational teams use terminology and contexts that parents can understand, while avoiding professional jargon. Furthermore, it is important that educational teams engage within active listening and positive dialogue, including comprehension checks to ensure that parents understand any and all discussions regarding their child. Parents should be encouraged to ask questions and engage in ongoing communications to increase understanding of their child's communication disorder and the educational process at all levels. Parents ongoing opportunities to engage in problem-solving discussions with educational teams will support their understanding of their child's communication disorder, the educational label or classification, how it manifests within communication contexts for their child, the assessment process as well as the intervention process. It is important that parents and educators say, "This does not make sense. Can you clarify this for me?"

It is crucial that parents have a thorough understanding regarding their child's communication disorder. Parents' participation within the collaborative team problem-solving process will increase their understanding of the processes of assessment, interventions, data collection as well as any dismissal procedures. It will increase their understanding and knowledge regarding the why, when, who, what and how. We know that parent training and professional collaboration are major components within evidence-based practices. Unfortunately, parents are not always involved within the team problem-solving process and often do not have a complete understanding of their child's communication disorder as well as their child's educational programming. Parents may be unclear regarding their child's communication disorder, their child's performance within the assessment process as well as current interventions. Parents may not fully understand why their child was dismissed from speech-language or communication services and/or may not agree with the dismissal process.

Educational teams or team members may have limitations in the amount of time they have to meet with parents to discuss students' programs. They may not have a sufficient amount of time to meet with parents to explain their child's communication disorder, the assessment and interventions processes as well as opportunities to provide crucial information. The collaborative team problem-solving model provides opportunities to address these issues and work through them as the team moves forward in supporting students, creating a shared knowledge base for educators and parents.

A study by Ash, Christopulos and Redmond (2020) concluded that mothers often lack information or understanding regarding their child's language disorder. This lack of information provided to mothers about their child's language disorder caused mothers long lasting psychological harm. They referred to this as "chronic sorrow". Their findings indicated that mothers' emotional distress regarding their child's language disorder continued for many years. They also found that when parents (mothers) do not receive explicit information regarding their child's language disorder, it creates negative perceptions regarding the speech-language profession and the therapy process. These negative perceptions are increased when there is a lack of agreement across speech-language pathologists as well as professional terms used to describe their child's disorder. They found that not only did mothers not understand the information they received from speech-language pathologists but also that some of the information received conflicted from what was told to them in previous discussions and/or experiences. A student may have a different speech-language pathologist as they move from grade to grade, preschool to elementary school, elementary school to junior high, junior high to high school. Their child may be receiving private speech-language therapy from a private agency, as well as at their school.

Trust is the foundation of positive, collaborative relationships. Lack of crucial information and knowledge regarding their students' language, speech, communication disorders as well as conflicting information across speech-language pathologists can create parents' mistrust. This in turn can create barriers to effective problem-solving and programming for students.

Parents' participation within problem-solving discussions along with their ability to effectively advocate for their child is dependent on a shared knowledge base and understanding of what their child's communication disorder is, what the educational classification means for their child, and how the team will assess and provide interventions.

Educational Teams

There are many different types of educational teams and team processes, with challenges and successes inherent within each model. Effective program development, as well as successful student outcomes, are dependent on how educational teams proceed through the collaborative process. What we call our teams is not as important as how we proceed through collaboration. It is important that parents and educational staff understand the type of educational teaming the school engages in as well as the procedures and processes of teaming within the students' programs. Educators may be a member of several different students' educational teams.

Each educational team is composed of several professionals within specific disciplines (e.g., Teacher, Special Education Teacher, Parent, Administrator, Occupational Therapist, Physical Therapist, Speech-language Pathologist, Autism Consultant, Para-professional, Social Worker, Psychologist, Vision Itinerant Teacher, Hearing Itinerant Teacher).

Ehren and Jackson (2003) discussed three different levels of teaming.

Level 1 teaming is a group of educators who work together for one single purpose. For example, teams meet annually for an Individual Educational Planning (IEP) Meeting. Other than meeting for the IEP meeting, ongoing collaboration does not take place. Within Level 1 teaming, individual team members independently complete data collection, assessments, write goals and implement interventions.

Level 2 teams share information, materials along with some decision making. They coordinate some of the workload; however, individual outcomes are dependent on individual efforts. Ehren and Jackson (2003) provided the following as an example of level 2 teams. Teachers meet with grade level chair leaders to discuss possible modification to curriculum for students who may be struggling with literacy acquisition. Outcomes are determined by individual teachers, as it is up to individual team members to implement suggestions and/or interventions or not.

Level 3 teams work collaboratively with interdependence among educational team members. Their interactions and collaboration are ongoing with outcomes dependent on group efforts. Student programming is dependent on team collaboration. Educational team members work together with the teacher on an ongoing basis to implement goals and objectives of the Individual Education Plan (IEP), promoting generalization of skills (Ehren & Jackson, 2003).

Approaches to Teaching

Multi-Disciplinary Approach. Educational team members conduct educational programming for students (assessment, data collection, interventions) independently from other team members. This model is often referred to as the "expert model" in that team members utilize their skills or their knowledge within their own discipline (e.g., communication) independent from each other (e.g., sensory, motor, cognitive processing, academics). Team members meet to provide knowledge, to exchange information regarding their specific domain area (e.g., communication). The multi-disciplinary approach can be seen as being fragmented. Goals from one discipline can actually conflict with goals from other disciplines (King-Sears, Janney & Snell, 2015).

Interdisciplinary Approach. Educational teams work within a more coordinated process during assessments, interventions, and programming procedures. However, team members implement team decisions independently and share results of their work with students at a team meeting. Individual team members (e.g., teachers) may choose to implement interventions and/or behavior plans or may choose to not implement interventions and/ or behavior plans. Students' programs can be fragmented and duplicated. Students may learn particular skills outside of the classroom, possibly within therapy rooms or special education resource rooms, and may not be taught to generalize and transfer those skills into all contexts (King-Sears, Janney & Snell, 2015).

Transdisciplinary Approach. Within this approach, educational teams work collaboratively throughout all phases of students' educational programming. Educational teams work collaboratively in decision making regarding students' programs. Working together (interdependence) is crucial to meeting students' needs. This model supports the collaborative team problem-solving model (King-Sears, Janney & Snell, 2015).

Collaboration vs. Teaming

There are significant differences between the educational team collaborative problem-solving model and teaming processes. Collaboration is an ongoing process. The educational team collaborative problem-solving model is based on everyone involved, the entire educational team (including parents) having a shared understanding or a shared knowledge base of the processes regarding common goals as well as shared decision making based on objective data. It is not one teacher or educational member deciding whether they will integrate an intervention, adaptation and/or modification or not. There is equality among all team members (including parents), meaning that everyone on the educational team has equal input within the decision making process when determining students' programs and outcomes. A collaborative problem-solving process creates shared responsibility among all of the educational team (including parents) when determining key decisions and accountability for outcomes. The collaborative educational team does not simply come to assessments or IEP meetings to exchange information. Through the problem-solving process, educational teams create shared understanding, shared goals, while working toward fidelity and consistency in implementation of processes at every level. Each team member brings relevant information regarding their specific domain. However, within the collaborative problem-solving model, knowledge, data and ideas from other stakeholders are actively listened to, processed and included within discussions to determine final outcomes. The collaborative problem-solving model creates coordination and collaboration between all educational services provided, such as assessments, goals, interventions, data collection and professional development (Friend & Cook, 2007).

This collaboration is especially crucial within the communication domain. Parents, teachers, social workers, principals, physical therapists, occupational therapists, gym teachers, art teachers, etc., have interacted with and observed students within dynamic communication environments in which the speech-language pathologist may not have. They bring important communication information to problem-solving discussions, which is crucial to integrate into students' total communication profiles. Without this input, there can be significant gaps within students' communication profiles that would impact interventions and students' success.

A special education director told parents that he could not make the teachers implement a behavior, communication plan or any of the interventions. This statement would not occur within a collaborative process. The entire educational team would have come to a shared understanding through shared knowledge of the student's strengths and needs and the importance of the behavior, communication plan and interventions. There would be shared understanding of why and how the plan and interventions would be implemented across all environments with fidelity and consistency.

In order for the collaborative process to be effective, team members must understand the benefits and "buy in" to the collaborative process. When team members do not have "buy in" or understand the collaborative process they may make statements such as, "Why should I spend so much time meeting with my team? I simply do not have the time! We waste too much time and get very little accomplished." In order for the collaborative process to be successful, there needs to be structure to the process. This structure must include establishing meeting protocols (such as establishing team meeting processes, rules, schedules, meeting goals) as well as ensuring adequate time for educational staff to meet. It is crucial that school administrators understand the collaborative process and provide needed support for the process to be successful. The collaborative team process can include a variety of ways teams can interact such as in-person meetings, phone meetings, telecommunications, emails and Google Documents. The important concept is that whatever communication interaction is employed, structures of meetings remain constant, data driven and child focused.

The reality of the school system is that there are various levels of teams and collaboration. It is important for parents to understand how their student's educational team collaborates in order to understand how the student's educational program, assessment as well as interventions are determined and how the educational team will implement them with consistency and fidelity. It is important for both educators and parents to work within their school's teaming process to effectively support a more collaborative process for students. Best practice is situational! This is also true within the collaborative team problem-solving model. Some teams may be more advanced within the collaborative process than others. What is the one thing that can be implemented today that will create a more collaborative process? The answer to this question is effective communication! How can we (both educators and parents) be more transparent, positive and effective within our own communication styles to facilitate effective collaboration?

It is crucial that interventions are based on objective data within dynamic environments, that team members, including parents, understand the student's level of functioning, understand the student's communication strengths and challenges and that interventions are implemented with consistency and fidelity. So how do educators and parents effectively support this? When we work within our current system, prioritize needed change and implement change through effective communications, we have started the process of effective collaboration. We can then build on this process and expand collaboration. What is the one thing we can do today that will make a difference in students' programming through collaboration?

Many educational staff are on several teams depending on their caseload. Some educational personnel, such as social workers, psychologists, speech-language pathologist, physical therapists, occupational therapists, autism consultants and hearing and vision itinerant teachers, often service several schools within the district. Educational staff who are hired by a special education cooperative may service several schools within different school districts.

There are teams in which team members have worked together for many years, and teams in which team members are new to working together. Educational personnel (e.g., Speech-Language Pathologist, Occupational Therapist, Physical therapists, vision or hearing itinerant) often receive their assignments and student caseloads at the beginning of the school year.

These are just a few possible barriers to the collaborative process. So, how do you work within your school system to effectively participate within a collaborative process? Ask yourself, what is the one thing I or my team (we) can do today that will increase collaboration and increase positive student outcomes?

Following is a list of questions parents and educational staff can ask to determine level of teaming and/or collaboration with current school system.

- Who are the team members on the students' team?
- What are the roles of each team member?
- When are the team members at the school?
- When does the team meet and how often?
- Does or how does the team collaborate within students' assessment process?

- Are students' communication skills assessed within dynamic communication environments? Do all team members have input into the assessment process and shared understanding of students' communication needs?

- Does the team collaborate regarding students' goals (at what level) in order that they are coordinated and do not conflict with each other?

- Does the team develop shared or common goals that support students across environments?

- How does the educational team monitor the interventions, modifications and adaptations that are implemented with consistency and fidelity across all environments?

- How does the team provide professional training that would support consistency and fidelity in the intervention process?

- How are para-professionals supported by the educational team?

Effective student outcomes are based on shared understandings at implementing the collaborative process. It is important that educational teams identify mutual goals for collaboration. Collaboration goals will provide a framework and structure to collaborative team meetings and discussions. This will allow teams the ability to remain on task, be efficient within the collaborative process and engage in collaborative discussions that result in effective shared decision making.

CHAPTER 4:

THE DYNAMIC COMMUNICATION PROCESS

ALL BEHAVIOR IS COMMUNCIATION! Throughout the chapters of this book we will examine and discuss the meaning behind this statement and the communication concepts that support this statement. We will discuss how to observe and understand the communication process, assess dynamic communication, and provide communication interventions to support students' communication success within academic and social contexts. Case study examples will be provided.

It is crucial that we (educators as well as parents) have a shared understanding, a shared knowledge base of the dynamic communication process. Perhaps you recall when I discussed that my parents did not see the necessity of learning sign language to communicate with my sister (who is profoundly deaf). They did not have the crucial knowledge regarding the dynamics of communication and the differences as well as the relationships between speech (one means of communication) and language.

I worked in an early intervention program (birth through age 2), as well as in preschool programs (ages 3 to 5 years) and elementary programs working with children who were hard of hearing or deaf and their families. The parents of these children expressed the same response as my parents. I want my child to talk! The first step in the intervention process was to provide these families with crucial information regarding the differences and the relationships between speech and language and an understanding of the dynamic communication process.

SPEECH

Speech is one component within the communication process. It refers to our ability to verbally produce meaningful sounds and to combine sounds to form words, phrases and sentences. Our speech articulators (lips, teeth, tongue, alveolar ridge, hard palate, velum or soft palate, uvula and the glottis) produce the speech sounds of language. We produce speech by movements of the articulators in coordination with respiration (breathing). Speech is one means of communication or one way we express our language. Speech is the most conventional means of communication. A student may have adequate or excellent abilities at producing speech, with excellent speech intelligibility; however, this does not mean the student has the ability to express himself or herself using appropriate language or that the student is an effective communicator. Students who present with excellent speech intelligibility can have receptive and/or expressive language disorders (within one or a combination of the five elements of language), communication disorders.

Speech delays and/or speech disorders can have a direct impact on academic and social success. There is a direct relationship between the severity of the speech delay or speech disorder and the level of impact it has on academic and social success. Students who present with speech delays and/or speech disorders may experience increased levels of communication anxiety. They may avoid speaking or interacting within various communication contexts (environments as well as persons). They may have difficulties expressing themselves. They may become anxious when they have to speak in front of a class, interacting within class discussions or when they have to give oral presentations. They may avoid social interactions with adults and/or peers. They may reduce the length and complexity of their language to increase listeners' understanding of their communications. Speech disorders can impact morphological, syntactic, semantic as well as pragmatic elements of language. Avoiding communication interactions can impact their active participation within learning and social experiences, which can directly impact receptive and expressive language development and pragmatic social interactions.

Case Study: Bob (Speech Disorder)

Introduction

Bob (a high school student) had a severe speech disorder (a severe articulation disorder as well as functional voice quality disorder) that significantly impacted his speech intelligibility along with his self-concept. His speech disorder impacted his expressive language and pragmatic language development. He would avoid talking and in fact spoke very little at school. After several years of intensive direct intervention to correct his articulation and voice disorder, his speech became intelligible.

Analysis

Intensive interventions to correct Bob's speech disorder gave him increased confidence to engage in social interactions. However, because he had avoided social interactions, he did not have the experiences that would have provided him with the needed expressive language and social pragmatic skills to engage within a variety of communication contexts (communication environments and communication partners). He had a communication reputation as a student who just did not talk or engage ("a very quiet student"). It was said that he did not want to interact and preferred to be alone. (Red flag!) His family would "talk for him". They would fill in what they thought he was saying, or would just nod as if they understood him. He wanted to interact; however, he did not have the skills to do so. This caused him a great deal of anxiety. He would internalize his anxiety and completely shut down.

Recommendations

The recommendations were to implement an expressive language, pragmatic social language intervention program that would allow him the ability to develop the expressive language and pragmatic interaction skills that he lacked.

44

Through this intervention program, he not only gained the needed expressive language and pragmatic language skills needed to engage in social interactions, he also gained self-confidence as a social communicator!

Speech Delay or Disorder

A speech delay occurs when speech is developing in the right sequence, but at a slower rate than normal speech development. A speech disorder is an impairment in the ability to produce speech sounds, within fluency or use of voice. A speech disorder can be functional, in which there is not a known cause. A child (or adult) may have a speech disorder due to structural and/or neurological deficit (such as a cleft palate, trauma or surgery). A differential diagnosis is crucial when assessing students' speech skills and speech intelligibility. Interventions and therapy programs will be significantly different for students who present with apraxia, dysarthria, articulation disorders, phonological disorders, voice disorders, stuttering and/or cluttering. There are students who may present with a combination of speech disorders.

An **articulation disorder** is a speech impairment in the ability to correctly use the speech articulators (lips, teeth, tongue, alveolar ridge, hard palate, velum or soft palate, uvula and the glottis) to produce speech sounds. The person may substitute one sound for another, omit a sound, add sounds, and/or distort speech sounds, which impacts or interferes with speech intelligibility. Incorrectly producing the /s/ sound, or substituting a /th/ sound for the /s/ sound, as well as distorting the /r/ sound are examples of articulation delays or disorders.

Apraxia is a neurogenic speech disorder with impairment in the person's ability to execute and coordinate movements of the speech musculature for the volitional production of speech. Apraxia is a speech disorder of motor planning. Apraxia "is an inability, unrelated to actual muscle weakness or pathology, to produce volitional movements and sequences of movements necessary for connected, intelligible speech" (Hickman, 1997, p. 1). A student who has apraxia of speech will demonstrate difficulties sequencing sounds in words, producing multisyllable words and producing words, phrases and sentences of increased length and complexity. Their speech may be unintelligible; they may demonstrate oral-motor groping behaviors.

Dysarthria is a neurogenic speech disorder originating within the central or peripheral nervous system. Respiration, articulation, phonation, resonation and/or prosody may be impacted. It may affect chewing, swallowing and movements of the jaw and tongue (Nicolosi, Harryman & Kresheck, 1996).

A child who has a **phonological disorder** has an impairment within the sound system of language. There is a language component to the speech disorder, in that the child continues to demonstrate processes that are found in the speech of younger children. We will discuss phonology as one of the five language elements later in this chapter. The goal of speech therapy is to remediate phonological processes (Hodson & Paden, 1983).

Fluency disorders are speech disorders that occur when there is a disruption in the flow of speech. **Stuttering** is one example of a fluency disorder. A stuttering disorder is an impairment in the ability to produce speech fluently. Young children go through a developmental age in which they can become dysfluent. All of us can stumble and become dysfluent at times. This does not necessarily mean that we stutter. We refer to dysfluencies in speech as stuttering disorders when the disturbance in the normal fluency of speech (both verbal and secondary behaviors) interrupt the person's ability to communicate within academic and/or social environments. The student (or adult) may demonstrate repetitions of sounds, prolongations of sounds and/or blocks in which the sound seems to "get stuck". The student (or adult) may experience anxiety, excessive tension and struggle with behaviors and secondary stuttering symptoms such as twitches, eye blinking and head nodding. Students' academic as well as social interactions and success may be significantly impacted in that the student may avoid speaking either in class or in social situations. Oral presentations and class discussions may be impacted.

Cluttering is another example of a fluency disorder. Cluttering is a disorder of speech and language processing. Speech may be extremely rapid, resulting in unorganized and often unintelligible speech. Speech patterns may appear very similar to a stuttering disorder. A cluttering diagnosis has a co-existing impairment in formulating language. The person will tend to talk too quickly, slur or omit syllables in longer words and demonstrate difficulties formulating language. They may be unaware of their speech difficulties (Daly, 1996).

A **voice disorder** is a speech disorder that involves deviations in vocal pitch, vocal intensity or the quality of a person's voice. A voice disorder may be organic or functional in etiology (Sapienza & Ruddy, 2018).

Speech: One Means of Communication

Speech is one means of communication or one way we express our language. Speech is the most conventional means of communication. Sign language, gestures, body language, facial expressions and communication devices are examples of other means of communication. Means of communication provide us with the ability to express language: our thoughts, our ideas, our needs, our emotions, etc. (communication intents). There are a variety of means in which we use to express ourselves. We all use various means or multiple means of communication throughout our day to express our language and to communicate. Speech is only one means of communication. We combine verbal speech, eye contact, facial expression, gestures as well as written language such as notes, texting, computers, depending on who we are talking to, the environment in which we are speaking, why we are speaking and the contexts. How many of us can get through our day without our iPhone, iPad, texting or use of our computers? Chart 1 outlines the various means of communication or the ways in which we express language.

CHART 1: THE MEANS OF COMMUNICATION

Verbal	Para Linguistics Paralanguage	Non-Verbal
• Speech • Vocalizations (non-speech: e.g., grunts) • Verbalizations	• Vocal Volume • Intonation • Vocal Pitch • Vocal Quality • Vocal Stress • Rate of speech	• Use of Gestures • Eye Gaze (joint attention, eye contact) • Facial Expressions • Head nods/shakes • Posture • Proximity (distance from speaker) • Physical manipulation • Body contact (e.g., hand shaking, touch) • Orientation (Head and body orientation when seated or standing) • Sign Language (Idiosyncratic; Formal Sign: ASL, Signed Exact English) • Augmentative or alternative communication

It is crucial that students have functional means of communication that allow them opportunities to fully express language at whatever developmental level they may be at. Some students with communication deficits, delays and/or challenges may require additional means of communication, such as visual language systems. Visual language systems (such as sign language, visual communication supports, voice output devices) will not only support language development and effective communication, but will not suppress any other means of communication (including speech). In fact, they can actually support speech development. (Silverman, 1996). Students will naturally combine various means of communication and will use the means of communication that is most efficient and accessible within specific communication contexts. Educators and parents should consider multiple means of communication as well as honoring or responding to all the ways students communicate (all of their means of communication). We need to encourage and enhance any and ALL means of communication intent and actual communication acts. This will facilitate students' receptive and expressive language development.

The use of multi-modality or multiple means of communication is the preferred practice in supporting students with communication disorders (Gibbons & Szarkowski, 2019). One means of communication may be effective in one situation and may not work at all in another. It is important that we understand and respond to all communications from students, no matter what means of communication they are employing at the time. Unfortunately, there may be situations in which the means of communication that is most accessible to students within specific communication contexts is that of "overt behaviors". By providing students with effective means of communication, we can replace "overt behaviors" with effective communication interactions.

We will be discussing these ideas and communication concepts in detail as we work through the dynamic communication process. Once we have a shared understanding, a shared knowledge base regarding the communication process, we can then apply this to successful interactions, assessments as well as interventions. We can also apply this knowledge within Universal Design of Instruction, use of adaptations, and modifications.

Educators may state, "I have no concerns regarding the student's language or communication skills as he has excellent verbal skills," when actually, the child has significant difficulties communicating and exhibits significant "overt and/or covert behavior" issues. Our ability to communicate effectively depends on both speech (one means of communication) and language skills. Stating that a student has a speech deficit does not mean that he/she has a language disorder. Furthermore, stating that a student has good or excellent speech or verbal skills does not mean that he/she has adequate language skills or that he/she is an effective communicator. It is crucial that educators and parents have an understanding (shared knowledge base) regarding the differences and the relationships between speech skills (one means of communication) and language skills.

Language

Language is another component of communication. It consists of a shared set of rules to express our ideas, emotions, beliefs, thoughts and concepts. Language is a socially shared rule system, in that the speaker and listener must understand the same set of rules. Different languages have different sets of rules (e.g., English, Spanish, American Sign Language, etc.). There are five components or elements of language: phonology, morphology, syntax, semantics and pragmatics.

Communication competence involves both receptive language and expressive language. Receptive language is our ability to comprehend or understand verbal and/or visual language. Expressive language is our use or production of language to communicate (through means of communication). Expressive language is our ability to communicate our perceptions, ideas, needs, wants, feelings or intentions to others. There is a dynamic relationship between receptive and expressive language. Our understanding of language or receptive language develops prior to expressive language, as comprehension or understanding precedes production or use.

Language Delay or Disorder

A language delay occurs when a child's language is developing in the right sequence but at a slower rate than normal language development. A language disorder is an impairment or disability within comprehension (receptive language) and/or use (expressive language). A student may have a language disorder in both receptive and expressive language. This impairment may be within spoken language (verbal speech), written language and/or other symbol systems. A language delay or disorder may involve one or a combination of the elements of language: phonology, morphology, syntax, semantics and/or pragmatics.

When parents are told that their child has a language delay or language disorder they often do not have a clear understanding of what it means for their child. This can also be true when teachers are told that a student in their class has a language disorder. They may not understand what this actually means for that particular student and how it manifests within academic and social curricula. It is crucial that parents and educators have a clear understanding of what language disorders are, what the specific language disorder is for an individual student and the impacts on academic and social curricula.

A language delay and/or language disorder can occur within one or any combination of the five different components or elements of language.

Five Components or Elements of Language

There are five different elements of language that directly refer to a specific domain of language knowledge. The five components or elements of language are interrelated and do not develop in isolation. Each of the five language components or elements are present in any interaction in which language is used. Because each element is present within any interaction, a language delay or language disorder in one element of language will impact performance in all of the elements of language.

CHART 2: THE COMPONENTS OR ELEMENTS OF LANGUAGE

The Components (Elements) of Language
FORM
Phonology (Phonological Knowledge): The study of the sound system of language.
Morphology (Morphemic Knowledge): The study of words and how they are formed.
Syntax (Syntactic Knowledge): The study of the rules that govern sentence structure.
CONTENT
Semantics (Semantic Knowledge): The study of the meaning of words.
USE
Pragmatics (Pragmatic Knowledge): The study of the rules that involve the use of language during interaction with other people.

Phonology (Phonological Knowledge)

Phonology is the study of the sound system of our language. There are two components within phonology: (1) a repertoire of sounds referred to as phonemes, and (2) a finite set of rules defining how these sounds or phonemes can be combined or sequenced (Hodson & Paden, 1983). Although there are 26 alphabet letters in the English language, there are 43 distinctive sounds or phonemes. Phonemes, the smallest linguistic unit of sounds, are combined with other phonemes to form words.

Perhaps you have been told your child has a phonological disorder. What does this mean? A phonological disorder is a language based disorder in that the student has difficulties applying phonological processes or rules of speech (phoneme) production. A student's speech may be significantly impaired, making it difficult to understand the student. Speech-language therapy goals would be developed to remediate phonological processes.

Morphology (Morphemic Knowledge)

Morphology is the study of words and how words are formed, understanding the parts of words. Words are made up of morphemes, the smallest units of meaning in a language. Morphemes are different from syllables. A word may have two or more syllables and only one morpheme. Each morpheme carries a meaning. There are two different types of morphemes, free morphemes and bound morphemes.

Free morphemes are morphemes that have meaning on their own; they can stand on their own. For example, the words "boy", "is", "house" and "yesterday" contain one morpheme. They have meaning on their own and broken down any further would lose that meaning.

Bound morphemes cannot stand on their own as they only have meaning when attached to a free morpheme. For example, when we add "-ed" to walk, we create past tense verb "walked". The -ed marker is a bound morpheme in that it only has meaning when attached to the verb "walk" to make it past tense. The word "walked" has two morphemes: walk and -ed. A second example is adding "-s" to "boy" to create the plural form, boys. The -s marker is a bound morpheme, as it only has meaning when attached to the noun "boy" to make it plural form, in this case -s means plural noun. The word "boys" also has two morphemes: boy and plural s.

An effective language user has the ability to use morphemes appropriately in words. A student who has a language delay or language disorder within the component or element of morphology would have difficulties with understanding and producing word endings such as past tense verbs (walked), plural nouns (books) or present progressive verbs (walking). A deficit in this area would impact academic and social contexts.

Syntax (Syntactic Knowledge)

Syntax is the study of the rules that govern how words are put together to create phrases and sentences in order to convey meaning. It refers to the rules of grammar. Every language has rules or a grammar in which words are combined to create sentences and phrases. Word order is important in creating meaning and also in understanding or comprehending the meaning of another's message. For example, the following two sentences have the same words, however, in different word order. This change in word order creates two separate sentences with two very different meanings: Did you hit Jack? Did Jack hit you?

A student who has a language delay or a language disorder in the element of syntax would have difficulties understanding and using a variety of sentence types. Their ability to complete written language assignments would be impacted. A deficit in this area would impact academic and social contexts.

Semantics (Semantic Knowledge)

Semantics refers to the study of the meaning of words. Semantic knowledge is closely tied to the development of conceptual knowledge. It refers to understanding and use of vocabulary, word meanings and concept development. Semantic knowledge is closely tied to general linguistic competence and to reading comprehension. Following are examples of semantic knowledge: word meanings, vocabulary, words that have multiple meanings, literal vs. figurative language, idioms, metaphors, sarcasm, slang, play on words, concrete vs. abstract word and concept knowledge, questions, classifications, comparisons, analogies, attributes, synonyms, and antonyms.

A student who has a language delay or language disorder within semantics would have difficulties understanding the language of others as well expressing themselves. They would have difficulty understanding concepts, vocabulary, as well as using them within their own language and application within social interactions and academic tasks. They may not understand or may misinterpret abstract language, figurative language, play on words, multiple meanings of words, idioms and sarcasm. They may not understand or misinterpret slang and differences within cultural language. Students' written language will reflect their level of semantic knowledge. A deficit within the element of semantics will impact verbal and written language. A deficit in this area would impact all academic and social contexts, as semantic skills are crucial to all curricular areas, understanding and expressing language.

Case Study: High School Reading Class (Semantic Language Disorder)

Introduction

As a speech-language pathologist, I team-taught with a special education reading teacher at the high school level. There were fourteen high school students within this classroom, all of whom had significant semantic and pragmatic language disorders. They were reading a book about a community in New York that was very different from the community in which they lived. The story had many instances of figurative language and play on words with which they were very unfamiliar. The students were engaged in a popular activity (popcorn reading) in which they took turns reading aloud from the book.

Analysis

The students were engaged in reading and all read fluently. However, they were not responding or answering questions from the teacher. It did not appear that they were comprehending or understanding the events of the story.

Recommendations

In order to support students' comprehension of the story, I modeled the strategy of Mind's Eye/Visualization. (Mind's Eye or visualization is an intervention to support students in processing and understanding language as well as to facilitate students' use of comprehension checks. (This intervention is discussed in Chapter 11.)

A student read an excerpt from the book that had the following sentence: "The cat was a wino." I raised my hand and said, "My Mind's Eye tells me that statement does not make sense." I drew a picture of a cat drinking wine on the board. Many of the students said, "Yeah, why would a cat drink wine?" I asked them to come up to the board and draw what their understanding of the statement was. Each of them said it did not make sense and drew a similar picture. I asked, "What if the cat was a man; how would that change your picture and your understanding?" I heard all kinds of exclamations, such as, "Oh, the man is a wino! The man drinks wine!" I then explained that the term cat refers to a man and that wino in this context meant that the man drinks too much wine. We went back and reread the chapter. This time the students actually understood and enjoyed what the story line was expressing!

Pragmatics (Pragmatic Knowledge)

Pragmatics is the study of the rules of conversation. Conversational rules involve the use of language during interactions with other people. Pragmatic language refers to the use of language for communication and is embedded in all academic, vocational, social and cultural contexts. It is the knowledge or the awareness of how to use language differently in different settings and situations. Pragmatic language is contextually based. We adjust our use of language based on who we are talking to, why we are talking and where we are. It involves shifting our language during formal vs. informal conversations. Pragmatics involves the communication skills (verbal and nonverbal) that allow us to interact effectively for a variety of reasons, across different environments (contexts) and with different people (communication partners).

Pragmatic language skills involve the ability to use language within a variety of communication contexts (communication partners and environments) within dynamic communication interactions. Pragmatics involve the ability to use a combination of means of communication (Chart 1), the ability to create shared communication intents (Chart 4), the ability to attend and at joint attention. Joint attention is a crucial communication skill that is developed very early. Joint attention is the ability to have a shared visual focus with a communication partner and to shift the visual focus to objects and back to the communication partner. An example of joint attention is when a baby interacts with his or her parents. A baby shifts visual focus from mom to the bottle and back to mom. A second example is during a classroom discussion, students employ joint attention when they visually focus on their teacher, shift their visual focus to the board, or book and to other students and then back to the teacher. They create and maintain shared visual focus.

Pragmatic language also involves abilities at initiating or starting conversations appropriately, turn-taking or taking turns during conversations. We take turns speaking and listening. It involves abilities at maintaining conversations or the ability to continue conversations, as well as abilities to repair communication breakdowns or misunderstandings. Pragmatic language also includes our abilities at contextual use of vocal tone, vocal volume, prosody, intonation, vocal quality, stress and the rate or speech appropriately within social interactions (environments as well as people).

A pragmatic language deficit would impact all academic, vocational and social contexts. A student who has a deficit within pragmatic language would demonstrate difficulties within communication interactions. Their ability to apply pragmatic or conversational rules may be inconsistent from one context to another due to differences between communication environments and communication partners. Students may not be able to shift their communication style to reflect formal vs. informal communication partners and/or environments. Students may also have deficits within one or a combination of the other four elements of language and/or speech deficits along with deficits in pragmatic language.

Many students who present with deficits within the pragmatic language element are often misinterpreted as students with behavior challenges.

Auditory Processing Disorders

The American-Speech-Language-Hearing Association (1993) defines auditory processing disorders (APD) as deficits in the information processing of audible signals not attributed to impaired peripheral hearing sensitivity or intellectual impairment. It is an impairment in the ability to process (understand) auditory information in the absence of (or without) a hearing impairment.

Auditory processing is the ability to make use of and understand or comprehend what is heard (verbal speech). It is the ability to identify sound, interpret sound and attach meaning to the sound. Auditory processing involves several different skills which are crucial to all academic curriculum areas.

Auditory localization is the ability to localize where the sound source is coming from. The child will turn his head toward the sound.

Auditory association is the ability to identify a sound with its source. The child knows the sound of a bell or the sound of his mother's voice.

Auditory attention is the ability to pay attention to certain or salient auditory stimuli and not to others, as well as the ability to maintain this attention. It includes the ability to pay attention to or focus on specific, important units of sounds, such as speech sounds, words, phrases, conversations, noises, etc.

Auditory blending is the ability to combine phonemes (speech sounds) of a word produced with pauses between them. It is the ability to combine isolated phonemes into words (e.g., c-a-t = cat).

Auditory closure is the ability to understand an entire message or a whole word when parts of it is missing.

Auditory discrimination is the ability to discriminate or hear differences between words and sounds that are auditorily similar. This is the ability to sort and distinguish sounds from each other and includes differentiating different speech sounds from other speech sounds as well as other sounds (e.g., cat vs. bat).

Auditory figure ground involves the ability to select relevant auditory information from irrelevant auditory information within the environment. It includes the ability to identify and listen to a speaker in the presence of competing background noise, to identify one speaker from another.

Auditory memory, sequential memory is the ability to store and recall auditory information of different lengths or numbers in the exact order.

There are many students who have difficulties processing auditory information within dynamic school environments, such as school classrooms, lunchrooms, gyms, and hallways, that impact their academic and social success. This difficulty processing auditory information can be frustrating, create anxiety and result in outward (overt) and inward (covert) behaviors. Students may process auditory information effectively when there is limited language input or language load, limited background noise or clutter, familiarity with the language content or with the communication partner. However, they do not have the same abilities at processing auditory information with increased language load or input, novel language content, unfamiliar communication partners and within dynamic communication situations. Students with learning disabilities, autism, language disorders, hearing impairments, intellectual deficit, cerebral palsy, or other deficits as well as children with a primary disability of communication disorder may have difficulties processing auditory information. A student who has difficulty processing auditory information within dynamic communication environments will miss crucial language input. They may become confused, frustrated, anxious, and may shut down or act out. So, what does that mean for students' educational programming? This question should be rephrased to, "What does this mean for my student?" as each student has individual strengths and challenges. It is crucial to understand each student's level of learning processes, language processing and ability to process auditory information within total school environments.

Universal Design of Instruction (UDI) is crucial in supporting students who have challenges processing auditory information. Implementing UDI supports all learning styles.

A student who has difficulty processing auditory information may present with one or a combination of the following:

- The student may demonstrate difficulty understanding the speech or language of others in noisy listening environments, such as the classroom, lunchroom, morning information coming over the classroom speaker, etc.

- The student may not understand or may misinterpret the verbal messages of others.

- The student may frequently ask for information to be repeated.

- The student may have difficulty attending (especially within noisy environments or when there is competing auditory input).

- The student may not respond or demonstrate a delay in responding to the verbal communications of others.

- The student may demonstrate difficulties following complex auditory directions.

- The student may avoid social interactions as they have difficulty following conversations within small and large group interactions.

- They may tune out auditory input (language) if it becomes too difficult to process.

Assessing a student's ability to process auditory information is one component within a comprehensive speech-language communication assessment. A school speech-language pathologist will complete a comprehensive communication evaluation to determine the student's needs within the communication domain (which would include how the child processes auditory language). It is important that this evaluation address any questions the educational team (including parents) have regarding the student's communications skills and include assessments within dynamic communication environments.

Educational teams may determine (through the dynamic assessment process) that a student has a deficit in the ability to process auditory information. An action plan would be developed (goals and interventions) based on individual student's needs. Interventions should support overall comprehension and functional communication within dynamic environments. Visual processing supports and interventions will facilitate students' abilities at processing language. Visual processing supports may include use of visualization, visual graphic organizers, and visual mind maps. Interventions may also include teaching the student "active listening", use of communication repair strategies, use of context cues to increase understanding, comprehension checks, preferential seating, FM technology, controlling background noise, and use of computers to support classroom activities. The intervention plan may also include allowing students increased processing time, giving students time to respond, breaking down oral directions and/or provide visual supports as you give oral directions.

Communication

Communication is the process in which we exchange information, ideas, needs and desires. We combine speech (or other means of communication) and the five elements of language to exchange information. Dynamic communication depends on the interactions between speech (or other means of communication) and language. There are four essential elements within the communication process: sender and receiver of the message, shared intents and shared means of communication. Successful communication interactions are dependent on the success of all four elements. One or more of the essential communication elements may be missing or impaired for students who present with speech and/or language delays or disorders. When one or more of the elements is missing, a communication breakdown may occur. In fact, communication breakdowns can and often do occur for all communicators (Kuder, 2013).

> **There are four essential elements within the communication process.**
>
> 1. The speaker sends the information (through a combination of means of communication).
>
> 2. The receiver (listener) decodes, comprehends or creates meaning of the message.
>
> 3. There is a shared intent to communicate.
>
> 4. There is a shared means of communication. We must have the ability to understand the means of communication used by our communication partner. For example, sign language is a means that not all of us share. Second language users often speak (verbalize) a language which we do not understand and do not share.

Communication Disorders

The American Speech Language Hearing Association (ASHA) defines communication disorders as impairments in a person's ability to receive, send, process and comprehend (understand) concepts. It involves verbal, nonverbal and graphic symbols. A communication disorder can range from a mild to a profound disorder. A communication disorder can occur within one or both of the components of communication: speech skills and/or language skills.

We artificially separate speech, language and communication in order to discuss and study each one. However, within dynamic conversations and interactions, speech (or other means of communication), language and communication are dynamically interrelated. Our communications—what we say and how we say it—are ever changing depending on the context (environment and person) we are communicating with or in. We change the way we speak, how we speak, the language we use depending on the context (where we are, what we are saying, who we are talking to, why we are communicating) as all communication is contextually based

CHART 3: COMMUNICATION – SPEECH – LANGUAGE

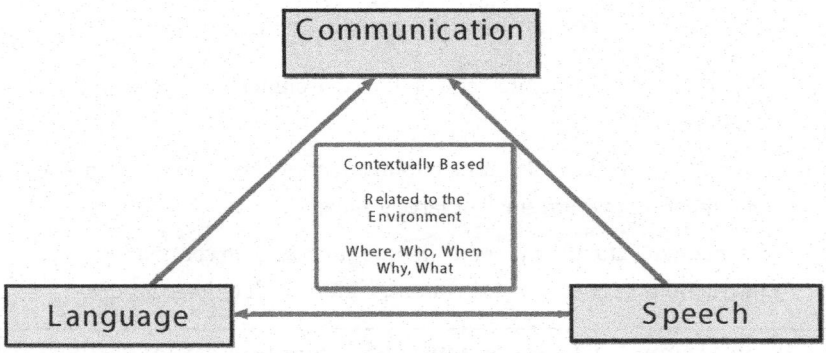

Shared Communication Intents (Speech Acts)

Shared communication intents, also referred to as speech acts, are the reasons why we are communicating. We use language for different reasons. Effective communication requires shared intents between speaker and listener. A student may have excellent verbal skills (speech skills) but have limited use or abilities at expressing a variety of communication intents. A student may be intelligent, bright, able to express him or herself in some communication contexts employing speech as the means of communication. However, the student may not be able to use speech as a means to communicate effectively or access appropriate language to express communication intents, such as: expressing emotions, wants, during highly stressful or anxious communication contexts, greeting peers and/or adults, explaining or retelling personal experiences, actions or behaviors, expressing or accepting help and/or criticism. It is important that educational personnel and parents understand what shared intents are and their impact on effective interactions as well as communication breakdowns. Chart 4 outlines a variety of communication intents or speech acts that we utilize within communication interactions, with various communication partners and within various communication environments. In other words, the reasons why we communicate!

CHART 4: COMMUNICATION INTENTS (SPEECH ACTS)

We attend to communication partners within various communication environments.

- We attend in order to interact with the environment and with communication partners.
- We attend to make and maintain joint attention, eye-contact in one-to-one situations, within small or large groups.
- We maintain attention (persist) in order to engage in communication interactions in one-to-one situations, within small or large groups.

We use requests when interacting with communication partners within various communication environments.

- We ask for attention, objects, actions and information from communication partners.
- We use questions forms (yes/no, wh-questions) along with intonation patterns to request.
- We ask for help, to have messages clarified, for permission and for approval from others.

We respond to requests from communication partners within various communication environments.

- We imitate the communications of others, both verbal and nonverbal, such as speech, sign language, facial expressions and body gestures.
- We label objects and actions of others.
- We comply with and/or refuse to comply with requests from communication partners.
- We express our wants and/or needs in response to requests from communication partners.
- We answer questions (yes/no questions, wh-questions) presented to us by communication partners.
- We provide information and describe things or happenings when requested by communication partners.

- We agree with, protest and/or argue with communication partners' statements.

- We clarify and/or add information to our language during communication interactions in response to non-verbal and verbal requests from communication partners.

- We accept criticism and or corrections from communication partners.

- We return greetings and say goodbye.

We use verbal and nonverbal means of communication to communicate our thoughts to others. We label and describe when providing information (language) to communication partners.

- We greet and say goodbye.

- We agree, disagree, apologize and/or protest.

- We tease and joke with communication partners.

- We criticize, attempt to convince and complement communication partners.

- We express our personal beliefs, emotions and feelings.

- We label and describe people (we know or do not know), objects (in or out of view), our actions as well as actions by others, our wants, our needs, our emotions and/or our feelings.

- We comment on and provide descriptions about people and events we have met and/or experienced, will meet and/or experience and have heard or read about.

- We retell or relate stories, personal events and happenings that we have experienced, heard about or read about in the present, past and/or future.

Communication Breakdowns

Communication breakdowns can occur within the communication process when our intents are not interpreted correctly by the listener or when we do not interpret others' intents correctly. Communication disorders will impact students' abilities at receiving (comprehending) messages as well as sending (expressing) messages. For example, a student with a hearing impairment may not hear, receive or understand the entire message. A student with a language disorder may not understand the information or may not be able to express themselves, impacting both receiving as well as sending messages. A student may have good speech or verbal skills; however, they may have significant impairments in receiving and/or sending messages (information, language).

Our communication effectiveness within the student-teacher dynamic relationship depends on our abilities to repair communication breakdowns. Have you successfully expressed your communication intents in a way that students can process and understand them? Have you successfully understood the communication intents of your students? The following case study is an example of how a student may have good verbal skills; however, may also have a significant language disorder resulting in significant communication breakdowns which result in overt behaviors (communications). Vicky demonstrated significant deficits using appropriate language to express herself as well as processing the speech acts or intents of the adults within the classroom. This resulted in challenging communications (overt behaviors) as her means of communicating her frustrations.

Case Study: Vicky (Communication Disorder)

Introduction

Vicky was an extremely bright kindergarten child with excellent verbal skills and an educational disability classification of autism. She received the following special education services: social work services, speech-language therapy and one-to-one para-educator support. The educational team requested team consultation to problem-solve possible interventions and to develop a Behavior Plan for Vicky, as she was having several verbal outbursts daily and would throw herself down on the floor. The educational team consultation began with a direct observation of Vicky within her kindergarten class. Vicky had a meltdown on the day of the observation

Observation

The students were participating within morning circle time. Vicky's teacher explained that she did not participate within morning circle because she would become disruptive. In lieu of participating within circle time, Vicky worked at her independent workstation writing in her journal and drawing a picture. Independent, academic work was a preferred activity for Vicky. She persisted at working independently at her desk writing and drawing about McDonald's. Her teacher and para-professional were unaware of what she was writing about.

The class broke up into several different groups. Vicky continued to work independently at her desk. On several occasions the teacher and para-professional provided Vicky verbal directions from across the room. Vicky did not respond to several of the directions. On other occasions she stopped working, looked up from her paper and demonstrated the following communication means: facial expressions, pointing to her paper, stopping drawing and looking at her paper or saying, "What about McDonald's?" Vicky did not receive a response by either the teacher or para-professional to any of her communications.

Vicky pointed to her paper (communication means) when she was verbally directed to go to the smartboard. The para-educator walked Vicky to the smartboard. Once at the smartboard, Vicky appeared to use a trial-and-error approach toward matching the rhyming pictures, by circling the smartboard pen until it grabbed a word. She visually looked across the room to the teacher and pointed to the board (communication means). However, Vicky did not verbally say anything. Neither the teacher nor the para-professional responded to her. Looking at the board, Vicky said, "What this rhyme with?" She repeated this several times; each time, she did not receive a response.

Vicky's teacher verbally directed her to go to her reading group. Vicky said, "What about McDonald's?" The teacher verbally told Vicky that they were not having McDonald's for lunch. Vicky again said, "What about McDonald's?" She repeated this several times. The teacher walked over to Vicky, took her by the hand and attempted to walk her to the reading table. Vicky looked at her desk, pointed (communication means) and this time screamed in a very loud voice, "What about McDonald's?" She then threw herself on the floor and began to scream and cry loudly, the only communication means that received any response from the adults in the room.

Analysis

Vicky's meltdown was a direct result of her inability to communicate a variety of communication intents, her inability to repair communication breakdowns as well as her teacher and para-professional missing important communication means used by Vicky: gesture, facial expressions, body posture and tone of voice. Vicky did not demonstrate or gain joint attention and/or visual attention prior to interacting with her teacher and para-professional. Vicky's deficit processing auditory language along with her expressive and pragmatic language deficits impacted her ability to process her teacher's and para-professional's verbal directions, attend within circle time and interact with her peers. Although Vicky demonstrated verbal skills, she was not able to express herself. Vicky became more and more frustrated with little to no ability to repair the breakdown.

Recommendations

*A visual processing intervention was immediately implemented to increase Vicky's ability to process language and decrease her frustration. A write-on board was placed within her visual field (without saying anything) with the following written on it: (1) reading group. (2) draw and write about McDonald's. (3) play-doh or sand table. (Remember, Vicky has strong academic skills.) I sat next to Vicky and waited for her to become calm. Once she became calm and visually looked at the board, the words were slowly read: "first, second, third". Vicky took the pen, circled "sand table," then walked to the reading table: **The power of visual processing!***

Team recommendations were to facilitate joint attention, active listening, language processing and expressive language by creating structure, consistency and predictability through Universal Design of Instruction as well as individual visual processing adaptations, interventions and supports across all school environments. Rather than excluding Vicky from morning circle, it was recommended that the educational team collaboratively implement Universal Design of Instruction, modification and adaptations. Visual processing interventions and visual communication supports would support Vicky's active engagement and participation within all learning experiences. (These interventions are discussed in Chapter 11.)

Impact of Communication Delays or Disorders

All communication disorders can present in a range or a continuum of severity from mild disorder to severe/profound disorder. There is a direct relationship between the severity level of the communication disorder and the impact regarding the challenges that the student may face.

Students with speech deficits, such as articulation disorder, apraxia of speech, stuttering, cluttering and voice disorders, along with the language element of phonological disorder may present challenges in their ability to express themselves clearly. Listeners may not understand their messages clearly. The level of severity of their speech disorder will impact the challenges that the student may face. They may begin to avoid speaking in school and avoid social situations. They may begin to reduce their language complexity, impacting syntax, morphology and semantic language levels. They may become passive communicators and that may impact their self-esteem. They may become frustrated and upset when they cannot express themselves clearly. Their speech deficit can eventually impact their pragmatic/social language development.

Students who present with an auditory processing disorder may have difficulty processing auditory information quickly and efficiently. They may demonstrate difficulties understanding the speech or language of others in noisy listening environments, such as the classroom, lunchroom, morning information coming over the classroom speaker, etc. They may not understand or may misinterpret the verbal messages of others. These students may frequently ask for information to be repeated. They may demonstrate difficulty following directions and complex auditory directions. They may have difficulty attending (especially within noisy environments or when there is competing auditory input). They may not respond or demonstrate a delay in responding to the verbal communications of others. They may avoid social interactions as they have difficulty following conversations within group interactions. They may tune out auditory input (language) if it becomes too difficult to process. All aspects of language will be impacted: syntax, morphology, phonology, semantics and pragmatic language development. These children may be mislabeled as students with Attention Deficit Disorders because of the difficulty attending to auditory information. However, their attention may significantly improve with increased abilities to attend when visual processing supports are provided across total school environments.

Students who demonstrate receptive and/or expressive language disorders may have difficulties that will have a significant impact on completing academic work and participating within social environments. It is important to understand the impact that communication disorders have on students' success within academic curricular and social interactions.

Following are some examples of the challenges our students may face:

- Students may avoid speaking in school and other social situations due to significant speech disorders such as apraxia, stuttering and voice disorders.

- Students may lack the vocabulary necessary to express their intents.

- Students may not be able to process auditory information quickly and efficiently within a variety of academic and social contexts.

- Students may not have the ability to recall words (word recall) quickly and effectively within dynamic communication interactions (including classroom environments).

- Students may have slow processing rates, with difficulty keeping up with dynamic conversation (as well as classroom experiences).

- Students may have challenges interacting with various communication partners.

- Students may not have the syntax or morphological skills necessary within verbal language or written language tasks.

- Students may have difficulties with story retelling, which creates challenges when sharing personal experiences and academic narratives.

- Students may have challenges understanding the rules of a given social situation or may apply rules in a concrete manner, not able to be flexible.

- Students may be passive within social interactions.

- Students may talk and write only about their interests, unable to incorporate interests of others.

- Students may have difficulty expressing their needs, even though they may have good verbal abilities.

- Students may avoid interactions or interact with only a few individuals.

- Students may have difficulties with nonverbal aspects of communication such as body language, joint attention, eye contact, facial expressions and tone of voice.

- Students may engage in one-sided, unending monologues about their topic of interest.

- Students may not have the communication skills in order to repair unsuccessful communications, communication breakdowns or misunderstandings.

- Students may demonstrate literal, concrete interpretation of language with difficulty understanding figurative, abstract language including understanding social slang and cultural language differences (social interactions and/or academic curriculum).

- Students may demonstrate difficulties integrating multiple concepts.

- Students may need more time to process new information.

- Students may misunderstand the nonverbal or verbal communications of peers and adults.

- Students may have difficulty with reading comprehension and story interpretation such as understanding the perspective of characters, understanding character development, character relationships, understanding social contexts (cultural differences), time concepts and story development.

CHAPTER 5:

ALL BEHAVIOR IS COMMUNICATION

All behavior is communication! The overt and/or covert behaviors of students are their best attempts at communication as well as their reactions to our communications. These verbal as well as nonverbal communications are their accessible means of communication within communication contexts. Do we have an impact on the communications (behaviors) of students? The answer to that is a resounding YES! Minahan and Rappaport (2012) state that the only behavior teachers can control is their own. When we change the way we interact with students, we can then support students in increasing positive, effective communications and reduce challenging behaviors (communications). When we interact with students who experience challenging behaviors, in positive, productive ways, we can create positive communication change. However, when we respond to students with ineffective and/or negative communications, we can increase overt and covert behaviors and actually intensify challenging behaviors. How we respond to students' behaviors (communications) can actually escalate or deescalate their levels of anxiety, frustrations, anger and the overt behavior itself. Our communications can either build a trusting relationship with our students or destroy a trusting relationship.

It is important to consider the students' perceptions of, and their processing of, our communication intents and not how we think they should have been processed or understood. *Did we create a shared understanding, shared intents of our message? Does the student have communication challenges that could misinterpret our message or even a portion of our message? Did we use a communication style that supported our intended message or that conflicted with our intended message?* It is important that we do not make assumptions that our message was clearly received by students or that we delivered our message in a way that our intents were clear, understood and processed by students.

Our students come to all learning experiences, environments and communication partners with previous experiences. Experiences build upon one another to create knowledge. Our knowledge is based on our experiences. The experiences the students have had impact where they are today and what they bring to current interactions, learning situations and environments. As with all of us, they have had positive experiences and perhaps negative and/ or challenging experiences within their educational career and within social interactions. Hopefully, the balance between the two is not an equal one and positive experiences highly outweigh negative or challenging experiences. However, for our students with communication disorders, this may not be the case. Too often, our students have experienced frustrating interactions with educational staff, peers and, yes, family members. We remember past interactions and how they made us feel. We (students, teachers as well as parents) often come to expect a certain communication style from each other and react as such. This is referred to as our communication reputation. The good news is that we can change negative communication reputations to positive communication reputations by creating positive interactions and experiences that build upon each other. We can teach students this concept within the intervention process and we can also support parents. We must reflect on how we can modify our own interactions to create positive experiences for students, parents and ourselves.

Educators and parents have the power to create positive learning communication experiences and environments that promote successful interactions for our students. Implementing interventions that support students' abilities within the communication process (understanding language and expressing themselves successfully) along with changing the way we communicate with students, can significantly decrease ineffective overt behaviors (communications) and increase students' success within the communication process and success within academic and social contexts. We have the power to change the balance to increase positive communication experiences for our students. We cannot eliminate or change past experiences, but what we can do is create positive experiences that build upon each other and create a new reality for our students. This new reality should clearly express, yes, you are accepted and loved unconditionally; and yes, you are in a nurturing, caring environment that supports you at every level. Educators and parents have great power to create a new reality that tells all of our students that they are important and have potential to live amazing, happy lives. We can break down communication barrier walls, brick by brick. However, we must be patient. It took a long time to build these walls and it can take even longer to break them down. Shared knowledge, honesty, trust, acceptance, tolerance, patience, creativity, kindness and love are the powerful tools that will help create the new reality for our students.

Students' verbal and nonverbal communication skills, as well as, paralinguistic skills (e.g., vocal volume, intonation, vocal pitch, vocal quality, vocal stress and rate of speech) can provide valuable information regarding students' level of comfort, stress, anxiety, frustration or anger. The more escalated students may be, either inwardly or outwardly, the more likely students will use behavior (non-verbal communications) in lieu of words to express themselves. The collaborative team problem-solving process ensures on-going discussions regarding students' communication intents and will identify challenges or gaps in educational and communication programs. Educational team collaboration will result in implementation of appropriate supports and interventions.

Reflection Question

- Do we pay attention to all the means or ways students attempt to communicate and provide effective communication responses?

The case study regarding Vicky (Communication Disorder) is a perfect example. Vicky's nonverbal means of communication were missed (facial expressions, pointing, body language), which eventually led to her yelling and throwing herself on the floor. This level of communication could not be ignored and the adults immediately responded to her, reinforcing this means of communication (behavior). How we respond to students' behaviors or communications can actually escalate or de-escalate their level of anxiety, frustrations, anger, and the behavior itself.

Differential diagnosis through collaborative dynamic assessment is crucial to effectively understand students' communication strengths and challenges and to effectively implement interventions and student programs. We need to understand the communication intents that led up to the behavior and communications. Incorrect or incomplete assessments can lead to incorrect assumptions and eventually ineffective programming for students. This can increase students' levels of anxiety and frustration and intensify barriers between students, instructional programs and educational personnel.

Reflection Questions

- How do peers respond to students' behaviors (communications)?

- How do educators and parents respond to students' behaviors (communications)?

- Do educators and parents model understanding and acceptance in order to facilitate trusting relationships?

The dynamic student-teacher relationship is a complex one, mirroring the dynamic communication process. As in any communication interaction, there can be communication misunderstandings and/or breakdowns. Our communication style has a direct impact on repairing these communication breakdowns and either increasing or decreasing effective, positive communications of our students. Looking at students' communications, both non-verbal and verbal (behaviors), from students' perspectives will allow us the opportunity to understand their communication intents. When we consider the possible communication intents students may be attempting, with or without knowledge, we are looking at interactions in positive ways. We no longer are judging students, but supporting students' communication process. Avoiding judgment statements and asking specific intervention questions allows us opportunities to gather pertinent information when developing programs to support students.

A teacher stated that a student was demonstrating specific behaviors because he wanted attention, so he needed to be ignored. Wait, perhaps he did need our attention and did not have the communication ability to gain it in any other way. Perhaps he was not able to initiate an interaction. Ignoring this student's communications may have created his need to increase his nonverbal communications, until we could not ignore them any longer. By ignoring students and not acknowledging their communication intents, we can actually increase students' levels of stress, anxiety, frustration and perhaps mistrust. When we look at the behavior or communication through the student's perspective and not on judgment assumptions, it allows educational teams the ability to develop appropriate intervention programs. *Why does the student use this means to gain attention? Does the student have the ability to gain attention through appropriate communication means using effective language within all five language elements? If not, what intervention would support his or her ability to do so?* We need to understand our students through their eyes. When we take time to listen to what they have to say, both nonverbally and verbally, they will blow you away! When you take the time to listen to what is beneath the overt behavior, you will find beautiful spirits and people who have great things to say. They just need support in doing so. They need to trust that we care enough to listen!

Our perceptions drive our interventions and the way we interact with students. An honest reflection of your own perceptions regarding students' behaviors (communications) will allow you the opportunity to create positive changes in the way you interact with students. *Do you see students as being manipulative, disrespectful or even odd? Do you create a nurturing communication environment that builds trust and allows students the opportunity to interact and take chances without being judged or ridiculed by both peers and adults?* Trust is the building block of all relationships and positive communication exchanges. *Do your students see you as someone who attempts to understand their anxieties, fears and anger and someone they can trust to work through challenges?*

J. Baker (2008, 2015) once described teaching as actually 90 percent tolerating our own discomfort long enough to understand what to do next. Educators often feel a level of increased anxiety when faced with students' escalating behaviors (ineffective communications). When we can take a step back and understand that it is not about us, but about the student's ability or inability to cope and communicate, we can then create positive interactions. These interactions may require changing the means or way we communicate with the student. It may require use of visual processing, or simply allowing the student time. For some reason we often feel we need to talk and because our own emotions may be escalated, our communication style may become ineffective and even add to existing barriers. Perhaps we feel that we need to fill every silent gap with a verbalization. Actually, the opposite is true. Let there be silent gaps in which students can breathe and process. Let there be silent gaps in which you can nonverbally communicate acceptance and kindness. The student may simply need us to be quiet, observe and listen. Be an active listener, a quiet observer. In order to create positive change and positive student outcomes, it is important to reflect on our own practice, our own interactions and interaction style with students.

Reflection Questions

- Am I taking the interactions with this student personally?
- Am I controlling my own emotions in order to support this student?
- Do I see this student's behaviors and communications as a threat to my own competence?
- Am I engaging in power struggles with students?

- Do I tend to avoid this student, hoping to avoid ineffective interactions?

- Do I understand and know this student's communication challenges?

- Am I judging this student on experiences other professionals have shared with me?

- Do I have the critical knowledge to support this student?

- Have I collaborated with the educational team in understanding and supporting this student through the collaborative problem-solving model?

- Am I in a cycle of daily negativity and confusion with the student?

- Do I require professional development to support my effectiveness with this student?

Communication Frustrations and Anxiety

Students with communication disorders experience challenges which can lead to frustration and anxiety. Students with various communication disorders can experience significant levels of overt and/or covert anxiety. This anxiety can then lead to fear. They may experience anxiety and fear of sensory experiences, fear of not being able to express themselves effectively, and/or not knowing how to act or communicate within social situations. They may demonstrate fear and anxiety when attempting to follow rules and may not even understand the rules or why there even is a rule. They may demonstrate anxiety in not knowing how to initiate interactions and fear being rejected or ridiculed. They may fear not being able to recall words or to articulate clearly and become embarrassed.

Students may develop their own strategies to deal with the what-ifs, the frustrations, the anxiety, and the fear. The strategies they have created may have worked for them in gaining needs, wants, desires and in reducing anxiety, frustration and pain, even if only for a moment. (Remember our friend Vicky. She learned that throwing herself on the floor would definitely get a response from the adults in the room). Students apply these self-created strategies, which are often reinforced by adults, in anticipation of future stressful and painful interactions and communication environments. These strategies may have worked in one setting, so they attempt to use them again and again. If it worked once, it must work again. Perhaps the strategies do not work, so they dig their heels in and escalate the strategies to higher levels.

This creates barriers, walls, along with mistrust between the student and communication partners. Perhaps students do not trust that we can provide them with a safe, nurturing environment in which they can take chances. Perhaps they do not trust that they can communicate and may not understand how or why they are not successful. Perhaps they do not trust that they can be successful and they expect failure at every level. Perhaps students know they will be judged and do not trust that they will have acceptance or unconditional love. Perhaps they fear every situation and environment because they do not know when or where they will experience unbearable sensory overload. Perhaps they fear being watched and ridiculed when attempting to physically navigate hallways, gym classes, classrooms and/or the playground. We can go on and on.

If students cannot express themselves in a quick and efficient manner, they may use means of communication that are accessible to them at the time, such as: yelling, acting out, crying and/or throwing themselves on the floor. When they do this, they immediately get our attention! If a behavior worked in the past (was reinforced), the student may revert to this behavior again, with increased intensity. It is crucial that interventions address the underlying communication disorder and not simply the observed behavior.

An occupational therapist stated that a child's behavior was not due to communication, but to sensory needs. Yes, there are students who experience significant sensory challenges. The overt behaviors that students exhibit are their means of communication, the way they express their distress of sensory experiences. Students may express themselves through nonverbal means. Or, through verbal speech, they may have the ability to express some communication intents within some communication contexts. However, in high anxiety communication situations or when their neurological system is in alarm state, they revert to communicating through nonverbal means. They simply cannot say to us, "I am having a high sensory experience that is distressing. This is way too much input for me." Through the collaborative process, the educational team will identify and provide interventions that support students' sensory needs across environments. These interventions will include necessary communication supports.

Communication is a 24-Hour, 7-Day a Week Process

Communication is a 24-hour, 7-day a week process; it occurs all day within many different communication contexts and with many different communication partners. We do not simply communicate during certain times of the day or during certain classes at school and then take breaks at other times. Educators provide students successful communication opportunities all day, within various communication environments and with various communication partners (adults and peers). You are probably saying of course to this statement. However, implementation of behavior plans, communication supports and/or interventions are often fragmented with great gaps and inconsistencies within various school environments or contexts. In addition, there are educational staff who work with students who are unaware of or do not understand the behavior plans, communication supports and/ or interventions, and therefore do not implement them. This will impact the success of students' programs and students' outcomes. Students' overt behaviors may escalate, resulting in changes in students' educational placement and/or programming.

The collaborative team problem-solving model would support consistency and fidelity by creating a shared knowledge base regarding why, what, when, who and how regarding the implementation of behavior plans, communication supports and interventions across total school environments. The collaborative team problem-solving model would maintain open dialogue between all team members (including parents) regarding student's communications across total school environments.

Relationships between Domain Areas

Chart 5 outlines skills within specific domain areas. These domain areas are interrelated and have an impact on each other within dynamic communication and school environments. The successful interaction of each domain area is crucial for academic, social and vocational success. We do not simply isolate communication from executive functioning, cognitive processing, sensory experiences, motor skills or emotional/social levels. Our ability to communicate effectively is not only impacted by the interrelatedness of the communication areas but by these areas as well. Communication success is also impacted by our ability to use and maintain executive functioning skills, our abilities at cognitive processing, sensory processing, motor skills and our emotional levels. When we identify a deficit in one area, the intervention process will be impacted by contextual situations that involve the use of required skills in all of the domain areas.

Educators should consider all domain areas when developing communication interventions and behavior plans. Is the student interacting with familiar communication partners that support and organize the needed executive functioning areas or unfamiliar communication partners? Is there a high level of cognitive processing required within the communication exchange? Does the child need to integrate motor planning while integrating the intervention within the communication domain? What sensory experiences are happening during the communication exchange and how do these sensory experiences change within different environments or contexts? These are just a few examples of why it is crucial that interventions and behavior plans consider dynamic contextual information across domain areas. We need to know our students and how they maintain and integrate skills across all domain areas.

CHART 5: ACADEMIC, SOCIAL AND VOCATIONAL SUCCESS

Academic, Social and Vocational Success				
The following domain areas interact within dynamic environments. Integration of each domain area is crucial for academic, social and vocational success.				
Communication	**Executive Functions**	**Cognitive Processes**	**Sensory**	**Motor**
Joint attention	Response Inhibition	Theory of Mind	Auditory	Fine Motor
Receptive Language	Working Memory	Flexible vs. Rigid	Visual	Gross Motor
Expressive Language	Emotional Control	Concrete vs. Abstract	Touch/Tactile	Muscle Tone
Auditory Processing	Flexibility	Fiction vs. Reality	Taste	Coordination
Discourse Skills	Sustained Attention	Contextual Interpretation	Smell	Balance
Speech	Task Initiation	Detail vs. Gestalt Processing	Proprioceptive	Dysgraphia
Means of Communication	Planning	Perspective Taking		Motor Planning
Shared Intents	Prioritization	Critical Thinking		Visual-Motor Integration
Social Thinking	Time Management	Problem Solving		Kinesthesia
Pragmatics	Goal-Directed Persistence	Central Cohesiveness		
Semantics	Metacognition			
Syntax				
Phonology				
Morphology				
Non-Verbal Language				
Suprasegmental (e.g., stress, rhythm)				

Students with communication disorders may present with social/emotional challenges. They may exhibit behaviors that are secondary to their communication disorder. These behaviors are the communication means by which students express their communication intents. These behaviors can be misinterpreted and incorrectly judged by educators and parents.

Educational teams may identify students with educational disability classifications of emotional disturbance or other health impairment. Educational staff work diligently to understand what triggers the overt behaviors without assessing the challenges or deficits underlying the observable behaviors.

Students may be given the educational classification of autism or Asperger's syndrome. Educational teams meet to problem-solve behavior concerns and to create educational behavior plans. The behavior plans may be developed without consideration to non-verbal and verbal communication deficits or other relevant domain areas. An assessment may be initiated. The educational team may report that they do not have concerns within the communication domain. As a result, the communication domain is not included within the assessment process. There are students identified with the educational classification of Autism Spectrum Disorder; however, unfortunately, their educational programs do not include crucial assessments and interventions within the communication domain.

Parents and educators must understand that **autism is a communication disorder** (non-verbal communication as well as verbal communication)! Autism is a developmental disability that significantly affects verbal and nonverbal communication as well as the ability to engage within social interactions. In order for a student to qualify under the educational disability classification of autism, they must demonstrate deficits within: (1) verbal communications, (2) non-verbal communications, (3) social interactions (reciprocal social interactions) (ISBE, 2009).

Students who are identified with an educational disability classification of autism, emotional disturbance or other health impairment require dynamic communication assessments to identify necessary communication interventions and supports.

Case Study: Emily

Introduction

*Emily was a seventh-grade student with an educational disability classification of autism. Emily was included within the seventh-grade regular education program; she received social work services and occupational therapy along with special education supports. Emily did not receive speech-language communication services. **(RED FLAG!)** Emily's mother requested consultation as her daughter was having significant behavior challenges within her seventh grade regular education program. Emily's mother had concerns regarding Emily's communication abilities, such as communicating her needs, social interactions with peers and adults, use of coping strategies as well as sensory needs. The educational team initiated Emily's three-year re-evaluation to address her behavior challenges. A review of her records was completed.*

Review of Emily's Records

*A review of Emily's records indicated that Emily had received a speech and language screening in first grade. The results of this screening indicated her speech and language skills were assessed to be within age-appropriate limits. Emily had not received speech-language services at school since that initial speech-language screening in first grade. (Emily was now in seventh grade with a diagnosis of Autism.) **(RED FLAG!)***

Emily's Seventh-Grade Re-Evaluation (Assessment)

Speech-language communication skills were not assessed as the educational team determined that Emily demonstrated age-appropriate language processing and communication skills. However, embedded within each of the educational reports (psychological report, occupational therapy report, social development study and medical review report) and throughout the newly developed Individual Education Plan (IEP) and Behavior Plan the educational team outlined the following concerns: "Emily demonstrated limited verbal inter-actions with peers, challenges with starting and maintaining conversations, challenges with paying attention to directions and instructions, social-com-munication challenges, slow processing speed, atypical social communications, off-topic exchanges, difficulty receiving criticism, inappropriate vocal tone, prosody, modulations, verbal aggression, blurting out and interrupts others, misinterprets social situations and struggles with grasping sarcasm and humor."

Assessment recommendations were that Emily should continue with social work services and occupational therapy along with special educa-tion supports.

Follow-up Meeting

Emily's behavior challenges continued, and in fact increased in intensity, dura-tion and frequency. Emily's mother requested a follow-up meeting with Emily's educational team to discuss Emily's IEP program, her Behavior Plan and her progress. She requested that all team members be present at the meeting, along with the speech-language pathologist. The meeting focused on a collab-orative discussion regarding the communication and executive functioning data that were reported throughout the current documents/reports and how the data that the education team reported directly related to communication and executive function domains. This discussion created a shared knowledge base. The problem-solving discussion then looked at the inclusion criteria that the team reported to identify autism as Emily's primary educational disability classification. There was a mismatch between the data reported by the educa-tional team and the intervention program, as communication and executive functioning interventions and supports were not assessed or included in her program. Furthermore, the speech-language pathologist was not included within any portion of the process.

Recommendations

The recommendations were that the educational team re-open Emily's three-year re-evaluation to include the speech-language communication domain *along with the executive functioning domain in order to identify strengths, deficits and to collaboratively develop a comprehensive communication, executive functioning intervention program. The team identified a need for the educational team to participate within professional development activities to increase team knowledge within dynamic communication and executive functioning assessments.*

In order for our students to be successful within academic and social environments and maintain appropriate behaviors (communications), they must be actively engaged and active participants within all communication environments. Our students must feel that they are active members of our school and classroom communities. The ability to engage in successful communication exchanges at many different levels is crucial to maintaining appropriate communications (behaviors) within all contexts.

The goal for all students is to replace any inappropriate behaviors or communications with flexible, functional communication and to support access to these skills. By replacing inappropriate behaviors (communications) with functional effective communication, students can successfully participate and actively engage within all academic and social environments. Again, the objective is to support all students in the ability to maintain functional use of communication and success within the communication process within all communication contexts. What do we mean by functional communication? Functional communication is the ability to express our wants, needs, feelings and ideas (communication intents) successfully in all communication contexts, environments and with all communication partners no matter where we are within the learning process.

The collaborative problem-solving model must be employed within the assessment and intervention process, including the development of behavior plans. The collaborative problem-solving model ensures that educational teams participate in on-going discussions regarding students' strengths and challenges. It further enhances the effective development of appropriate interventions, supports and behavior plans.

Educational Classifications and Medical Diagnoses

Educators and medical professionals provide students with educational as well as medical classifications, labels, diagnoses that often become the focus of our discussions. Of course, diagnoses and educational classifications are important information; however, we know that a label does not determine who we are. Each one of us is a unique individual. Any label or diagnosis can manifest itself differently for different students. In fact, there are students who do not fit into any specific category; they may not meet all the criteria on the checklist and yet, we know they have communication challenges. Our discussions regarding behavior and communication applies to all students, whatever educational classification or medical diagnosis they may have or not have. When we look beyond the educational classification, the diagnosis and at the profile of individual students, we are then able to provide successful programming and interventions. When we look at each individual student's strengths, needs, challenges, successes, experiences, interests, anxieties and communications, we can then develop individualized student communication and educational profiles. This provides educators and parents opportunities to design communication and educational programs that make sense for the individual student. Educational and/or medical labels, diagnoses and/or classifications do not drive students' programs. Students' individual communication and educational profiles must always be the driving force when designing student programming.

Our discussions regarding communication will apply to the following students.

- Students with limited communication competence
- Students with communication delays and/or disorders (diagnosed or undiagnosed)
- Students with speech delays and/or disorders
- Students with language delays and/or disorders

- Students who are on the autism spectrum (Asperger's syndrome; high, moderate, low functioning autism)
- Students who have intellectual impairments
- Pre-verbal or emergent-verbal students
- Students who have good verbal skills, with significant communication deficits/challenges
- Students who have multiple disabilities
- Students with developmental delays
- Students with hearing impairments, or who are deaf
- Students with visual impairments
- Students who have physical impairments
- Students who have cerebral palsy
- Students considered to have attention deficit disorders
- Students considered to have an emotional disturbance
- Students considered as having behavior disorders and/or challenges
- Students who have learning disabilities
- Students who have had traumatic experiences
- Student who are medically fragile
- Students who are health impaired
- Students in which English is not their first language; ELL students
- Students without an identified disability
- Gifted student

CHAPTER 6:

EXECUTIVE FUNCTION SKILLS

Students who present with executive function deficits will have challenges within academic experiences and assignments (both individual as well as small and large groups, short-term assignments as well as long-term assignments). They may demonstrate communication challenges which may be misjudged by peers and adults as inappropriate behaviors.

Case Study: Billy (Executive Functions)

Introduction

Billy was a third-grade student within the regular education program; he did not receive special education services. Billy's teacher contacted his parents requesting that they come to school to meet with him as Billy was having behavior challenges at school.

Teacher's and Parents' Concerns

Billy's teacher reported that he was manipulative and would do only what he chose to do. He was disrespectful toward his teachers and argued with them. His parents were shocked as this did not sound like their son. His teachers reported that Billy did not follow assignment directions, did not complete his schoolwork and did not do his homework. When he did complete his homework, he did not turn it in. His teachers reported that Billy refused to transition from a preferred activity to another activity. His teacher further reported that he arrived late to his classes, past the bell. Billy appeared disorganized within his classes; he refused to keep his school supplies organized within his desk. He preferred to keep them in a basket under his desk and would have a meltdown when told he could not keep them there.

Billy's parents were frustrated and did not know how to help their son. They dreaded nightly homework time. Their fun-loving child erupted into angry rages or simply tuned out and shut down. They felt that his nightly struggles were impacting their family dynamics. They were very concerned and did not know how to motivate their son into caring about his schoolwork

Case Study: Noah (Executive Functions)

Introduction

Noah was a seventh-grade student within the regular education program; he did not receive special education services. The principal at Noah's school contacted his parents requesting that they come to school to meet with the educational team as Noah was having some behavior challenges at school.

Teachers' and Parents' Concerns

Noah's teachers reported that although he was a bright student, he was having difficulties paying attention to details, organizing himself and following through on instructions. He was constantly losing his books, pencils and homework. He was not allowed to take out library books from the school library, as he had lost several library books. He was getting into arguments with his peers in the classroom and in the lunchroom.

Noah's parent reported that he would talk excessively, interrupted others and was having difficulty organizing and keeping his room tidy.

Both Noah's teachers and parents reported that Noah was generally a pleasant and compliant student who did not require much discipline. However, he did not like school and would not apply himself to his schoolwork.

Billy and Noah exhibited deficits within the executive function domain along with communication challenges. However, the educators in both cases referred to the challenges that Billy and Noah were presenting as either behavior challenges or behavior issues. Students who present with deficits and/or challenges within the executive function domain are often misjudged as students who present with behavior challenges. It is crucial that parents and educators have a shared understanding or shared knowledge base regarding executive function skills and their impact within academic tasks and social communication interactions.

Executive function skills allow us the ability to complete daily tasks at school, home, work and within the community. We employ executive function skills when we complete assignments, clean our home, perform chores, follow schedules, inhibit our responses, plan short-term and long-term projects, manage our leisure time, develop and follow through on short-term and long-term goals, organize our schoolwork and materials, as well as inhibit inappropriate communications and/or behaviors (Dawson & Guare, 2010).

Executive function skills allow us the ability to process, plan and carry out procedures in order to complete tasks. The more difficult the task, the more we rely on our executive function skills. School assignments as well as social interactions present significant challenges for our students with executive function deficits as well as communication disorders. Dynamic communication interactions are high level executive function processes in that they are dependent on our ability to integrate and combine executive function skills and access language in a quick and efficient manner.

Executive Function Skills

Within the resource *Executive Skills in Children and Adolescents: A Practical Guide to Assessment and Intervention,* Dawson and Guare (2010) outlined eleven different executive function skills. *(This is a valuable resource for educational teams as they move forward within the collaborative model in assessing and supporting students with executive functioning disorders.)*

The eleven executive function tasks are interrelated within academic tasks as well as dynamic communications. Following are brief summaries of each executive function skill. Examples are provided as to how deficits within each skill may manifest and impact academic success as well as effective communication.

Response inhibition involves our ability to think before we act or speak. When we can resist the urge to say or do something (use our filters), we can then think about how our actions, our communications (both verbal and nonverbal), impact social interactions.

Students who demonstrate deficits within response inhibition may blurt out in class; they may verbalize every thought they have. They may say whatever they are thinking and may verbalize every idea they have, even if it is inappropriate or can be hurtful. We often refer to this as not having or using a filter. They may use word choices along with communication styles that may be perceived as rude and/or disrespectful. Students may argue with peers and teachers, and may make inappropriate statements to teachers and peers. Students with deficits within Theory of Mind have difficulty with response inhibition; they may not understand that what they say may have an impact on the listener. (Theory of Mind is discussed in Chapter 7.)

Working memory is the ability to hold information in our memory. Working memory allows us to use past experiences and apply them to current situations or to use them in the future.

Students who present with deficits within working memory may forget directions that were given by the teacher and may be perceived as ignoring the teacher. Students may forget that they have completed homework and/or that the homework is in their backpack and may not turn the homework in. Students may forget the verbal prompts and reminders from adults. They may have difficulty holding concepts in their mind and may not be able to complete tasks such as mental math, comparisons of concepts, explaining similarities and differences between concepts.

Emotional control is the ability to control our emotions. Emotional control allows us opportunities at completing or achieving goals and tasks. It also allows us the ability to control and manage our behaviors (communications).

Students who demonstrate deficits within emotional control may shut down during stressful academic tasks, such as tests or difficult assignments. They may become frustrated and may use inappropriate language. They may yell at an adult or peers when upset.

Sustained attention refers to the ability to maintain attention to a situation or task (including communication interactions) with or without distractions, as well as when the student may be fatigued or bored. The inability to sustain attention does not necessarily mean that the student has an attention deficit disorder. In fact, many students who have difficulties within this area respond well to interventions that are individually based on a student's profile, structured, consistent, implemented with fidelity and include visual processing supports. Their ability to sustain attention can increase significantly.

Students may appear bored within the classroom or within a communication interaction and may not maintain active listening or attention to the speaker and/or conversation. They may shut down in class and not be actively engaged. They may demonstrate difficulties maintaining attention to academic tasks or may not complete tasks in a timely manner. Students may walk away during a communication interaction and may not attend or respond appropriately during communication interactions (including classroom discussions).

Planning and prioritization is the ability to create a plan in order to reach a goal or to complete a task. In order to do this, we need to be able to identify what is important, to be able to prioritize, and then to determine what we need to focus on at the moment. We do this when we know we are going to enter a discussion or interaction. We think about what we are going to say and perhaps how we will say it. We often plan and practice challenging conversations, such as a discussion with a teacher and/or principal, job interview, school meetings and/or evaluation meetings.

Students who present with deficits within planning and prioritization may present with difficulties organizing and presenting oral presentation, class projects, as well as individual and group projects. They may not be able to create an outline for a project or may have difficulty completing multi-step assignments. Such students may have difficulty engaging in conversations.

Flexibility is the ability to change or revise our plans when there may be changes or new information (e.g., We have to cancel a planned family vacation due to weather or illness. School is closed for an extended length of time due to Covid-19. There was a fire drill during an academic lesson.). Flexibility is understanding that there is not just one way to do things or to say things. Flexibility allows us the ability to accept that there are many ways to do things (Cannon, Kenworthy, Alexander, Werner & Anthony, 2011).

Students who have deficits or challenges with flexibility may become overtly upset when a teacher tells him or her that they need to change, fix or correct their paper due to errors. They may become upset when an activity has to be canceled due to unknown obstacle, such as weather, when their teacher is absent or when a fire drill interrupts their schedule. A child may become upset and argue when a vocabulary word is used in a different meaning.

Case Study: Intermediate Student (Flexibility)

An intermediate level student became upset when a math teacher was talking about the math concept "compass." His understanding was that a compass was a device for determining the direction we are traveling in. He was in the Boy Scouts and that was his experience of the meaning of compass. He began to argue with the teacher, telling her that she was wrong and should learn what compass meant!

Students may learn a rule once and not be able to adapt when the rule is changed. For example, a student learns the rules for playing the game Uno; there are many different ways to play the game. The student cannot accept different rules when playing Uno with someone new, who has a different set of rules. Students may learn a rule in one class and apply that rule to all his/her classes, for example, putting toys away in a specific way, not allowing them to be put away any other way. A student may greet a specific communication partner (e.g., teacher) with one type of greeting and not be able to change it. The student may get stuck in a negative communication loop with a specific teacher, and not being able to change it (e.g., always expecting a positive and/or negative interaction and initiates each interaction as such).

Case Study: Donny (Flexibility)

Introduction

Donny was a sixth grade-student entering junior high with a diagnosis of Asperger's syndrome. The educational team met to discuss his transition from fifth grade to junior high school. There were at least fifteen educators along with his parents at the transition meeting. (Reg Flag!) The fifth-grade team reported that Donny was doing a "wonderful job" in fifth grade and they did not expect any difficulties at the junior high level. The team reported that "He was doing fine; he was highly verbal and in fact was extremely verbally manipulative." It was also reported that he would require minimal interventions at the junior high level.

Danny had several behavior incidences on his first day of junior high school (sixth grade).

Behavior Incident

Donny was curled up in a ball sitting in the corner of the hallway, the vice principal was standing over him verbally telling him (in a loud voice) to get up and get to the school office. Donny yelled back, "It's not my fault; she is a liar!"

Events Leading to this incident

Donny went to his first class in which the teacher told the class the homework rule was that they would not lose points if the assignment was late, just as long as they turned it in. He then went to his math class, in which the teacher explained that they would lose points for late assignments. Donny blurted out, "You are a liar!" The teacher told Donny to go to the office.

He left the room yelling that she was a liar, went to a corner of the hallway and refused to go to the office.

Analysis

From Donny's perspective the teacher must be lying, because the rule was that you do not lose points if your homework is late. He did not have the flexibility to change that rule in his mind from one class to another. Deficits within flexibility, poor emotional control and deficits accessing language during highly emotional situations led to his verbal outburst. From his perspective, what he did and said was very appropriate.

Recommendations

The immediate intervention to support Donny was to STOP TALKING TO HIM and ask the vice principal to please walk away in order to break the negative interaction cycle. The speech-language pathologist placed a visual support within Donny's visual field, sat quietly and waited. Once Donny was calm, visually looked at the visual support and then looked at the speech pathologist (joint attention), she asked him if he wanted to see the speech office.

*The speech-language pathologist introduced the process of making conversations visual (this intervention is discussed in Chapter 11). She took out a paper and began to write and draw information about herself and asked him to do the same. Once they were engaged in a visual conversation, she began to draw a chart. At the top of each row, she wrote his classes in order. Under each class, she wrote **rules for this _____class**. Through visual processing they wrote the rules regarding homework for each class. She left spaces for those classes he did not know the rule. She walked with him to the next class. His* *detective job for the day was to fill in each blank. He completed that. At the end of the day he came back to the speech office and they reviewed each class. His response was, "I think I will always do my math homework first, just in case I do not have time to finish all my homework!":* **The power of visual processing!**

Team recommendations were to schedule (as soon as possible) a collaborative team problem-solving meeting to discuss strengths and challenges within communication, cognitive processes and executive functioning domains. Further recommendations were to create structure, predictability and consistency through visual processing interventions and supports across all school environments.

Task initiation is the ability to begin a task in a timely fashion. Students who present with deficits or challenges within task initiation may not begin class and/or homework assignments. They may daydream and avoid beginning a task and may be perceived as procrastinating or not wanting to work. They may be perceived as being unmotivated or unwilling to work. Students may not initiate communication interactions quickly and efficiently. Unfortunately, students are often labeled or judged as being lazy.

Case Study: Billy (Task Initiation)

Introduction

Billy was a senior high school student with an educational disability classification of autism. He attended a technical program at the local junior college as part of his senior high school program. He was highly motivated within this program. Billy demonstrated challenges completing reports within his language arts/reading program as well completing his projects within his junior college technical program.

Discussion

Billy and I had a discussion regarding one of his assignments. He said he just couldn't seem to get things done. He looked at me and said, "You know, I am just really a lazy student." However, Billy was in no way a lazy student. I asked him why he said that and he replied that he had heard it all of his life. Can you imagine how this impacted his self-concept at so many levels? Yikes! Do we really do that to students? I explained to Billy that he was in no way lazy. We then discussed executive functioning and what that meant. He yelled, "Yes, that's me!"

Analysis

Billy had excellent verbal skills. However, his communication style was awkward within prosody, semantic content (concrete), and demonstrated deficits within his ability to apply social pragmatic language within dynamic communications. Billy demonstrated communication anxiety; he would shut down and would not ask for help. Billy also demonstrated significant deficits within the executive functioning domain: task initiation, organization, sustained attention and time management.

Recommendations

A visual processing plan was developed with Billy and his teachers. This visual processing plan supported Billy in initiating his assignments (short-term and long-term projects), his ability to persist at completing his assignments as well as supporting his organizational skills. The visual plan made time concepts visual for him. He successfully completed his senior year!

Organization is the ability to create a system in order to keep track of materials, information, supplies, etc. There are actually two levels to this skill. One is actually keeping the system and the second is using and maintaining the system.

Students who present with deficits or challenges with organization may have difficulties organizing school papers, assignments, homework and long-term assignments. Parents, teachers and/or para-professionals may support the student in organizing a binder, only to find the next day that it is either lost, or papers are missing. Students may not be able to keep desks or rooms organized. Students may not write down assignments in their homework assignment books, or if they do, may not follow through on completing assignments.

Time management is the ability to estimate how much time it will take to complete a task, to make sure you allow sufficient time and to be able to monitor the concept of passing time. This skill also involves the idea of a sense of time passing. Many of our students can tell time; however, they do not have an internal concept of the passing of time. They may say, "This is taking forever!"

Students may not realize how long they have been talking and monopolize the conversation. They may not complete assignments on time or may not want to initiate an assignment because they think it will take so long.

Goal-directed persistence is the ability to have a goal and to follow through with all of the steps needed to complete this goal without being distracted by other interests.

Students who present with deficits or challenges within this area may not be able to complete assignments, specifically assignments with multi-steps.

Metacognition is the ability to reflect on oneself, to problem solve, to self-monitor and to self-evaluate. This is a formal operational or higher level skill. Students may have difficulties within problem-solving situations and may have challenges or be unable to self-monitor behavior (communications). Students may have difficulty implementing study strategies. They may have difficulties at self-evaluation and may struggle answering adults' questions such as, "Why did you...?" They may have challenges within problem-solving processes that involve their own behaviors (communications). They may be able to apply appropriate problem-solving to role playing or test book examples, but unable to do so within their own dynamic communication environments. This is an extremely important concept within assessment and intervention processes. There are numerous social, communication and/

or behavior assessments as well as intervention programs in which educators ask students to examine a social scenario and provide possible communication solutions. The student may be able to complete this task; however, they may not be able to apply the same communication logic within their own dynamic communications.

CHAPTER 7

COGNITIVE PROCESSES

Cognitive processes play a large role in the effectiveness of students' communication skills and directly impact students' overt and covert behaviors. Deficits within a cognitive processing area, or combination of cognitive processing areas, will have a direct impact on students' abilities at processing language, accessing language effectively and efficiently as well as expressive language abilities. Each cognitive processing area plays a crucial role in students' abilities to maintain healthy relationships and effective interactions. When we understand students' levels within each of the cognitive processing areas, we can support them through effective interventions. The areas of cognitive processes include: Theory of Mind, flexible vs. rigid thinking, concrete vs. abstraction, fiction vs. reality or fact, contextual interpretation, detail vs. gestalt processing, perspective taking, critical thinking, problem-solving and central cohesiveness.

Theory of Mind (ToM)

Case Study: Mike (Theory of Mind)

Introduction

Mike was a fourth-grade student within the regular education program. He did not receive special education services. The school principal contacted Mike's parents to attend a meeting at school to discuss behavior concerns.

Teachers' Concerns

Mike's teachers reported concerns regarding his classroom performance. They reported that he was argumentative and would tell teachers they were wrong. He refused adult assistance and used a disrespectful tone of voice when speaking to them. Mike shouted out in class and would yell, "That is not fair!" He argued with his peers as well as his teachers. Mike screamed and yelled at his peers during a game of "UNO," stating that they did not know how to play. His peers were using rules for playing the game that were different from what he used for playing the same game at home.

Case Study: Tommy (Theory of Mind)

Introduction

Tommy was a second-grade student within the regular education program. He did not receive special education services. Tommy began to receive poor grades on his assignments and began to refuse to go to school. A meeting was scheduled with Tommy's parents and his teachers to discuss his behavior challenges and his poor grades.

Teachers' and Parents' Concerns

Tommy's teachers reported that he was demonstrating significant behavior issues at school. He was having difficulties interacting with his peers and teacher. He argued with his peers. They further reported that he displayed negative responses to his peers' ideas and would blurt out, "You are dumb!" He was refusing to follow classroom rules, stating they were wrong. Tommy would become upset at school and would hide under his desk, covering his head with his coat. He did not appear to notice his peers observing him.

Both Mike and Tommy demonstrated deficits within **Theory of Mind (ToM)**. It is important to understand what ToM is and its relationship to communication. A student who demonstrates deficits within ToM will demonstrate communication deficits, especially in the elements of semantics and pragmatics. ToM falls under the cognitive processing domain. ToM is understanding that not everyone thinks the same way as you do and that we understand that what we do or don't do will impact others' decisions to want to talk to us, be a friend or engage in relationships (Kowalski, 2010).

The term Theory of Mind (ToM) is often interchanged with the terms perspective taking and social cognition. Ashley (2007) discusses ToM as the ability to make attributions, the ability to create thoughts about others, or the process by which we make judgments regarding how our behaviors impact others. When we use Theory of Mind, "We make sense of what people say and do and predict what they will do next" (Ashley, 2007, p. 107). ToM allows us the ability to monitor our behavior in order to have successful interactions.

Social language is based on speakers' and listeners' understandings that not everyone has the same beliefs, purposes, needs, wants, feelings, perspectives, interests and opinions and that they can be different from our own. We can have a discussion in which we do not agree on a topic, idea or perspective. Every social interaction requires use of ToM by both the speaker and the listener.

Students who present with deficits within Theory of Mind may demonstrate challenges or deficits in understanding and use of appropriate semantic and pragmatic content, as well as understanding and processing communications of others. They may have difficulty understanding, discussing and accepting emotions, beliefs, ideas, thoughts, and opinions that are different from their own. Adults may misinterpret students' errors within social interactions (both informal and formal) as students being manipulative, rude, insensitive, disrespectful, and/or uncaring.

Case Study: Tony (Theory of Mind)

Introduction

Tony was an eight-grade student with a diagnosis of Asperger's syndrome. He was an extremely bright student who demonstrated significant deficits within Theory of Mind.

Theory of Mind Deficit

During a speech-language therapy session, Tony made the following statement using a very interesting tone of voice, "I do not understand how a very intelligent woman like you can actually believe in a deity that lives on a cloud." I wear my Christian cross most days and he could not understand how I could believe in God. To him, the idea of God was what he could concretely experience-the idea of God in movies or books, God depicted as a beautiful being looking down from the clouds. He could not understand any abstract understanding of God. His level of cognitive processing led to an abrupt communication style with choice of words, inflection and nonverbal body language that one might take as insulting.

As Tony demonstrated, students with deficits within **ToM** may have significant challenges taking the perspective of others and may not be able to understand both sides regarding beliefs or both sides in a disagreement. They may insist that they are right and will argue incessantly. They may appear blunt within their communication style and can appear to be insulting or rude.

Students with deficits within **ToM** may have difficulties understanding the intentions of others and/or may misinterpret them. They may think or say everyone is against them or are being unfair. They may have difficulties understanding slang, gender and/or cultural differences in communications. They may have difficulty understanding emotions of others (peers and adults) as well as predicting the behavior and emotional state of others. They may lack the understanding that their communications (non-verbal and verbal) impact how others think and/or feel. These challenges, along with difficulties explaining their own behavior (communications), may result in misunderstandings and/or verbal and nonverbal confrontations.

Students with deficits within **ToM** may demonstrate significant challenges within problem-solving situations and in predicting what might happen if, "I do or say this". They may have difficulty differentiating fiction from fact. They may be able to read about or discuss a social scenario and discuss given solutions. However, they may not be able to apply the same solutions or logic to their own interactions.

Students who experience deficits within **ToM** may experience academic challenges. They may have challenges understanding or using narratives, explanations, descriptions and persuasion within academic tasks as well as within personal interactions. They may have difficulty understanding the perspective within stories, characters and character development. This may impact their ability to understand or comprehend storylines and narratives; as well as, their ability to complete written assignments.

Students who have a deficit within Theory of Mind may present and be perceived as students with behavior challenges. They can be perceived as rude. They can be very blunt in their communication style, not understanding that what they say or do impacts the other person. What is on their mind comes out of their mouth with absolutely no filter. They may say exactly what they think, such as looking at a woman and stating, "You are really fat".

Students' who have deficits within Theory of Mind may want to do things that they find interesting and may refuse to engage in classroom topics and/or activities they find irrelevant. This includes insisting that they write only about what they like and not what the directions require. They may see no reason to write or read about what the teacher assigns. They may have difficulty understanding why they need to be interested in what other people are interested in and can be blunt in expressing this. They may present with unusual prosody: vocal tone, intonation pattern, vocal intensity and rate of speech.

Students who have deficits within **ToM** may use inappropriate hygiene or exhibit body functions (e.g., flatulence, picking their nose or pimples, belching) without understanding how others see these actions.

Educational staff often attempt to problem solve within a logic level students cannot process or understand. They may not understand and process the consequences that they may receive from adults and see them as completely unfair. This may lead to frustration, embarrassment, confusion, anger and actually escalate inappropriate behaviors (communications). They may provide too much information or not enough information, or provide information that they believe to be factual.

Case Study: Ethan (Theory of Mind)

Introduction

Ethan was a high school student enrolled in the regular education program. He did not receive special educational services. He was involved in a behavioral incident on the school campus.

Behavior Incident

Ethan was involved in an aggressive argument with a student on the school campus. This verbal argument escalated to a physical altercation. Ethan was taken to the principal's office. Ethan was asked to explain his actions. He explained the incident from his thought process, his perspective. He was told he was not cooperating and was given a consequence. Ethan was so distraught by the educational staff, in his mind, calling him a liar that he had a complete meltdown. He began to scream and use very inappropriate word choices. His parents were called to the school and he was given a one day out of school suspension. Ethan had no idea why he was suspended. When he returned to school, his first action was to confront the teacher who called him (in his mind) a liar and begin the cycle all over again. Does this sound familiar to anyone? Do you have students who are stuck in a cycle of behavior? In this student's mind, he was right.

Supporting Students with Deficits within Theory of Mind

Students' communication styles reflect their disability and not a personality flaw! Listen (active listening) and understand them from their perspective not ours, without any judgments. Become an active listener and work collaboratively with your educational team (including parents) in developing and understanding complete profiles for students within all domain areas. It is important to understand that their communication style is not about us and that we do not take their communications and communication style personally. Unfortunately, many educators and parents do and they engage in heated verbal interactions with students. The most important intervention is to stop talking, stop engaging within negative communication loops and to implement consistent and explicit visual processing supports.

These students may present with good verbal skills; however, this does not mean they are effective communicators. When we use verbal speech to attempt to process with these students, they often become frustrated and argumentative as they need to let us know we are WRONG, and they are RIGHT. They will hold on tight to their ideas. Unfortunately, too many adults get into verbal power struggles with these students. You will never win, if that is what you are attempting to do.

There are several very effective visual processing strategies that can support these students and help them work through and develop effective communication skills. As we just discussed, stop talking! Stop engaging in ineffective verbal communication exchanges. Remember my story about my sister who is deaf. She would close her eyes and stop engaging in arguments with me. The argument would stop because the communication loop was interrupted! Employ active listening from their perspective; make use of visual processing techniques such as visualization, making conversations visual and mind mapping. Make rules, directions and explanations visual. Explicitly explain visually the why for the student. Make use of the thinking like a scientist intervention in which facts are presented through visual processing and connections between ideas are facilitated. (These interventions are discussed in Chapter 11.)

Case Study: Kevin (Theory of Mind)

Introduction

Kevin was a very bright seventh-grade student. Kevin had deficits within communication and executive functioning domains as well as Theory of Mind deficit.

Theory of Mind Deficit

Kevin refused to show his teacher his math work or the steps to reaching an answer to a math problem. His teacher would explain that it was important that he show the steps within the process. However, Kevin found no reason to do so, as he knew the answer. He would argue this incessantly!

Recommendations

Kevin was very motivated by his grades and the number of points he would receive for assignments. The recommendations were to make directions to Kevin's assignments visually explicit and such that they made sense to Kevin. Kevin's teacher changed the directions to the math assignment to explicitly specify how he would receive his points and grade. He would receive one point for the correct answer and would receive four points when he showed the steps to the answer. Kevin now had a reason to show his work-the extra points. If he did not show the points, he would not get a good grade on his assignment. He included the steps to the math questions!

CHAPTER 8:

COMMUNICATION ASSESSMENT

The Power of Observation and Active Listening

Speech-language pathologists assess students' communication skills to determine whether students have deficits within the communication domain, to identify needed communication goals, objectives, interventions and supports as well as to monitor students' progress and generalization of communication skills across communication contexts (environments and persons). Dynamic communication assessment is the first step toward developing effective programming and interventions for students with communication disorders. Speech, the five elements of language (syntax, morphology, phonology, semantics, pragmatics) and contextual information are interrelated within dynamic communication environments. Each communication area is addressed within assessment questions that determine assessment components as well as communication contexts.

The collaborative problem-solving model ensures that communication assessments are coordinated through educational team collaboration and that educational programming and interventions are determined through shared decision making based on assessment data.

The evaluation process can be a stressful and anxious time for parents and students. In fact, it can be stressful for educators as well. The collaborative team problem-solving model supports educators, parents and students through the evaluation process by creating trusting relationships in which educational teams (including parents) work toward understanding students, their strengths and challenges. The collaborative problem-solving model establishes policies and procedures in which the assessment process can remain student centered and data driven. Throughout the assessment process it is crucial that educational teams build trusting relationships with parents, students and each other, in order to have meaningful, honest discussions regarding students' strengths, challenges and needs.

Parents, as members of the educational team, participate throughout the assessment process. The collaborative team problem-solving model includes crucial information from parents within assessment discussions. It is important to understand our students' parents' perspectives within the assessment process without any judgments. Educators have not walked in parents' shoes and have not had the everyday experiences that they have had with their child. Parents have seen their child in the best of times and in challenging times and all that goes in between. Honor, respect and appreciate their experiences, as they have raised and loved their child. They come to the problem-solving table with knowledge about their child that educators may not have. Parents need to feel that they can trust that the educational staff will engage in data based problem-solving discussions that will support comprehensive assessments, leading to effective educational programs, supports and interventions for their child. The collaborative model allows educational teams opportunities to engage in interactive styles that facilitate trust, understanding and support.

It is also important that parents honor, respect and appreciate the knowledge, expertise and experiences that educators have. Educational personnel are professionals who are committed to supporting all students' success. It is important for parents to understand educators' perspective without any judgement. Parents have not walked in educators' shoes either (at least in the experiences of the school environment with their child). Educators have experiences with their child in a different environment, different contexts and within different sets of rules. Parents' interactions with educational personnel can be positive and informative by asking for objective data and clarifications when they do not understand. Parents can ask educational personnel questions in a positive, effective communication style that will result in positive problem-solving discussions.

When parents and educators work collaboratively within meaningful student-centered discussions, based on objective data, effective assessments can be conducted that will lead to effective programming for students. The collaborative process facilitates relationships, based on underlying trust, in which the focus of educational teams' goals is to conduct assessments and develop educational programming, interventions and supports that will provide positive learning experiences for students. Collaboration increases opportunities that assessments will be coordinated and complete and examine students' entire communication and educational profiles.

Students are crucial members of the collaborative process and deserve the same respect and appreciation for the experiences they have had or have not had. When educational personnel and parents think outside our box of knowledge or what we think the student is doing, communicating or not, we are then able to understand communication from the students' perspectives. It is important to look at and understand communication through our students' eyes, no matter what level of functioning they may be at.

In addition, it is as important that educators afford the same respect of each other and create trusting environments in which honest problem-solving discussions can occur. No one should feel judged by any statements, suggestions or questions they may have.

Differential Diagnosis

Individuals with Disabilities Education Act (IDEA) 2004 mandates that school districts conduct assessments to determine whether students have a disability under one of the 14 educational disability classifications, to identify any deficit areas, along with strengths and challenges of individual students, in order to develop individualized effective educational programs, supports and interventions.

IDEA 2004 defines the term "child with a disability" to mean a child *"with intellectual disabilities, hearing impairments (including deafness), speech or language impairments, visual impairments (including blindness), serious emotional disturbance (referred to in this chapter as 'emotional disturbance'), orthopedic impairments, autism, traumatic brain injury, other health impairments, or specific learning disabilities; and who, by reason thereof, needs special education and related services."* IDEA expanded on this definition to include *"The term 'child with a disability' for a child aged 3 through 9 (or any subset of that age range, including ages 3 through 5), may, at the discretion of the State and the local educational agency, include a child experiencing developmental delays, as defined by the State and as measured by appropriate diagnostic instruments and procedures, in one or more of the following areas: physical development; cognitive development; communication development; social or emotional development; or adaptive development; and who, by reason thereof, needs special education and related services."* [20 U.S.C. §1401(3)]

IDEA 2004 mandates school districts implement a variety of assessment tools in order to gather relevant, functional, developmental and academic information about the student. This includes information provided by the parents. *"In conducting the evaluation, the local educational agency shall ... use a variety of assessment tools and strategies to gather relevant functional, developmental, and academic information, including information provided by the parents, that may assist in determining ... whether the child is a child with a disability; and the content of the child's individualized education program ... not use any single measure or assessment as the sole criterion for determining an appropriate educational program for the child...".* [20 U.S. C § 1414 (b) (2) (A)]

Effective assessment procedures begin within the collaborative team problem-solving process, in which educational teams (including parents) collaborate regarding screening, assessment questions, domain meetings, assessment procedures and contexts. In addition, the educational team collaborates on assessment results as well as educational programming. However, the assessment process does not end there, as it is interrelated with the intervention process. Assessments and interventions create an ongoing loop. We continue to collect data and adjust students' programs, supports and interventions as they progress or not.

Chart 6 demonstrates the dynamic collaborative assessment-intervention loop. There is an ongoing relationship between assessment and intervention. Assessments begin with assessment questions, which then determine the assessment procedures (data collection) as well as assessment instruments. This objective data drives educational programing, supports and interventions. Data are collected to determine the effectiveness of the educational programming, supports and interventions. New evaluation (data) questions are formed. Additional data are collected.

CHART 6: DYNAMIC ASSESSMENT – INTERVENTION LOOP

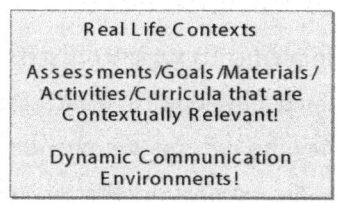

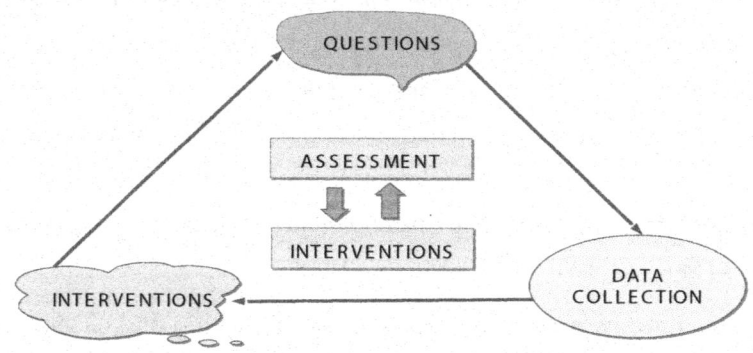

Request for an Evaluation (Assessment)

All school districts have a process in which all children, birth through 21 years of age, go through screening procedures to identify students who may need special education services (ISBE, 2009). If a student does not pass a screening instrument, the educational staff will contact parents to determine what if any additional action should be taken. Students' speech-language skills are screened to determine possible communication delays or deficits. Speech-language screening instruments and procedures vary from district to district. It is possible that a student can pass a speech-language screening and still have deficits within the communication domain. This may occur because speech-language screening instruments may not address or include all communication areas within critical contexts; the screening instruments may be limited in scope and contexts.

A referral for an evaluation can be requested by the school district (teacher, or any other educational personnel). A referral is the process of asking for an evaluation. Parents' consent is required prior to the district conducting an evaluation. [20 U.S. C. §1401 (3)]

Parents have the right to request an evaluation for their child. Parents do not pay for any evaluation that the district administers, as the evaluation is a component within Free and Appropriate Public Education (FAPE). Parents' request for an evaluation must be done in writing; a verbal request is not sufficient. A parent may request an evaluation if their child has been struggling in school within academic, functional and social contexts. An evaluation would determine if the student's difficulties are due to a disability and if the student qualifies for special education services from the district: *"… either a parent of a child, or a state educational agency, other state agency, or local educational agency may initiate a request for an initial evaluation to determine if the child is a child with a disability."* [20 U.S. C. § 1414 (B)]

The date of a parent's referral or request is documented. The school district has fourteen days from the written request to decide if it will proceed with the parents' request for an evaluation or not. *"If the district determines that the evaluation is not necessary, it must notify the parents in writing of the decision not to evaluate and the reasons for the decision"* (ISBE, 2009).

Parents have a right to challenge the district's decision through requesting a due process hearing. A due process hearing is a formal means of conflict resolution available to both parents and school districts. A due process hearing is conducted in a manner that is similar to an adversarial court proceeding. It is conducted before a neutral arbitrator who will render a decision at the conclusion of the hearing (ISBE, 2009). Parents and/or school districts can have a wide range of disagreements or disputes as they collaborate in providing assessments, programming, supports and interventions for students. Fortunately, most disputes can be resolved when educational teams (including parents) work within the collaborative problem-solving model. The collaborative model allows educational teams ample ongoing opportunities to meet and participate in data driven discussions and conflict resolutions. However, there are times when disputes require a formal proceeding to be resolved. A detailed explanation of due process can be found within the ISBE, 2009 document: *Educational Rights and Responsibilities: Understanding Special Education in Illinois.* (The Board of Education for each state can provide the criteria for due process proceedings.)

Due process requires a great deal of time and financial obligation. Due process proceedings can break down positive collaborative working relationships and communications. The amount of time parents and educators spend on a due process proceeding would take away from planning students' programs, teaching and parenting. The process is stressful and tedious for all involved and can increase levels of anxiety for parents, educators and students. **Due process should be the last resort that both parents and school districts turn to for dispute resolution.**

The Assessment Process

Domain Meetings

Once a referral for assessment (from either educational staff or parents) has been accepted by the school district, the educational team will schedule a domain meeting. The assessment process begins at the domain meeting.

Educational teams review any existing evaluation information that is currently available on the student in order to determine whether this information is sufficient to determine the student's eligibility or continued eligibility for special educational services. If not, educational teams would then determine what additional information is needed. (Examples of existing information may come from outside agencies, private therapy assessments and/or reports, parents, district testing, medical reports and/or classroom performance.) Parents have the right to request that the school district complete an evaluation to determine students' eligibility. The evaluation must be completed within sixty days after the school district receives signed consent from parents for the evaluation. [20 U.S.C. §1414 (C)] Consent for the evaluation is signed by the parents at the end of the domain meeting.

The purpose of a domain meeting is to determine what if any additional information is needed in order to determine: students' eligibility for special educational services, the educational disability classification or if a student continues to be eligible for special education services.

Goals for domain meetings are to

1. Determine if additional information is needed to determine whether a student is eligible for special education services or continues to be eligible for special education services.

2. Determine what domain areas, need to be assessed as well as assessment components.

IDEA (2004) mandates that educational teams examine all areas of student's functioning when completing initial evaluations and making determinations regarding whether the student is a student with a disability, as well as to determine total educational needs. The domain meeting facilitator (usually a district administrator) will facilitate an educational team discussion (which includes parents) within each domain area (refer to Chart 7) to determine if the specific domain would be relevant to the evaluation process. The following three questions are discussed in detail and corroborated with objective data within each domain area:

1. *What is the existing information about the child?*

2. *What additional evaluation data are needed?*

3. *What sources will be used to gather the data?*

Educational Disability Classifications
(IDEA, 2006, Sec. 300.8, (c))

(Refer to Appendix 2 for a definition of each disability classification.)

Autism	*Emotional Disturbance*
Specific Learning Disability	*Intellectual Disability*
Hearing Impairment	*Deaf-Blindness*
Deafness	*Multiple Disabilities*
Visual Impairment – including blindness	*Speech or Language Impairment*
Orthopedic Impairment	*Traumatic Brain Injury*
Developmental Delay	*Other Health Impairment*

The assessment process determines whether students are eligible for special education services and under what educational disability classification. The communication assessment will determine whether students have a speech-language communication disability and whether students qualify for speech-language (communication) educational services. A comprehensive speech-language communication assessment is required to determine students' communication abilities and/or deficits as well as qualifications for speech-language communication services. IDEA 2004 mandates that students are eligible for speech-language therapy services when they have a speech-language communication deficit that has an adverse impact on academic and/or functional performance within total school settings.

Speech or language impairment can be identified as students' primary educational disability classification or secondary educational disability classification. Students who are identified under another educational disability classification (e.g., specific learning disability, hearing impairment, developmental delay, autism, etc.) may present with communication deficits and receive speech-language services as resource support, without speech-language impairment being identified as the primary or secondary educational disability classification. *It is important for educational teams to determine if additional communication information (data collection and/or communication assessments) is necessary within the communication domain to identify communication deficits, needed communication programming, services, supports and/or interventions.*

CHART 7: ASSESSMENT DOMAIN AREAS

Academic Achievement: Current or past academic achievement data pertinent to current educational performance.
Functional Performance: Current or past functional performance data pertinent to current functional performance
Cognitive Functioning: Data regarding cognitive ability, how the child takes in information, understands information and expresses information.
Communication: Information regarding communication abilities (language, articulation, voice, fluency) affecting educational performance.
Health: Current or past medical difficulties affecting academic performance.
Hearing/Vision: Auditory/visual problems that would interfere with testing or educational performance. Dates and results of last hearing/vision test.
Motor Abilities: Fine and gross motor coordination difficulties, functional mobility or strength and endurance issues affecting educational performance.
Social/Emotional Status: Information regarding how the environment affects educational performance (life history, adaptive behavior, independent functioning, personal and social responsibility and cultural background.)

Educational teams may determine what specific domain areas should be assessed or not (e.g., communication domain) without a comprehensive detailed discussion that is substantiated with objective data. For example, the meeting facilitator will ask general questions within the three areas of: (1) What is the existing information? (2) Do we need additional information? (3) What sources will be used to gather the data? The responses from the educational staff may not include objective data, may not be comprehensive within all domain areas and may not address critical contexts. *"If the IEP Team and other qualified professionals, as appropriate, determine that no additional data are needed to determine whether the child is a child with a disability or continues to be a child with a disability and to determine the child's educational needs, the local educational agency ... shall notify the child's parents of that determination and the reasons for the determination; and shall notify the parents of their right to request an assessment to determine whether the child is a child or continues to be a child with a disability and to determine the child's educational needs..."* [20 U.S.C. §1414 (A)(i)(ii)]

Example Domain Meeting Discussions: Communication Domain

Example 1: *Existing Information.* The educational team does not report any concerns regarding the student's communication skills. They state that the student does fine in class. The educational team decides that there is no need for **additional information** within the communication domain. A speech and language assessment is not required and there is no need to gather additional communication information.

The problem with this recommendation is that the educational team members may not have crucial knowledge regarding all the areas of communication and all the critical contexts as well as the impact on academic, functional and social success. Explicit objective data regarding the student's ability to communicate effectively across all communication partners and contexts were not provided and discussed.

Example 2: *Existing Information.* The speech-language pathologist may report that the student has met current IEP speech-language goals. The student does not require further speech-language services as speech-language goals have been met. It is determined that there is no need to gather *additional information* within the communication domain. No additional communication assessment or data are required, with recommendations to dismiss the student from speech-language services.

The problem with this recommendation is that the speech-language goal area may have targeted one component of communication. Success of the goal may not indicate success within speech, all five language elements and within all communication contexts. The student's success within one goal area does not ensure communication success within all speech and language elements and within dynamic environments within all communication contexts

Example 3: *Existing Information.* The speech-language pathologist may report that the student passed a speech-language screening and therefore, there are no concerns within the communication domain. It is determined that there is no need to gather **additional information** within the communication domain as the student passed the speech-language screening instrument. Communication assessment is not required.

The problem with this recommendation is that it is possible that a student can pass a speech-language screening and still have deficits within the communication domain. The screening instrument may not include all communication areas within crucial contexts. The speech-language screening instrument may be limited in scope and contexts. *"The screening of a student by a teacher or specialist to determine appropriate instructional strategies for curriculum implementation shall not be considered to be an evaluation for eligibility for special education and related services."* [20 U.S.C. §1401(E)]

Example 4: *Existing Information.* The speech-language pathologist may report that the educational team reported concerns within the communication area and may include specific concerns from educational staff and/or parents. ***Needed Additional Information:*** The educational team may determine that a speech-language evaluation is relevant and necessary. ***Sources from which data will be obtained:*** The speech-language pathologist will complete a speech-language evaluation.

The problem with this recommendation is that it does not specify assessment questions or explicitly state what the components of the speech-language assessment will be and within what contexts. Speech-language pathologists can complete speech-language assessments and overlook crucial communication areas, which result in not identifying significant communication disorders. This can occur when speech-language pathologists administer specific formal assessment tools in which they do not have a thorough understanding of what the specific test actually assesses, as well as if the results from a particular test will support the student's communication and educational programming. Do the results from a particular formal communication assessment target and answer the assessment questions, resulting in effective communication programming for the student? Furthermore, this can occur when crucial contexts are not assessed, or when the speech-language pathologist has limited input from educational team (including parents). Assessment is not one-size-fits-all.

Assessment Questions

The assessment process begins when educational teams ask probing questions to determine the required assessment components within relevant domain areas. The assessment questions further determine assessment contexts along with specific assessment tools and assessment procedures. The assessment questions provide educational teams assessment goals that directly relate to students' challenges and strengths. They allow educational teams opportunities to collect assessment data in an effective, efficient and objective manner.

Assessment questions allow educational teams collaboration opportunities regarding why, what, how, when and who in gathering pertinent, meaningful assessment data within relevant environments for individual students. Assessment questions should be discussed for each of the domain areas.

It is important to note that educational personnel often report and document pertinent communication information within the other domain areas. For example, under social-emotional status, the team may report difficulties with interactions or expressing emotions or other communication intents. It may be reported under academic achievement that the student has difficulty within reading and writing assignments (which may be language based) or that the student does not participate in classroom discussions. The educational team may report concerns regarding students' behavior. Their descriptions regarding the behavior may in fact identify communication challenges. This information is crucial in determining communication deficits and needed supports. The collaboration process would facilitate a discussion between educational personnel and parents in which all relevant information is included into the student's assessment profile.

Our discussion will focus on the communication domain. However, communication is impacted by each domain area; all domain areas are interrelated. The assessment process begins with assessment questions within each domain area: communication, academic achievement, executive functions, cognitive processing and motor and sensory integration.

Following is a list of example communication questions educational teams may present and discuss at formal domain meetings. *(This is not a complete list of possible questions and not all of the questions will be pertinent for every student.)*

- What is the primary language of the student's home, general cultural identification and mode of communication? What language is spoken in the student's home? What language is used most comfortably and frequently by the student (e.g., language spoken, sign language)?

- Would this student require a bilingual evaluation and/or an interpreter?

- Do the parents require an interpreter at educational meetings?

- What is the student's level of hearing and vision acuity?

- What information does the team currently have regarding the student's communication skills?

- Did the student receive speech-language services at the preschool level or elementary level? If so, what assessments were completed and what were the student's goal areas? Does the student have previous IEPs? Was the student dismissed from speech-language services? If so, why was it recommended that speech-language services be discontinued?

- Has the student received previous communication assessments either at school or from an outside agency? What were the components of the assessment and in what contexts? What were the results and recommendations?

- Does the student receive private speech-language services? What are the goal areas?

- Do the parents have communication reports from private agencies?

- Does the student receive counseling support from either school personnel or an outside agency? What are the goals of the counseling sessions?

- Do the parents have any concerns within the communication area? If so, what are they?

- Does the student experience behavior issues at school? If so, what are they, when do they occur and how often?

- Do educational staff have concerns regarding the student's communication skills? If so, explicitly describe them.

- What is the student's level of speech intelligibility across communication contexts? Do peers and/or adults have difficulties understanding the student's speech skills?

- How does the student express herself or himself across school environments with peers and adults?

- Does the student demonstrate difficulties expressing himself or herself verbally and/or in written form?

- How does the student process auditory information within various environments (structured, non-structured, quiet, noisy or with increased language load)?

- How effective is the student in expressing himself or herself across all environments with all communication partners? Adults vs. peers? Formal vs. informal? Structured vs. unstructured? Social? Academic? Vocational?

- How does the student communicate within diverse communication contexts?

- How does the student initiate communications with peers and/or adults?

- How does the student process language (visual vs. auditory language)?

- How does the student interact with peers in various environments?

- Does the student demonstrate breakdowns within the communication process? If so, at what level?

- Does the student avoid communication situations?

- How does the student perform within written language assignments?

- Does the student actively engage and participate within classroom discussions, either one-on- one, small group and/or large group?

- How does the student interact with adults and peer?

IDEA 2004: Academic, Social, Vocational Impact

Educational staff may express that the student's communication deficits or challenges are not impacting his or her academic performance as the student is maintaining passing grades. Because of this, the student does not qualify for services from the speech-language pathologist or educational team within the communication domain. The educational staff may acknowledge that the student may have challenges expressing himself or herself, communicating within various environments and interacting with peers and/or adults. They may discuss educational challenges within the reading and writing domain. Educators may acknowledge and have concerns regarding the fact that the student is demonstrating behavior challenges. However, it is not until the behavior challenges become severe, overt, consistent and interfere with classroom management that the educational team may seek consultation. Unfortunately, the speech-language pathologist may not be included within the team discussion regarding the student's behaviors (communications). A behavior plan may be developed; however, it may not address the underlying causes of the overt behaviors, that of ineffective communication abilities. The behavior plan may have a reinforcement system that may be difficult for the student to consistently achieve due to communication deficits, as well as deficits within the domains of executive functioning, cognitive processing, sensory and motor skills. The challenges within these domains may lead to covert and/or overt anxiety, stress, frustrations, depression and eventually into "overt behaviors". Educational staff may not understand (have crucial knowledge) that the student's overt behaviors have a direct connection and are a result of communication deficits, which in turn have a direct impact on academic and social success. Overt behaviors (communications) have a significant impact on students' academic and social success, whether the student is maintaining passing grades or not.

IDEA 2004 brought about important changes regarding evaluations, specifically regarding students' eligibility for special educational services, including speech-language communication domain. The fact that students may be receiving passing grades and that the educational team may report that the communication deficits do not impact the student academically are not acceptable reasons for students to be denied speech-language communication services and supports.

IDEA 2004 mandates that students qualify for special education services, including speech-language communication services, when deficits impact students' performance and success within academic and/or functional areas. IDEA 2004 mandates that schools may not focus predominantly or exclusively on academic skills in determining whether students qualify for special education services, but must consider all areas of students' functioning within total school settings. Furthermore, communication adverse effects must be determined on a case-by-case basis, based on the unique individual needs of a particular student. Students' eligibility for speech-language communication services must be determined by the impact of the communication disorder within the total school setting, and not just the academic setting (Estomin, Flynn, Mele-McCarthy, Rudebusch & Witmire, 2007a). Stating that communication challenges are not impacting educational performance is not a sufficient response to deny students' eligibility for services (Kowalski, 2010), [20 U.S.C. § 300.107 (a), 300.117].

Academic achievement refers to students' performance within academic areas such as math, reading, language arts, science, history, along with art, music, gym class, computer class and library. In order for the educational team to determine whether students' communication deficits impact academic performance, it is crucial that they understand the connection between speech, language, communication and the areas of academic performance, such as literacy skills, along with a thorough understanding of the academic curricular. Communication skills, receptive and expressive language skills as well as speech skills provide an important foundation for literacy skills, are embedded throughout academic curricular as well as social interactions.

Functional performance refers to skills that are not considered academic or related to students' academic performance or achievement such as grades and test scores. Functional skills are skills that are used within everyday life experiences (including social skills and communication interactions). Examples of functional communication, interpersonal skills and contexts are social conversations, peer and/or adult interactions, group discussions, school clubs, athletics, recess, play interactions, assemblies, field trips and after school activities. An adverse effect on functional performance is present when the communication disorder limits students' performance or participation within any interpersonal activities within the total school setting (Estomin, Flynn, Mele-McCarthy, Rudebusch & Witmire, 2007a).

These changes have significant implications regarding collaborative communication assessments. The collaborative educational team process facilitates discussions regarding impacts of communication deficits on students' academic and functional success. If a collaborative team discussion has not occurred; it can be initiated. Should the school district decide not to proceed with an evaluation, providing parents with written notification, parents can request a collaborative team meeting to discuss their concerns regarding the district's decision. Parents can request that a speech-language pathologist attend this meeting, along with additional educational team members. Parents can begin the discussion by voicing concerns and asking questions. Questions are an excellent way to begin a collaborative discussion. It is important that the discussion regarding the assessment questions remain student centered and data driven. In the absence of an agreement, parents have the right to challenge the school district's decision by initiating a due process proceeding.

Following are examples of questions parents and/or educators may ask at collaborative educational team meetings:

- Why did the school district determine a communication evaluation was not necessary? What data was this decision based on? Who determined that the communication evaluation was not necessary?

- What information, objective data, does the educational team currently have regarding the student's communication skills and within what environments or contexts?

- What objective data does the team have regarding student's functional communication performance and student's active participation within total school settings?

- Could the student's challenges within the academic curricular be related to language or communication deficits?

- Could the student's overt behaviors be related to communication deficits or challenges?

- What are the possible communication intents of the student's behavior?

- Would providing communication supports and increasing communication competence replace and/or reduce ineffective communications (overt behaviors)?

- Would providing communication supports and increasing communication competence impact student's success within the academic program?

- Has the student been an active participant in the educational learning process? What does that active participation look like for this student? How does the student engage with peers and adults?

- What challenges does the student demonstrate within interactive communications with both peers and adults?

An incorrect or incomplete diagnosis can result not only in ineffective programming but can increase levels of frustration, stress, anxiety, fear and embarrassment that students and/or the students' parents are experiencing. Misdiagnosis and/or misclassification along with incorrect or incomplete information directly impacts students' success within academic and functional contexts and can be devasting and impact students' success for many years. Students can be misdiagnosed due to incomplete assessment components. There are students who have significant communication deficits who are identified as students with attention deficit disorder (other health impaired), as students with behavior and/or emotional disturbance as well as students with intellectual impairments. *(Note: There are many students who do appropriately qualify under these educational disability classifications. A comprehensive collaborative assessment process would facilitate accurate differential diagnosis and identification of educational disability classifications, effective student programming, interventions and supports.)* Communication assessment is a crucial consideration within all educational classifications.

Educators may identify students' educational disability classification without the critical knowledge base of how communication impacts all areas of performance. This can result in incomplete student communication and educational profiles. In addition, incomplete student communication profiles can be the result of assessing the communication skills for all students with the same diagnostic battery. Communication assessment is not one size fit all! Communication assessment should be based on the unique needs of a particular student. There are students who require communication interventions and supports; however, because of incomplete assessment processes they do not receive the proper supports. For example, a student may be diagnosed with an attention deficit disorder and may be given medication to address his/her needs. However, a calming sensory treatment plan along with visual processing communication interventions may appropriately address the student's needs in lieu of medication. A student may be labeled as a student with behavior challenges, in which a behavior plan is development and implemented. The success of the behavior plan may be difficult due to communication, executive functioning or cognitive processing deficits. Communication, executive function and/or cognitive processing interventions and supports may address the student's needs and should be included within any behavior plan.

In addition, there are students in which communication deficits were identified; however, they did not quality for services, as they were already meeting their potential. This is referred to as discrepancy formula or cognitive referencing, which resulted in denial of needed services to students whose achievement in certain areas may be commensurate with their overall

IQ score. The American Speech-Language-Hearing Association has eliminated discrepancy formula (cognitive referencing) when identifying communication disorders or determining eligibility for services due to serious "theoretical and statistical flaws on the practice of comparing results of standardized tests" (Estomin, Flynn, Mele-McCarthy, Rudebusch & Witmire, 2007, p. 57). Furthermore, there are limitations within results obtained from formal standardized communication assessments.

Communication recommended eligibility determinations are an integral part of the collaborative team problem-solving process. However, at times, communication eligibility and recommendations are determined by speech-language pathologists with minimal collaboration with educational teams. It is crucial that speech-language pathologists participate within the collaborative problem-solving process.

It is essential that speech-language pathologists collaborate with educational teams (including parents) in determining communication eligibility and communication recommendations for many reasons, including the following:

The speech-language pathologist may have had limited time interacting with the student in a variety of communication contexts (communication environments, partners)
The speech-language pathologist may have limited time assigned to work within the school environment, to a particular school
The knowledge level the speech-language pathologist has in understanding the relationship between speech, language, communication to academic and social success
The knowledge level the speech-language pathologist has regarding academic and social curricular
The knowledge level the speech-language pathologist has regarding the relationship between communication and overt and/or covert behaviors

| The experience level the speech-language pathologist has had in completing dynamic communication assessments |
| The amount of time the speech-language pathologist has to complete comprehensive communication assessments |

Speech-language pathologists' collaboration with educational teams (including parents), in determining qualifications and communication supports and interventions is essential. It is crucial that speech-language communication eligibility determination is completed with educational team collaboration in order to develop a complete communication profile of students' academic as well as functional communication performance within total school settings. IDEA 2004 mandates that communication eligibility must be determined from a variety of sources (formal assessments, informal measures, dynamic environments and communication partners) and that all communication information is objectively documented and compiled to create students' total communication profiles.

Case Study: Frank (Assessment)

Introduction

Frank was a third-grade student within the regular education program. Frank struggled with his schoolwork. His parents worked with him every night for hours to complete his homework, which resulted in him receiving passing grades on his assignments. Frank's parents met with his teachers to discuss their concerns regarding Frank's difficulties expressing himself and his frustrations when completing his homework. His parents reported that they felt he was stuttering and requested that their school district provide speech-language services for Frank. The school district reassured Frank's parents that he was doing fine in school, he was receiving passing grades and that he did not qualify for speech language services.

Frank's parents felt that along with his stuttering, his difficulties expressing himself were also increasing. Frank's mother talked with her doctor regarding her concerns and Frank's symptoms. The doctor wrote a prescription for stuttering therapy. **(Red Flag!)** *Frank's mother gave the prescription to the school speech-language pathologist, who then completed a speech-language assessment.*

Initial Speech-Language Assessment

The speech-language pathologist completed a speech-language evaluation (based on the doctor's prescription for stuttering therapy) in which the only component of the assessment was a formal standardized stuttering assessment. His scores on the stuttering assessment indicated that he had a stuttering disorder. Frank qualified as a student with a stuttering disorder as he demonstrated dysfluencies when he initiated language along with eye-blinking behaviors. Frank qualified under speech-language (fluency) educational disability classification. A speech-language program was developed to decrease stuttering behaviors and increase fluent speech. The only problem was that he did not have a stuttering disorder.

Frank's difficulties expressing himself continued, along with eye-blinking behaviors. His parents requested that he receive a language assessment. The speech-language pathologist included a formal standardized language assessment. Frank passed this formal standardized assessment for expressive language; however, he continued to demonstrate challenges expressing himself within dynamic conversations and his eye-blinking behaviors continued to increase. Frank began to interact less at school and did not participate within classroom discussions.

Collaborative Educational Team Meeting

A collaborative educational team problem-solving meeting was scheduled. The team discussed Frank's academic performance as well as his communication effectiveness within all school contexts. The information provided within this meeting, as well as the information provided by Frank's parents, was included within Frank's total communication and education profiles.

The educational team identified that Frank had significant challenges expressing himself verbally as well as within written language assignments.

The team identified the following: word searching behaviors and difficulties formulating and organizing language, along with delayed processing time. It appeared that his eye-blinking was consistent with his language struggles as his language disorder caused severe anxiety. He appeared to internalize his anxiety and the only overt expression was that of eye-blinking. The team further identified that Frank's dysfluent speech was a direct result of his inability to recall words quickly and efficiently in dynamic environments along with his challenges with organization and formulation of his thoughts (language) and excessive anxiety. His teacher reported that he had significant difficulties brainstorming, organizing and expressing his ideas within written assignments. (However, she did not have the crucial knowledge that his challenges within writing assignments were language based.)

Collaborative Team Recommendations

A comprehensive language-based strategy intervention program along with social work services were recommended. The following interventions and strategies were recommended across communication and academic environments: word retrieval strategies, visual processing strategies, explicit graphic organizers, use of prior knowledge, pausing and phrasing, visualization (mind's eye), visual supports, mind maps, comprehension checks, narrative interventions as well as story maps.

Assessing Speech-Language, Communication Skills: English Language Learners

IDEA (2004) along with IDEA Part B (2006) mandates appropriate services to culturally and linguistically diverse (CLD) populations. IDEA mandates that children cannot be identified as a child with a disability if the determinant factor is limited English proficiency [20 U.S.C. §1414 (b)(5)(C)]. IDEA further requires that schools and educational teams administer and conduct assessments along with any other evaluation materials in the "language and form most likely to yield accurate information, unless it is not feasible to provide or administer" [20 U.S.C. §1414(b)(3)(A)(ii)].

The Illinois State Board of Education (ISBE, 2002) outlined specific guidelines for evaluations (assessments) as well as providing educational services for students who are English language learners with disabilities. ISBE's guidelines explicitly outline requirements that educators and service providers (e.g., speech-language pathologists) must follow when assessing English language learners with disabilities or when determining if an English language learner has a disability (e.g., communication disorder). The guidelines explicitly outline requirements that assessments and IEPs are culturally and linguistically (conducted in the primary language of students) appropriate.

The American Speech-Language-Hearing Association (n.d., p. 2) made the following statement in regard to assessing English language learner (ELL) students: *"It is important for speech-language pathologists and audiologists to carefully review the child's language history to determine the language of assessment. Assessments and other evaluation materials must be provided in the child's native language or other mode of communication unless it is clearly not feasible to do so. If it is determined that the child should be evaluated in a language other than English, the speech-language pathologist must use all available resources, including interpreters when necessary, to appropriately evaluate the child."*

"Before a child is given a case study evaluation, the local school district shall determine the primary language of the child's home, general cultural identification and mode of communication" (ISBE, 2002, p. 1). Evaluations must be conducted, "To ensure that it is linguistically, culturally, racially and sexually nondiscriminatory... the language used within the evaluation must be consistent with the child's primary language of the home or other mode of communication" (ISBE, 2002, p. 2). The tests that are used within the assessment process must be relevant to ELL student's culture. Students who are hearing impaired should be administered assessments through visual communication techniques along with use of interpreters.

IDEA (2004) allows for variances from standard testing procedures when necessary when assessing ELL students. A qualified bilingual speech-language pathologist or bilingual specialist can support educational teams within the assessments process. Interpreters and translators can support educational teams when bilingual speech-language pathologists or bilingual specialists are not available.

Communication assessments for ELL students begin with collaborative educational team assessment questions in order to determine communication assessment components. Assessment questions determine why, when, when, where, how and who should complete specific components. Both formal and informal assessment procedures are considered within the complete assessment plan. It is important that educators observe and assess students' communication skills across communitive contexts (environments and persons). Dynamic communication assessments will provide information regarding students' abilities at communicating with peers, adults and interactions within various environments. It is important to determine whether parents require interpreter support to communicate with the educational team.

Dynamic Communication Assessment

Communication is a dynamic process. We alter or change our speech, our language, the way we express ourselves depending on the context, the communication environment and the communication partner. Vermeulen (2012) describes contexts as what is going on in the environment (outside and inside our brain) that influence our way of giving meaning to things. The external contexts are: the situations, where we are, who we are talking to and what is happening within the environment at the time. The internal contexts are: our ideas, knowledge, experiences and feelings that we have stored in our long-term memory.

The external and internal contexts influence one another and are inseparable. Our internal contexts, our stored language (our knowledge), determine our interactions within external contexts (the communication situations and communication partners). Nothing has a fixed meaning as meanings change according to the contexts. Changing or altering interactions styles, depending on communication contexts, can be difficult for students with communication disorders. This has important implications regarding communication assessment processes and procedures.

Students may not have comprehended (understood) language presented within dynamic interactions (academic and/or social). They may not have efficiently stored relevant contextual information (language) within their long-term memory, which will impact their ability to retrieve language quickly and effectively. Communication disorders may impact students' abilities at maintaining active engagement and participation within different contextual learning and social experiences. This in turn will impact their learning, knowledge and language growth. A student with a communication disorder may be able to access language, retrieve and use appropriate language in one context and not another, with one communication partner or within one communication environment and not another. Educators have made comments such as, "He can do it when he wants to!" What exactly does that mean? Statements such as this should be changed into assessment questions. Assessment questions will provide educational teams opportunities at gathering pertinent assessment information resulting in effective programming for students. Why can he or why does he do it in this environment and not others?

It is possible for speech-language pathologists to complete speech-language, communication assessments and miss or not identify significant communication disorders. This can occur when speech-language pathologists complete formal communication assessments without input and collaboration from the educational team, including parents. This can occur when the communication assessment is conducted within a quiet speech therapy office without addressing dynamic communication contexts (environments and communication partners).

Speech-language pathologists may administer a specific diagnostic assessment tool or process to all students who have been referred for a communication case study assessment. This may be due to the availability of assessment tools within the school district, as well as to the amount of time speech-language pathologists have to assess individual students. It is crucial that speech-language pathologists have a thorough understanding of what each communication assessment tool is actually assessing, as well as if the results from a formal language assessment will support students' communication and educational programming. An average standard score or percentile rank does not provide educational teams with relevant information if the assessment tool does not assess needed crucial communication skills. Will the information or the results from a particular formal communication assessment target and answer the assessment questions, resulting in effective students' communication programming? **Communication assessment are not a one-size-fits-all!**

Following are examples of dynamic communication contexts that may be included within assessment discussions and evaluation processes.

- Variety of different classrooms the student may attend throughout the day (e.g., regular education classroom, homeroom, art class, reading class, computer class, gym class, library, etc.)

- School hallway, school lunchroom, school office, nurse's office

- Playground, school assemblies

- Quiet, noisy environments, environments with excessive reverberation

- Unscheduled events: fire drills, tornado drills, school closing due to weather

- Community experiences and/or environments (e.g., field trips); school bus

- Environments and/or communication partners with increased anxiety, stress levels

- Large classroom groups, small classroom groups, one on one work, cooperative peer groups

- Formal vs. informal communication environments and/or communication partners

- One on one discussion vs. multiple communication partners

- Familiar vs. novel communication environments and communication partners

- Communications with peers; communications with adults

- Sensory factors; level of emotionality

- Level of stored language experiences with relevant concepts and vocabulary.

IDEA 2004 mandates that assessment procedures address both academic as well as functional communication performance. Effective, comprehensive communication assessments, which include students' functional communication performance, necessitate taking communication assessments out of therapy rooms and into dynamic communication environments, as well as within collaborative team problem-solving discussions. A combination of formal, standardized assessments, along with dynamic communication assessments will provide educational teams a complete profile of students' communication performance within academic as well as functional environments. *"In conducting the evaluation, the local educational agency shall ... use a variety of assessment tools and strategies to gather relevant functional, developmental and academic information, including information provided by the parents that may assist in determining... whether the child is a child with a disability; and the content of the child's individualized education program... not use any single measure or assessment as the sole criterion for determining an appropriate educational program for the child..."* [20 U.S. C § 1414 (b) (2) (A)].

Dynamic communication assessments begin with collaborative educational team assessment questions in order to determine communication assessment components. Assessment questions determine why, when, when, where, how and who should complete specific components. Both formal and informal assessment procedures should be considered within the complete assessment plan.

Formal Standardized Communication Assessments

Speech-language pathologists administer formal, standardized communication assessments to evaluate students' speech-language communication skills. Standardized assessments compare and rank individual student's scores in relation to same-aged peers. Most standardized tests are referred to as norm referenced tests, in that students' test results are compared to the results of a statistically selected group of test takers of the same age or grade. Standardized communication assessments provide information regarding whether test takers perform better or worse than hypothetical average students. One challenge with norm referenced tests is that the norms for specific standardized assessments may not include students from a variety of socioeconomic and/or cultural groups. Furthermore, the norms often do not include students with special needs or disabilities. Consequently, these assessments may not adequately assess students from diverse cultural and social backgrounds and/or students with disabilities.

Students' scores are ranked on a bell curve or a distribution of scores that resembles, when graphed, the outline of a bell. Standard scores, percentile scores, along with overall language performance scores can be provided, comparing these scores to same age or grade peers.

Formal, standardized assessments evaluate students' speech, language and communication skills within a one-to-one setting. They involve specific processes and procedures for administration, scoring and interpretation. There are a variety of formal standardized assessments available to speech-language pathologists to select from when assessing communication skills. Specific assessment tools may target specific communication skills or a combination of skills such as receptive and expressive language skills within the five elements of language (pragmatics, phonology, semantics, morphology, syntax), voice, stuttering and speech. Speech-language pathologists may have limited formal communication assessment tools available within their school district's speech-language program. This may result in administrating the same test battery or same communication assessment tool to every student referred for a communication assessment. Caution should be taken to ensure that the availability or access to specific testing materials does not determine how speech-language pathologists select assessment tools. When selecting formal communication assessment tests, it is important that speech-language pathologists have a thorough understanding of what communication skills each specific test is actually assessing, whether the results from a particular assessment tool will support students' communication and educational programming. Will the information or the results from a particular formal communication assessment target and answer the assessment questions, resulting in effective student communication programming?

Formal, standardized communication assessments can provide valuable information within students' complete communication profile. However, they do have limitations and should be one component within the total communication assessment process. A child may obtain average to above average scores on a standardized, formal language, communication and speech assessment and have significant language communication deficits.

Formal, standardized communication assessments evaluate language, communication knowledge and use along with processing language at the word, sentence or paragraph level without addressing the use of language communication functionally. Formal assessments isolate each element of language; they isolate specific communication skills. For example, a comprehensive receptive and/or expressive language assessment may have specific subtests that assess syntax, morphology, semantics as well as listening skills. However, within dynamic communication contexts, both academic and social, all five language elements are interrelated and each element has an impact on the other language elements.

Standardized tests do not reflect and/or describe students' spontaneous communication abilities or challenges. They often minimize the student's need to apply executive functioning skills. In fact, educators may actually adapt the environment or the communication situation in order for the student to be successful without knowing it. Communication success is dependent on timing and interpretation. It is also dependent on the ability to listen and respond to speakers' words in context, while simultaneously interpreting the meaning and intention of the message through both verbal and nonverbal communication cues. Standardized tests do not look at the dynamic communication process. Evaluators provide quiet, calm environments. Adults can help create communication success and often compensate for students' weaknesses to prevent awkward moments, even during assessments, without realizing they are doing so (Winner, 2007).

In the real world of academics and communication interactions, skills are not isolated. All five elements of language as well as our speech skills are interrelated. Students must rely on their own executive functioning skills within spontaneous communication interactions. Students are required to combine various skills and to process information in noisy environments. Students are required to multi-task, attend to salient information, disregard background noise, integrate language at various levels, process, organize and formulate language very quickly. This can be a very daunting task for students with communication disorders.

Formal assessments may not distinguish between students' communication interactions with adults, peers, within familiar and unfamiliar contexts, with known and unknown language contexts, persons and environments. Formal assessments may not distinguish between calm vs. stressful communication environments. Formal assessments do not assess students' means of communication and their ability to use a variety of shared communication intents, as well as discourse skills within dynamic communication environments. In other words, formal communication assessments may not assess students' communication skills within real life dynamic communication environments.

Evaluation Questions Determine Data Collection

Communication assessments will include one or a combination of the following communication assessment components. Identified assessment components are a direct response to educational teams' assessment questions. What data are needed to answer the evaluation questions?

Within the collaborative model, other members of the educational team (including parents) may support the speech-language pathologist in collecting critical communication information and data. The speech-language pathologist works collaboratively with the educational team in determining how the data will be gathered, where the data will be gathered as well as who will gather the data. Members of the educational team may be able to provide critical communication information within contexts that speech-language pathologists do not have access to.

Following is a list of possible evaluation components:

- Review of student's educational records
- Review of outside agency reports
- Academic and social data collection
- Hearing and vision screening (Note: This is a component of every communication assessment.)
- Auditory processing assessment
- Observations
- Language sample (mean length of utterance)
- Dynamic communication sample
- Communication assistive technology assessment
- Pragmatic language assessment within dynamic communication contexts
- Questionnaires, interviews (parents, student, educational staff) and/or checklists

- Developmental scales

- Story retelling; narratives

- Formal receptive language and/or expressive language assessment (five elements of language)

- Fluency assessment

- Voice assessment

- Differential diagnosis of speech (articulation, phonological, apraxia, oral motor skills)

An educational team case study communication assessment is not a question of right or wrong regarding administration of assessment components. It is a matter of whether the assessment is complete or incomplete. In other words, does the team have enough data, and the appropriate data, to answer the assessment questions? Does the team need additional assessment information? If additional data are required, the following questions may need to be answered:

- What additional data are needed?

- Where should the data be gathered?

- Who should collect the data?

- Are informal and/or formal components required?

- How should the data be collected and analyzed?

Know Your Students

The first step in supporting our students is to understand them from their perspectives. How do they see and interact with the world? Appropriate programming, interventions, supports and student success depend on educators understanding students through collaboration, objective observations, data collections and assessments. Individual student profiles drive students' communication and educational programs, interventions and supports.

We begin the process of knowing our students through observations and active listening. Dr. Barry M. Prizant (2015) discusses the importance of understanding students' perspectives and experiences. He tells us to listen carefully, observe carefully and continually ask why.

Moore (2002) discusses the importance of observing students' language and communication skills within natural communication settings, as their language disorders can be subtle. These subtle language disorders become apparent when educators observe and analyze them within natural settings. It is in dynamic communication environments in which students' true communication abilities are observed. Moore further emphasizes the importance of assessing students' language skills through observations in many different settings and by several different specialists, including speech language pathologists, teachers, social workers and psychologists.

The American Speech Language Hearing Association (ASHA) highlights the importance that communication assessments are contextually based and involve multiple settings and communication partners. ASHA further discusses the need for multiple observations, checklists, structured tasks and assessment measures to adequately assess communication skills and not the use of a single assessment tool.

Language Samples

A language sample can be one component within a speech-language evaluation. A language sample can provide a great deal of information in regard to students' overall language skills. A language sample measures the mean length of utterance (MLU) in regard to the number of morphemes within 100 utterances spoken by the student. Each word is broken down into morphemes.

Morphology is the element of language that pertains to the study of words and how words are formed. Words are made up of morphemes (the smallest unit of meaning in a word). There are free morphemes (morphemes that have meaning on their own and they can stand alone) and bound morphemes (morphemes that only have meaning when attached to a free morpheme). Evaluators, speech-language pathologists or other educational personnel, observe students interacting with peers and/or adults and transcribe what students are verbalizing, students' utterances. Each word students produce is broken down into morphemes. One hundred utterances are selected and the morphemes in each utterance are counted. Students' language utterances are transcribed and then calculated to determine the average number of morphemes that students produced in the utterance. The Mean Length of Utterance (MLU), is the average number of morphemes within the 100 utterances. The MLU is calculated by dividing the total number of morphemes within the 100 utterances by 100. (Example Language Sample Observation Forms are provided at the end of this chapter.)

For example, a student who had 430 morphemes within 100 utterances, would have a MLU of 4.30.

M LU = Total number of morphemes: **430**

Total number of Utterances: **100 (MLU. = 4.30)**

Brown (1973) described five stages of language development based on Mean Length of Utterance scores.

Stage 1: MLU 1.0 to 2.0 (12 to 26 Months)

Stage II: MLU 2.0 to 2.5 (27 to 30 Months)

Stage III: MLU 2.5 to 3.0 (31 to 34 Months)

Stage IV: MLU 3.0 to 3.75 (35 to 40 Months)

Stage V: MLU 3.75 to 4.5 (41 to 46 Months)

Mean Length of Utterance can be one indicator of a language delay or disorder. MLU provides important language information in regard to grammatical and sentence structures. The child's score is compared to same-age norms. Speech-language pathologists can collaborate with educational teams by providing professional training and demonstrate how to observe students and transcribe their utterances. Educational teams can then use this contextual information within the student's total communication profile.

Although Mean Length of Utterance provides valuable communication information, it is not sufficient when assessing students' overall communication skills. MLU scores do not provide crucial information regarding students' abilities at using a variety of shared communication intents or to understand and use nonverbal aspects of communication. MLU does not provide information regarding students' use of various means of communication, their abilities at language flexibility or processing language quickly and efficiently. MLU does not provide a complete profile of students' receptive and/or expressive language abilities within the five elements of language (phonology, morphology, syntax, semantics and pragmatics). MLU does not address students' abilities to recall vocabulary quickly and efficiently; to adapt communication to dynamic communication contexts and/or to communicate effectively with a variety of communication partners and environments. MLU does not address students' abilities to interact successfully with adults, peers, under conditions of calm/stress or order/chaos.

A student may obtain a Mean Length of Utterance Score that falls within normal age norms and still have communication deficits that impact academic, social and/or vocational skills. Similarly, a student may obtain scores on a standardized language assessment and still have communication deficits. It is important that speech-language pathologists conduct Dynamic Communication Assessments, in which calculating Mean Length of Utterance (MLU) and administration of formal language assessments are components within the total assessment process.

Communication Samples

Communication samples go beyond calculating Mean Length of Utterance and formal language and speech assessments. Language, speech, voice, prosody and communication are contextually based, influenced by the context of the communication interaction. When completing communication samples, we assess real life, natural contexts. Assessments are taken out of therapy rooms and into the classrooms, hallways, playgrounds and homes. When we assess communication within dynamic, changing communication environments, we get a more accurate picture of our students' abilities at being successful communicators within academic, social and vocational environments.

Communication samples provide descriptions of students' functional speech, language and communication skills across environments and across communication partners (academic as well as social contexts). Communication samples look beyond surface grammatical and morphological structures.

Following is a list of some of the communication skills that may be observed and assessed within communication samples:

- Nonverbal and verbal communications

- Means of communication

- Communication intents; shared intents

- Adult interactions vs. peer interactions

- Formal vs. informal communications

- Known vs. novel communication contexts

- Reciprocal interactions as well as the content of these interactions

- Repair strategies

- Semantic knowledge and use

- Abstract vs. concrete language use

- Discourse skills

- Executive functioning skills

- Language processing

- Joint attention, active listening

- Communication engagement

- Play skills
- Cognitive processing skills

Objective observations are completed to gather information regarding students' functional language abilities within various communication contexts. Multiple observations are completed within various communication contexts (environments and with various communication partners). We must observe students within real life contexts and interactions. We must take communication assessments out of therapy rooms and into dynamic communication contexts. Observations should include as many contexts as possible, such as: various classrooms, lunchroom, playground, gym class, hallways, home, assemblies, bus, field trips, formal vs. informal, structured vs. non-structured, stressful communication environments, calm communication environments, peer and adult interactions. It is not logistically possible for speech-language pathologists to observe students within all of the contexts. Within the collaborative team process, speech-language pathologists collaborate with educational team members (including parents) in collecting observation data.

Students' dynamic use of language can be observed during the following tasks:

- Performance within sequence picture tasks; picture tasks
- Story retelling (personal, academic, non-structured, structured)
- Narratives; verbal explanations; expressing ideas, thoughts and opinions
- Verbal brainstorming activities;
- Explain how to complete tasks; for example, how to make a sandwich, fix a bed, play a game
- Organize and write a sentence, paragraph or story

Case Study: Tommy (Assessment)

Introduction

Tommy (a third-grade student within the regular education program) was demonstrating behavior challenges. Tommy had a 504 plan with a goal to monitor behavior. (A 504 plan provides accommodations to children in school who have a condition that gets in the way of learning. It is not a special education support.)

Review of Tommy's School Records

Educational records indicated that Tommy had received special educational services within a district based preschool program under the IDEA disability classification of Developmental Delay, with identified needs in the areas of play, social interactions and expressive language. Tommy attended this preschool program for two years then transitioned into kindergarten. At age six, the educational team completed Tommy's three-year re-evaluation with the goal to dismiss him from special education services, as he was maintaining average grades within the academic program. The educational team determined that the communication domain was the only area that required re-assessment.

The speech-language pathologist administered Tommy a formal language assessment, a speech assessment and a language sample (Mean Length of Utterance). He received average scores on all the subtests of the formal language assessment. Tommy's Mean Length of Utterance (MLU) fell within the average range. Tommy was dismissed from speech-language services and the educational team determined that he no longer qualified for special education services and no longer required an Individual Education Program.

The principal voiced her concerns in the areas of peer interactions, attention and behavior. Tommy's mother expressed concerns in that she felt Tommy had difficulties with understanding people, following directions and carrying on a conversation. However, the speech-language pathologist assured her that his scores fell within the normal range and he did not have a language and communication disorder. However, to address the principal's and Tommy's mother's concerns, the educational team developed a 504 plan with the goal to monitor Tommy's behavior. Throughout Tommy's first and second grade years, he maintained passing grades, although he continued to struggle with completing tasks, peer interactions and work completion.

Behavior Concerns (Third-Grade)

Tommy's third grade teachers reported concerns regarding Tommy's abilities to begin and complete his work independently, along with peer interactions. Tommy would not ask for help and would insist that his work was done correctly. He would appear to be frustrated and would argue with his teacher. He would not initiate written assignment and would refuse to write when directed by his teachers. He began to talk back and yell, "I don't know" at his teachers. Tommy was not engaged within classroom discussions and did not follow his teachers' directions. Tommy was not completing his homework and when he did, he did not turn it in. Tommy began to get into arguments with his peers on the playground and refused to work within classroom cooperative groups. He began to refuse to get ready for school and to go to school. By the third month of school, Tommy would cry daily at school. His crying escalated into yelling and going under the classroom table or his desk and he would refuse to get out. At several in-school events, Tommy became upset and sat in the middle of the auditorium, crying and refusing to move.

Recommendations

After several school co-plan meetings and discussions with Tommy's mother, the educational team determined that an evaluation was necessary to assess skills across domains. The team began the assessment process by asking pertinent evaluation questions (at the domain evaluation meeting) to determine when, what, where and how data would be gathered. The educational team completed a dynamic communication assessment, executive functioning assessment and social-emotional assessment of Tommy, along with an educational profile. The team collected data to determine the frequency, intensity of behaviors and the antecedent to the behaviors along with any reinforcement.

The speech-language pathologist administered a formal language assessment. Tommy received average scores on all the subtests. The speech-language pathologist (in collaboration with the educational team) completed several student, parent, and teacher interviews and gathered information within dynamic communication environments and with various communication partners (structured vs. unstructured settings, formal vs. informal settings, playground, lunchroom, several different classrooms, etc.). The speech-language pathologist assessed Tommy's ability to complete narrative tasks, story retelling and verbal brainstorming. He was asked to explain how to complete tasks, play a game and tell stories within sequential order.

Results of The Assessment

A profile was developed that outlined Tommy's areas of strength and his areas of specific needs or deficits. The educational team determined that Tommy had strong abilities at following tasks when visual supports were provided and that he accessed any visual supports that were naturally provided within the environment. He was able to participate in cooperative group activities when an adult provided structure and when there were visual supports.

Tommy demonstrated deficits in the areas of verbal and non-verbal communications, social interactions, sensory integration, and executive functioning as well as Theory of Mind. He further demonstrated significant deficits in the areas of language organization, formulation, initiation and retrieval. His sensory profile indicated difficulties with auditory sensitivities and with movements and body in space (proprioceptive). His peer and adult interactions were significantly impaired. As the team gathered information and continued an open-dialogue with Tommy's mother, they determined that an Autism Rating scale would be completed. The data from this assessment indicated a very high probability for an educational classification of autism. The educational team qualified Tommy for special education services under the IDEA disability classification of autism and developed an individual education program to address his needs in the areas of language processing, expressive language, pragmatic language, sensory integration, executive functioning and emotional regulation.

Pragmatic Checklists – Pragmatic Protocols

There should be a specific goal or focus when completing student observations in order to collect relevant and pertinent data. The goal or focus should have a direct relationship to the assessment questions. It would be a daunting task to attempt to gather data on all pragmatic skills, communication interactions, executive functions and/or cognitive processes within one observation. Actually, this would not be plausible. It is important to have a clear goal as to what pragmatic skills, communication skills, cognitive processing skills and/or executive functioning skills will be the focus or goal of the observation as well as in what specific dynamic environment the observation will take place. This data can be compared to the data obtained from additional focused observations within other dynamic environments.

There are a variety of checklists and protocols available to support dynamic observations. Checklists are valuable tools in supporting observations within various communication environments, contexts as well as collaborative educational team discussions. Most checklists will have a list of skills, a rating scale as to if and how the student demonstrated skills and contextual information, such as where the student was, who the student was interacting with and if there were any observed concerns.

The following checklists and protocols support observations of dynamic communications, cognitive processes as well as executive functioning skills within dynamic interactive environments (academic and social). These resources support and facilitate focused observations, based on observation goals, within various environments.

Educational teams' decisions to include any checklist, protocol and/or assessment process should be based on individual student needs and be in response to the assessment questions.

Classroom Assessment Checklists: The resource *Conducting Educationally Relevant Evaluation: Technical Assistance for Speech-Language Pathologists* (Estomin et.al., 2007a) includes several classroom performance checklists, in which classroom communication information can be obtained from teachers. These checklists can be completed by several or all of students' teachers; the information compiled and discussed within collaborative team discussions. The checklists provide valuable information regarding a student's total communication profile.

Pragmatic Protocol: Prutting and Kittchner (1987) developed the *Pragmatic Protocol.* This is an instrument for students ages 5 and older. It examines children's use of language to signify conversational intent. Students are observed within natural contexts. Observers rate how students perform within 30 pragmatic aspects of language, which were extrapolated from the developmental child language literature as well as adult literature. The ratings consist of appropriate, inappropriate and no opportunity to observe, along with opportunities for the observer to document examples and comments. This pragmatic protocol assists educators in creating a profile of students' communication abilities. Detailed descriptions of each of the 30 aspects of language are provided.

The Conversational Effectiveness Profile – Revised: Kowalski (2010) developed *The Conversational Effectiveness Profile – Revised* to assess the unique communication skills of students with Asperger's syndrome and related disorders. This profile provides a comprehensive analysis of communication skills: Social Interactions, Social Communication, Social-Emotional Regulation. This assessment effectively assesses students' communication skills.

To complete this profile, the evaluator observes and/or interacts with students within various contexts. This profile also allows for collaboration with individuals who are familiar with the student. The *Conversational Effectiveness Profile* consists of the following domains: (1) Social Interaction domain. (2) Social Communication domain. (3) Social-Emotional Regulation. A three-point scale is used to rate the student's conversational effectiveness, both as a speaker and as a listener. *(1) Appropriate (2) Somewhat appropriate (3) Extremely inappropriate*

Checklist of Communicative Functions and Means: Weatherby (1995) developed a checklist of communication functions and means to determine the ways in which a nonverbal child or child with limited verbal skills communicates. Each communication function can be expressed in a variety of means. Weatherby divided functions under three areas: Behavioral Regulation, Social Interaction and Joint Attention. Observations are documented regarding students' use of various means of communication: physical manipulation, giving, pointing, showing, gaze shift, proximity, head nod/ head shake, facial expressions, self-injury, aggression, tantrum, crying/ whining, vocalizing, immediate echo, delayed echo, creative one word and creative multi-word.

This resource is extremely valuable when observing the nonverbal and verbal communications of children and the data obtained provides information within students' total communication profile.

The Social Thinking® Dynamic Assessment Protocol: Winner (2007) developed *The Social Thinking® Dynamic Assessment Protocol* to assess students' social cognitive/social language skills. This instrument is a valuable tool when assessing students' pragmatic language skills, social interactive functions as well as students' ability to apply social knowledge to academic curriculum. There are eight components to *The Social Thinking® Dynamic Assessment:* (1) Getting to know the student; (2) Questionnaire for Teachers and Related Services Professionals; (3) Writing sample: Asking for help; (4) The double interview; (5) Thinking with your eyes; (6) Sequencing pictures; (7) Social scenario pictures; (8) Assessing organizational skills.

Dynamic Assessment: (Ward, 2012) developed informal assessment procedures to assess students' communication and executive functioning skills. Evaluators observe students as they interact within various dynamic tasks. Dynamic communication and executive functioning skills are observed. Data obtained provides a profile of students' strengths and deficit areas. Observations are made of students as they participate within the following dynamic tasks:

1. Mature make-believe play skills: The student is observed as he/she interacts with various props.

2. Oral discourse skills: The student is asked to retell an experience or summarize a story, movie, book or how to play a game.

3. Working memory and self-regulation: The student is engaged in playing a game.

4. Writing: The student is asked to write a summary of a movie or a story. The student is also observed within the writing process as they use a graphic organizer as well as responding to open-ended questions.

5. Open Response: The student is asked to brainstorm or complete a graphic organizer.

6. Task Performance: The student is observed as he/she makes a craft, cooks and/organizes materials.

Executive Skills in Children and Adolescents: A Practical Guide to Assessment and Intervention: Dawson and Guare (2010) developed this valuable resource for educational teams as they move forward within the collaborative model when assessing students' executive function skills. It directly connects assessment to the intervention process.

In addition to the above assessment checklists, protocols and profiles, along with any other assessment components within individual student's assessment battery, the educational team may determine that observations should focus on specific, identified interactive, pragmatic skills in order to answer specific educational assessment questions. The following pragmatic interaction questions are a compilation of pragmatic skills. It is important to answer each of the questions in relation to specific communication contexts (environments and communication partners).

CHART 8: MEANS OF COMMUNICATION OBSERVATION FORM

(How did the student communicate within various environments?)

(What means or combination of means of communication did the student use?)

Means of Communication	Specific Communications Observed	Communication Contexts (Environment, Partner, Activity.)
Gestures		
Eye – Gaze Joint Attention		
Facial Expressions		
Head Nods/ Shakes		
Posture		
Proximity		
Physical Manipulation		
Body Contact		
Orientation		
Para-linguistics: Vocal Volume, intonation, pitch, stress, vocal quality, vocal rate.		
Vocalizations: (non-speech, e.g., grunts)		
Sign Language: Idiosyncratic, Formal Sign (ASL, Signed Exact English)		
Verbalizations (Verbal speech)		
Augmentation Communication Device (Technology)		
Visual Communication Supports.		
Crying, meltdown, other behaviors		

CHART 9: PRAGMATIC OBSERVATION FORM

(Did the student effectively understand or use the following pragmatic, interactive language skills within the contexts observed? Explain how the child either used or did not use each of these skills.)

OBSERVATION QUESTIONS	CONTEXT	DESCRIPTION DATA
Was the student engaged in communication interactions with adults and or peers? (How?) Was the student actively engaged within the classroom or social activity and or interaction? Was the student a passive observer?		
Did the student demonstrate joint attention? (Where and how?)		
Did the student understand (process) and respond to body language used by others? (How?) Did student use body language? (How)		
Did the student understand and use appropriate physical boundaries or physical space during interactions?		
Did the student process and understand changes in vocal intensity, tone of voice, facial expressions used by others (adults and/or peers)?		
Did the student attend to the speaker, persist at attention and respond appropriately?		
Did the student obtain attention in an appropriate manner and at appropriate times with peers and/or adults?		
Did the student actively listen to the speaker talk (adult and/or peer) without interrupting? (How?)		
Did the student initiate interactions with adults and/or peers? (How?)		

Did the student maintain interactions with adults and/or peers while maintaining the topic of discussion? (How?)		
Did the student engage in conversational turn-taking with adults and/ or peers? (How?)		
Did the student initiate greetings with adults and/or peers? (How?)		
Did the student terminate conversations with adults and/or peers? (How?)		
Did the student request help, clarification, permission or assistance with adult and/ or peers? (How?)		
Did the student provide salient information (concepts, vocabulary, referents) during communication interactions for listener comprehension? (How?)		
Did the student express, needs, wants, feelings and/or opinions successfully and in appropriate ways? (How?)		
Did the student use polite social routines with adults and or peers? (How?)		
Did the student respond to requests, questions, comments and opinions of adults and/or peers? (How?)		
Did the student adjust communication style in reflection of communication partners (adults and/or peers?), adjust language content and style? (How?)		
Did the student formulate, organize and express ideas in an organized, efficient and effective manner? (How?)		
Did the student engage in interactive turn taking during conversations with more than one communication partner?		

CHART 10: OBSERVATIONS OF BEHAVIOR

The following observation questions can guide the educational observer in maintaining focus on the observation goals and assessment questions. Observe the student within formal as well as informal education environments. The questions can also be the focus of education teams' problem-solving discussions at education team problem-solving meetings. Responses from educational staff should be documented within the assessment document in order to be included within the students' complete assessment profile.

Means of communication used by the student
• **Non-verbal,** • **Verbal,** • **Communication device** • **Visual Communication systems**

Visual communication system or communication device
• **Does the student have a visual communication system or communication device?** • **Was the system available to the student within all communication contexts, environments? (Explain)** • **How did the student access the communication system or communication device?** • **How did the adults and or peers interact with the student (communication system/device)?**

How does the student's ability to attend compare to his/her classmates or peers?
• **Was the student an active participant within the classroom discussion? Or passive?** • **What percentage of time did the student demonstrate on-task vs. off-task behavior?** • **Did the student respond to teacher's questions/comments? (Explain)** • **Did the student respond to peer question/comments? (Explain)** • **Did the student visually follow the speaker during classroom discussions?**

- Did the student follow classroom teacher directions and/or instructions? (Explain)
- What conditions improved the student's ability attend?
- What conditions impacted the student's ability to attend?
- Was the student able to maintain attention in the
    - Presence of background noise?
    - Sustain attention over time?
- How did the student engage in independent work?
- What supports were in place during independent work, group work, classroom discussions? (Explain)
- Did the student interact with peers in the classroom? (Explain)

TASK PRESENTATION - CLASSROOM SUPPORTS

- Were there any visual supports available to student? (e.g., schedules, smartboard, graphic organizers, charts, visual schedules, visual processing supports)?
- Did the student attend to the visual supports?
- What was the level of linguistic complexity within the academic task?
- What was the level of concreteness/abstractness within the academic task?
- What was the rate of interactions (teachers and or peers)? Did differing the rate of speed increase positive student outcomes?

DID THE STUDENT USE STRATEGIES?
(How did he/she problem solve?)

- Did the student ask questions? What types?
- Did the student request repetition, clarification?
- Did the student appear to problem solve? How?
- Did the student indicate he/she did not understand?

What is the student's learning style?

- Modality Strengths
- Modality Weaknesses

CHART 11: LANGUAGE SAMPLE FORM

Language Sample Form (MLU)

Context	Child's Utterance	Number of Morphemes

CHART 12: CLASSROOM OBSERVATION FORM

CLASSROOM OBSERVATION

Student: School: Date:

Context: Observer:

Activity	Teacher Presentation	Student's Engagement	Student's Communications
Be explicit and objective in the description of the lesson or activity.	How did the teacher present the lesson, the activity? (e.g., visual, verbal, manipulative, multi-modality, etc.) What was the length and complexity of teacher talk, teacher directions?	Was the student actively engaged or passive? Did the student interact with the teacher and/or peers? Did the student demonstrate atypical behaviors, [verbal and/or nonverbal]?	Describe the student's communications: Verbal and/or Nonverbal

CHART 13: CLASSROOM OBSERVATION FORM

Student:_____

School/ District:_____

Date:_____

CONTEXT SITUATION ACTIVITY	STUDENT COMMUNICATION (Verbal and nonverbal)	TEACHER RESPONSE CONSEQUENCE

CHAPTER 9:

THE INDIVIDUAL EDUCATION PROGRAM (IEP)

The Individuals with Disabilities Education Act (IDEA) 2004 identified the purpose of special education and special education services to *"ensure that all children with disabilities have available to them a free appropriate public education"* that is *"designed to meet their unique needs and prepare them for further education, employment and/or independent living"* (Sec. 300.1 (a)). Consequently, students' communication goal outcomes should result in facilitation and development of functional, useful, effective and successful communication skills within academic, functional, social and vocational contexts. The ultimate goal for all students is independent functioning and living, whether continuing their education, employment or within independent living communities. Students must be active participants and actively engaged within the learning process in order for this to occur. Just getting through the school day or school year is NOT acceptable!

There are too many students who leave our high schools and are unable to successfully maintain employment, continue their education, or function within independent living communities due to lack of communication skills, executive functioning skills, cognitive processing skills as well as independent living skills. Successful individual education programs reflect goals, interventions and supports that facilitate skill development, resulting in students' independent functioning. How do students' individual education programs (IEP), including assessments, placement options, goals, interventions, supports and related services, support short-term as well as long-term communication success and independence?

We will discuss the IEP process in relation to the speech-language communication domain. However, it is important to understand that each and every domain area is interrelated and crucial to the student's overall development as well as communication success. The process and integration of the collaborative problem-solving process remains constant for each of the domain areas.

Once the educational team determines that the student is eligible for special education services under one of the educational disability classifications, the educational team will develop an Individual Education Program (IEP) to address the areas of deficits (e.g., communication). The Individual Education Program (IEP) is developed at an IEP Meeting. (*Note: The IEP meeting may begin immediately following the assessment meeting, or can occur on a separate day and time.*)

An Individual Education Program (IEP) "is a written statement of the educational program designed to meet the student's needs and is developed by the educational team." (ISBE, 2009, p. 34). The IEP explicitly outlines educational placement, any related services, special education programming, supports, interventions, goals and objectives that students with disabilities are legally entitled to receive.

Parents will receive a formal invitation to attend either the assessment meeting and/or the IEP meeting. Parents can bring family members, a private educational service provider (e.g., speech-language pathologist, physical therapist), a private evaluator as well as an educational consultant to the IEP meeting and/or the evaluation meeting. If parents would like someone to attend the IEP meeting who is not on the list of attendees, parents can ask (in writing) that the person participate (ISBE, 2009). It is important that parents and the school district know who will be at the meeting.

The following individuals are required to attend IEP meetings:

- Parents

- Student: The student may attend and participate if the parent(s) decide he/she should be present.

- General Education Teacher

- Special Education Teacher

- School Administrator: It is important that the school administrator has a thorough understanding of the general education curricular to ensure that the IEP will be effectively implemented. Furthermore, this person must have authority to commit school and school district resources.

- Evaluation Personnel: This person must be able to explain evaluations and/or test results.

- Others with knowledge or special expertise about the student.

- Parents or the school may bring other people to the IEP meeting such as community service providers, advocates, lawyers, a friend for support, etc.

What Parents Should Bring to an Evaluation Meeting and/or an Individual Education Program (IEP) meeting.

Parents can ask their school district to send all IEP documents, assessment documents, assessment reports or any other pertinent documents to them to review prior to any meeting (five days in advance). Parents should review these documents, prepare comments and/or questions and bring them to the meeting. It is important that parents, as well as educators, have a written list of questions and concerns regarding students' speech-language communication strengths, challenges and needed supports. IEP meetings as well as evaluation meetings can be stressful and/or anxious times for parents. Our ability to express ourselves can be impacted by our emotional levels. Discussing our children can be a very emotional experience. Have you ever left a meeting and thought, "I wish I would have said or asked...? I really did not understand what he or she was saying!" Yes, we all have. A written list of questions and/or concerns will allow you the opportunity to remain focused and engage in positive problem-solving discussions.

It is important for parents to take their own notes at meetings. (You can audio record the meeting. However, you must inform the educational team that you will be audio recording the meeting.) There will be an administrator documenting information within the IEP document. It is possible that pertinent information may be missed and not recorded within the IEP document. Parents should make sure that any concerns they may have voiced at assessment or IEP meetings are recorded accurately within the IEP document. Ask the administrator if he or she has written down your concerns and questions and where they are documented. Parents can ask administrators to read the information aloud in order to ensure that the information was documented correctly. Parents should take time before signing the IEP to review the information. Educational teams often allow an hour for an IEP meeting. However, if the IEP cannot be completed within this time period, parents can ask to continue the meeting at a later date. It is important that parents as well as educators do not feel rushed.

It is important that parents bring any medical records they may have or any outside agency documents, assessments or reports. (Parents may want to provide this information to the educational team prior to the IEP meeting, giving them ample time to review the information.) Parents should bring their child's previous IEP documents and any written correspondence that they have received from school personnel (including emails, teachers' letters, report cards, progress reports, IEP update information). It is a good idea for parents to keep a binder (perhaps one for each school year) in which parents can keep all school correspondence as well as their child's IEP, IEP updates and any medical records. Download all email correspondence and keep these in your binder in the order you received them. Bring this binder with you to the meetings.

> If parents are not satisfied with the final IEP document, they can reject the IEP plan. If parents reject the IEP plan, do not sign the IEP and follow up by sending a written explanation to the school district that explicitly outlines why you reject the IEP plan. Ask for a follow up IEP meeting. If parents are satisfied with the IEP document, they should sign the document and the IEP plan will become effective.

Present Level of Performance

The present level of performance is a crucial component within the IEP process. This area explicitly outlines the needed supports, accommodations, modifications and adult prompts, along with interventions that were provided to the student to meet goals and objectives. Present level of performance describes, in depth, students' levels of communication functioning. (Each domain area identified would have additional present levels of performance.) The communication domain present level of performance should provide explicit, objective data regarding progress on students' communication goals.

It is important that the information written is in depth, specific, and based on objective data. Statements such as, "Tommy does well communicating in my class" or "Tommy is doing a great job working toward meeting his communication goals" are not acceptable. Each relevant area of a student's communication deficit should be reflected within the present level of performance.

The following data/information may be included within the present level of communication performance:

- Any relevant current communication assessments and/or data collection
- Explicit progress on communication goals; data reported:

- ○ **Unacceptable Data**: "Johnny is doing a nice job working on his interaction skills. He is doing a better job interacting with his peers."

- ○ **Acceptable, Objective Data**: "Johnny greeted a peer as he walked into the classroom without an adult prompt, using appropriate word choice. Johnny stated, 'Hi Bill, how are you?' He looked toward Bill as he greeted him."

- ○ **Acceptable, Objective Data**: "Johnny correctly produced the /s/ sound in all positions of words with 80% accuracy during three consecutive speech sessions."

- An explicit description and explanation regarding interventions and strategies that were implemented and their success. A statement regarding consistency in the use of the interventions and/ or strategies across communication environments and partners. This information identifies necessary consultation supports and/ or professional training for educational staff.

- Specific objective information regarding implementation of visual processing and visual communication supports.

- Specific, explicit information regarding the types of adult prompts that were employed (what prompts, why, where, how often and who). This information provides data in order to develop a plan to reduce prompts and increase communication independence.

- Assistive technology supports and progress or effectiveness. An objective statement reporting data regarding the consistency of use of technology across communication environments and partners. This information will support programming and needed training for educational staff:

  - ○ Access to academic and social curriculum

  - ○ Augmentative communication (visual communication supports, communication boards, communication devices)

- Other pertinent objective communication information and/or data.

Goals and Benchmarks

The annual communication goals target communication skills that students can achieve within the school year. The benchmarks (also referred to as short-term objectives) are the steps students will achieve to meet the annual or long-term goals. Students may have several annual goals within the communication domain as well as within the other domain areas (e.g., academic goals, occupational goals, physical therapy goals, occupational goals, social work goals, transition goals). Each professional is responsible for developing goals under his or her domain based on the evaluation information as well as current student progress. For instance, the speech-language pathologist will develop goals within the communication domain; the teacher will develop educational goals; the physical therapist will develop physical therapy goals, etc. Our discussion will focus on communication goals and objectives. However, within the collaborative team process, educational staff collaborate and coordinate goal areas, writing integrated goals across domain areas, in order to increase progress.

There are educational teams in which professionals independently write goals for specific domains (e.g., communication, social-emotional, educational). They share goals at the IEP meeting with minimum prior communication or collaboration with other members of the educational team. Within this model, there is little expectation that all educational personnel have responsibility at implementation of goals or the associated skill areas.

There are educational teams that work within the collaborative team model. Educational teams collaborate, prioritizes students' goal areas and write integrated goals that support each area or domain. Within this model, the expectations are that all goals are supported and integrated by all educational personnel. There is a shared understanding of the goals and the required supports and interventions. Within this collaborative process, parents are involved within the goal development discussion prior to the IEP meeting, as their input regarding the students' communication skills is crucial in determining goals, objectives and contexts of implementation. The expectation would be that all educational personnel working with students not only understand the "why" behind the goals, objectives and interventions, but that they would be responsible in implementing needed supports and interventions in order to increase students' communication competence.

The collaborative process regarding goal development is crucial in order to ensure that goals for the different domain areas support and do not conflict with goals within the other domain areas. For instance, a teacher may have a goal in which the student will write a three-paragraph essay. However, the student may not have the verbal and/or written language abilities and/or the executive functioning skills to complete this task. An integrated goal would consider each of these domain areas.

There are important IEP components that directly relate to communication needs, services, supports and interventions. These areas should be discussed in detail and pertinent information documented objectively and explicitly within the IEP Document.

Consideration of Special Factors.

The following areas should be discussed in detail in relation to needed communication supports. It is important that these areas are implemented throughout students' school day (as well as during after school activities) and by all educational personnel.

- Does the student require assistive devices and/or services? This would include any communication systems and/or communication device that the student uses.

- Communication needs including students who are deaf/hard of hearing. This would include use of sign language interpreter, use of sign language, FM systems, environmental adaptations

- English learner status—language needs.

- Blind/visually impaired—provision of Braille instruction.

- Does the student's behavior impede student's learning or that of others? If yes, then the educational team must consider a functional behavior plan. It is important that any functional behavioral intervention plan considers students' communication profiles and discusses in detail how students communicate within dynamic communication contexts. It is also important that speech-language pathologists be active participants within this discussion.

- Does the student require accommodations for the IEP to meet his/her linguistic and cultural needs? This would include students who are deaf/hard of hearing and English language learning students.

- Special education and related services will be provided in a language or mode of communication other than or in addition to English. The IEP also provides a discussion regarding the opportunities for the student to have direct communication/interactions with peers and professional personnel in the child's language and communication mode. For example, do educational professionals and peers have opportunities to interact with students who have speech generated communication devices and/or systems, employ American Sign Language or Signed Exact English as their mode of communication? Do these students have peer groups to interact with? This discussion is crucial when educational teams discuss placement options and professional training needs.

Supplementary Aids, Accommodations and Modifications.

It is important that educational teams have discussions regarding communication aids, accommodations and modifications that are required in order for students to make progress toward their annual goals and within the general education curriculum, to participate within extracurricular and other non-academic activities. It is important that educational teams explicitly outline students' requirements in order for them to be successful communicators across communication contexts. Furthermore, students' action plans should explicitly outline how educational teams will implement supplementary aids, accommodations, modifications and supports with consistency and fidelity.

It is crucial that all educational personnel who work with students understand the accommodations, modifications and supports and are provided any needed professional development and training in order to ensure consistency and fidelity of implementation across communication contexts. The communication accommodations, modifications and supports should be explicitly outlined within the IEP document.

Supports for School Personnel.

Unfortunately, this area is not always given full attention and discussion by educational teams. However, it is crucial that any school personnel who are working with students receive adequate program trainings and support (e.g., communication device, voice output system, visual processing, visual communications, specific interventions, prompts). It is important that school personnel trainings and supports are explicitly outlined within the IEP. The IEP should outline when the trainings and/or supports will be provided, by whom, in what locations and when.

> *"Each public agency must ensure that a continuum of alternative placement is available to meet the needs of children with disabilities for special education and related services ... instruction in regular classes, special classes, special schools, home instruction, instruction in hospitals and institutions... provision for supplementary services (such as resource room or itinerant instruction) to be provided in conjunction with regular class placement." [IDEA Part B 300-115 (a)(b)]*

Educational Placement

A discussion regarding educational placement, where the child will be educated, as well as needed services, should occur after educational teams have discussed students' goals, objectives (benchmarks), services, needed supports and interventions. Educational placement is individually based on the students' needs and made each year at students' Individual Education Program (IEP) meeting.

Educational Placement Options	Related Education Services
General Education with no Supplementary Aids	Special Education School Psychologist
General Education with Supplementary Aids	Speech-Language Services Social Work Autism Consultation
Special Education and Related Services • Within the General Education Classroom • Outside General Education Classes	Occupational Therapy Physical Therapy
Resource Rooms (Special Class)	Assistive Technology
Special Classes (Self-Contained Classroom)	Vision Itinerant Services
Special Schools	Hearing Itinerant Services
Home/Hospital Instruction	Interpreter (Bilingual; Sign Language) Other:_____

Service Delivery Options

Service delivery refers to the manner in which related services are provided to students. The following are determined at the IEP meeting.

- **Type of service**: (e.g., direct services, small group, whole group, collaboration, consultation)

- **The location:** Where the services will be provided (e.g., therapy room, classroom, school environments, community-based, home-based)

- **The frequency:** How often the services (e.g., speech-language) are provided, such as daily, twice a week

- **Length of time**: How long each session will last (ex: 20 minutes, 30 minutes, 40 minutes, etc.)

Our discussion will focus on the speech-language communication domain. However, the information applies to all areas of related services (e.g., occupational therapy, physical therapy). School districts must provide a continuum of service delivery options dependent on individual student's needs. One service delivery model should not be used exclusively. There is not a one-size-fits-all to service delivery. Ongoing collaboration is a crucial component within all service delivery models. Service delivery models should be determined through a collaborative team discussion regarding options that would support students' progress toward meeting goals, objectives (benchmarks) and facilitate positive student outcomes. Service delivery is a dynamic process that should be adjusted as students' needs change. A popular speech-language service delivery option is for students to receive 20 minutes of speech-language services twice weekly. This delivery option is often continued from year to year without consideration to changes in students' needs. There should be an ongoing collaborative discussion regarding any changes or adjustments to service delivery models based on students' current goals and needs; not on popular practice.

The following statements from speech-language pathologists or educational teams do not address individual student needs and do not comply with the requirements that districts provide a continuum of service options:

- I have one social language group and it does not fit into the student's schedule.

- All of my students receive 40 minutes of speech-language services weekly.

- I do not have time to collaborate with the student's team. I am not at the school when they meet.

- I go into all my classes and work with all the students. I do not have time to work with students one on one.

- All of my students receive pull-out therapy services. I do not work within classrooms because I do not have the time to do so.

Parents often discuss concerns regarding the number of direct minutes the student is receiving in services per week (e.g., 40 vs. 60 minutes of speech-language therapy). Although the number of minutes provided weekly is important, it is more important to understand the intervention process and how progress is monitored. Is the student making progress toward meeting short-term and long-term objectives and successful communication skills? Providing 60 vs. 40 minutes of speech-language therapy alone will not guarantee students' progress.

A combination of service delivery options, based on individual students' needs, facilitate positive student outcomes. A student may receive a combination of any of the following service delivery options:

Consultation: Speech-language pathologists collaborate with the educational team regarding students' programs, services, supports, etc. Consultation is a direct component within the collaborative team model and is a part of every student's speech-language communication program.

Pull Out Services: Speech-language pathologists provide direct services to students individually or in small groups in either a speech therapy room or other locations within the school, that are outside of the classroom.

Classroom Based: Speech-language pathologists provide services within the classroom. This model is also referred to as an integrated model, curriculum-based model and/or team teaching model. The speech-language pathologist works collaboratively with the teacher and shares responsibilities for planning, teaching, integrating interventions and supports, monitoring, progress and shared decision making (Estomin et.al., 2007b). Please note that this model does not mean the speech-language pathologist goes into the classroom at a specific time without a clear plan or goal as to her/his role within the process. It is not the speech-language pathologist walking around the room monitoring children.

Community-Based: The speech-language pathologist provides services in the community and/or student's home. The goal would focus on increasing the student's abilities at functional communication skills.

Self-Contained Program: The speech-language pathologist is the classroom teacher. The SLP provides both academic and social curriculum instruction as well as speech-language communication interventions and supports.

Indirect Services: The speech-language pathologist performs student specific activities that support and facilitate students' communication success and implementation of interventions, supports and communication systems within educational programs and environments. Examples of indirect services are adaptations and/or modification to the curriculum, school environment, assistive technology/augmentative communication support (Estomin, et.al., 2007b).

The speech-language pathologist and educational team will recommend the number of minutes the speech-language pathologist will provide speech-language services, the service delivery model and whether the services are provided inside or outside of the classroom. This will be documented within the IEP document.

The following questions can facilitate a collaborative discussion regarding service delivery options:

- How will the speech-language pathologist provide consultation and collaborate with the educational team? What will that look like on a daily, weekly or monthly basis?

- How was the amount of time determined (e.g., 40 minutes per week)? How will this amount of time support my student's success in meeting communication goals?

- How will you provide services outside of the classroom? What will those services look like?

- How will you provide services within the classroom? What will those services look like?

- Why do you recommend pull-out therapy services? What will pull-out services look like for my student? Why were pull-out therapy services not recommended?

- Why do you recommend one-to-one therapy? What will one-to-one therapy services look like for my student? Why was one-to-one therapy not recommended?

- Why do you recommend group therapy? What will group therapy services look like for my student? How will the members of the group be determined? Why will my student be in this specific group? Why was group therapy not recommended?

- How will you work with my student within the classroom-based service delivery option? What does this look like? How will this facilitate goal areas?

- Would a combination of service delivery options better support the student's goals?

- How do the recommended service delivery options ensure consistency and fidelity regarding implementation of needed communication interventions and supports across total school settings and contexts?

- How do the recommended service delivery options ensure communication success?

Inclusive Education: Active Engagement
- Active Participation

Parents often state that they want their child to be included within the child's home school and want an inclusive program for their child. Do parents fully understand what being fully included means for their child and their child's active engagement within the learning process? What does inclusion mean? What is inclusive education? Inclusion will mean something different for individual students. It is not a one-size-fits-all model. All students (those with disabilities and those without) are included within the school environment, as inclusion looks different for each child.

There are school districts that pride themselves in stating that they are a fully inclusive district. What does it mean when a district makes this statement? IDEA, 2004 mandates the necessity for a continuum of placement options based on individual student needs.

Before we begin our discussion regarding inclusion or inclusive education, let us revisit our discussion regarding the concept that all learning involves active engagement and active participation within all learning activities and experiences. Learning within school experiences involves active engagement and participation within academic, functional and social curricula. It is participation within experiences that students create learning. Learning is a journey that connects one experience to another.

A discussion regarding the educational process and the educational product is crucial to our understanding of inclusive education. The educational process is all that students do, participate in and engage in. It is the actual learning. The educational product is the grade, the spelling sentences, the math paper, the completed research paper, the completed test, the five paragraph essay, the diploma, etc. The student's active engagement in the educational process leads to learning. Unfortunately, there are many instances in which a student completes an educational product without true learning occurring because they were not engaged in the educational process. A grade, a homework paper, a final report, a test grade, a diploma has no meaning without the learning behind the product through active engagement within the process. A discussion between these two concepts is crucial when discussing students' Individual Education Program (IEP) and educational placement options in order to ensure that students continue to be engaged within the learning process throughout their educational career.

There are too many students at various ability levels who have earned high school diplomas yet who do not have the necessary communication skills, executive functioning skills and/or independent living skills in order to be successful adults. They are unable to go on to higher education, seek and maintain employment or live independently. Perhaps they completed many educational products over the years without complete active engagement or participation within the educational process.

Case Study: Tim (Inclusion)

Introduction

*Tim was an eight-grade student who had a diagnosis of Asperger's syndrome. He was described by his teachers as a very bright student. Tim had an Individual Education Plan; he was fully included throughout his entire school day. When asked the following questions: "How independent is Tim in completing his work in school?" and "What does being fully included mean for Tim?" his resource teacher stated that Tim completed all assignments in school and was receiving excellent grades. The resource teacher stated that he went to each class and completed the same assignments that the other students completed. The only difficulty Tim was having was that he would not complete his homework assignments, which was bringing his grades down. When asked if he received any modifications or adaptations, the resource teacher responded no, but that he did have one-to-one para-educator support. (**RED FLAG!**) Why does Tim have para-educator support? How does the para-educator support Tim? The resource teacher stated that he had always had a one-to-one para-educator supporting him, but did not know what that support looked like. (**Another RED FLAG here!**) The initial recommendation was that Tim be observed within his classes prior to a problem-solving meeting.*

Observation

The observation of Tim began within his first period class. The students began to enter the room. Tim entered the classroom a few minutes later, wearing his coat and hat and not carrying a bookbag. He walked to a desk and sat down. He did not engage in any interactions with his peers. (The other students in the class were informally interacting as the teacher was up in the front of the room preparing material for the class.) The para-educator followed Tim into the classroom, carrying his bookbag. She sat at a desk next to Tim and began to take out books and folders from his bookbag. When the teacher collected homework papers, the para-educator handed the teacher Tim's paper. The para-educator then told Tim that he needed to take off his coat and hat and hang them up in his locker. Tim complied, left the room and returned a few minutes later without wearing his hat and coat.

The para-educator took notes and gave them to Tim; she asked the teacher questions for Tim. Tim sat passively throughout the class. He did not talk to his teacher or his peers in the class at any point. Tim did not participate within the class discussion and he did not take notes himself. This continued throughout this class. At the end of the class, the para-educator took Tim's homework assignment book, wrote down his homework assignment, and put his homework assignment book in his backpack. The class was dismissed. Tim did not leave until the para-educator told him to go to his next class.

Reflection Questions:

- *Was Tim fully included within this class?*
- *Is this an example of inclusive education?*

Of course, the answer to both of these questions is NO! Tim was physically in the class; however, he was not engaged nor did he participate in any of the learning activities. However, his para-educator was fully engaged. Tim was not a participant within the educational process; however, his para-educator was. Tim did not have ownership of his learning. Tim's grades could not have reflected learning as he was not an active participant within the learning process. However, his para-educator was. You may be thinking that this is an unusual situation. However, it is not. There are many instances that are similar to Tim's, the para-educators doing, actively engaged, while the students sit passively.

Case Study: Sam (Inclusion)

Sam was a kindergarten child with a diagnosis of Down's syndrome in a school district that prided themselves in stating that they were a fully included district. What this meant for Sam was that he physically attended the same kindergarten class as his same-aged peers. It did not mean that Sam was actively engaged or participated in educational experiences or that he was actively engaged within the educational learning process throughout his school day. In fact, Sam spent most of his school day walking the hallway with his one-to-one para-educator. When he was in the classroom completing an activity, the para-educator completed most of the work and then Sam handed in the final product.

Reflection Questions:

- *Was Sam fully included within this class?*
- *Is this an example of inclusive education?*

Of course, the answer again is NO! Sam was not engaged in learning experiences or the learning process. Inclusion does not mean simply physically being in a class or on a class list.

Tim and Sam were not engaged in the process of learning. Inclusive education goes beyond being physically included in the classroom. Inclusion involves complete active participation within the learning process throughout the school day. Inclusive education means active engagement, active members of the group and of the learning process. Neither Tim nor Sam was a part of their group or engaged within the learning process.

Inclusion is a philosophy as much as it is a practice. It is believing that everyone is more alike than different and that differences make classrooms and classroom experiences richer for all students. All children, with and without disabilities, families and education professionals benefit when children are educated together. We know that all children learn social skills, gain a sense of confidence and independence and exhibit more appropriate behavior when there is diversity in our classrooms. All children benefit when they feel a sense of belonging to the classroom community (Brillante, 2017). However, this is not so if students are merely passive observers within the classroom.

Special educators and special education directors may report that a student has made progress because the student got through the day just fine without a behavior incident. What exactly does that mean? When asked how the student participated and how engaged the student was within classroom learning experiences, they often respond that they did not know, but there were no behavior incidents. Of course, it is extremely important that students' behavior incidents decrease as effective communications increase. However, it is crucial that interventions and supports increase students' active participation, engagement and learning. Physically being in a class without a behavior incident is not enough. Both Sam and Tim did not demonstrate any behavior incidents; however, they did not demonstrate active engagement within the learning process.

Inclusion is supporting students with and without disabilities within educational classrooms in order that they are active participants within the learning process. The crucial word here is supporting and not simply placing a student in a regular education classroom. Students with disabilities attend the same school as their siblings and neighbors; they attend general education classes with chronologically age-appropriate peers. However, students with disabilities have individualized and relevant learning objectives with appropriate modifications and adaptations. They are provided with the necessary supports to actively participate within the learning process, learning activities and within school routines (Brillante, 2017).

Inclusion is NOT a-one-size-fits-all model requiring that all students (with or without a disability) spend every minute of the school day in general education classrooms. The amount of time a student spends in the regular education classroom depends on individual student needs, in order to be successful and active within the learning process. A student might participate within the general education classroom with their peers, who do not have disabilities, for part of the school day rather than all day. Inclusion does not mean that students with disabilities never receive small-group or individualized instruction or that they only learn the core curriculum. It does not mean students with disabilities are placed in general education classes and sit passively.

Least Restrictive Environment (LRE)

Individuals with Disabilities Education Act (IDEA), 2004, utilizes the terms natural environment and least restrictive environment to describe the preferred setting for educating children with disabilities, instead of the terms full inclusion or inclusion. Least Restrictive Environment (LRE) ensures that children are educated with their same-aged peers who do not have disabilities to the maximum extent possible. Least Restrictive Environment (LRE) not only changes from child to child but may change over time (semester to semester, year to year) for a particular child. LRE can include more than one placement. In other words, the child may be in the regular education classroom for part of the day, and receive services out of the regular education classroom for part of the day, depending on the student's needs (e.g., resource room, special education classroom, therapy programs, community support, etc.).

The goal of Least Restrictive Environment is to provide children with as much access to programs with their peers as possible while maintaining active engagement and participation within the learning process.

Each district should offer a continuum of placement options. Placement options should be reviewed and discussed at every Individual Education Meeting (IEP Meeting), as students' needs change from year to year. Are school districts that pride themselves in stating that they are a fully inclusive district providing a needed continuum of services for all students? Are these school districts making placement decisions based on individual student's needs?

Parents and educators should ask questions at students' IEP meetings when discussing placement options and Least Restrictive Environment (LRE).

The following questions will support a collaborative discussion when determining appropriate educational placement and least restrictive environment for a student: (Reminder: The discussion regarding placement should be held after the student's goals and objectives have been determined.)

- What was the student's educational placement this past school year?

- How much time was spent in the regular education classroom? What were other placement environments, school environments, that the student attended. When and where?

- How successful was the student within this placement? What does the objective data tell us?

- What supports did the student receive this past year? Were there adaptations, modifications, and if so, how were they implemented? What adult prompts were provided the student and in what environments?

- How much of the school day was the student actively engaged within the learning process this past school year? What does the objective data tell us?

- In which classroom activities and learning experiences did the student experience active engagement and what supports were needed for the student's success?

- Did the student have full access to all learning experiences?

- Which classroom activities and learning experiences would require adaptations and modifications for full active participation?

- Did/will the student require adapted curriculum goals?

- Can the student's IEP goals be achieved within the regular classroom environment? Would a combination of school environments be necessary for the student to meet goals and objectives and engage in the learning process? What would this look like?

- Can changes to the classroom environment or lesson location facilitate full active participation within the learning process?

- What materials and personal and support structures are needed to ensure active participation within the learning process? What, where, when and how?

- Does the student require adjusted pacing of lessons, adjusted content and/or adjusted evaluation criteria or grading? Can this be met within the regular education program?

Best practice is situational. What can be accomplished for a student in one classroom or school, may not be possible in another classroom or school. This is true when we look at least restrictive environments and inclusive education. There may be program barriers to including students or to ensuring that a comprehensive program which explicitly outlines appropriate supports for a student are implemented. The barriers may vary from one educational environment to another. These barriers are seldom student centered; however, they have significant impacts on the success of students' active engagement within inclusive environments and success within educational and social curricula. It is important to have an objective, honest discussion regarding possible program and staff barriers that may impact students' achievement within specific school placement options.

Unfortunately, there are educational personnel who do not think students (with or without a disability) should be in their class for a variety of reasons. Also, parents may believe that no matter what, their child should be in a particular environment, such as being fully included within the regular education program or within a special education program, school and/or classroom. Both of these examples may demonstrate a lack of crucial knowledge in making such decisions. Philosophical beliefs, attitudes and knowledge bases of educators and parents have crucial impacts on educational placement. The collaborative problem-solving model would facilitate discussions to increase shared knowledge base and understanding.

Other programs, staff and/or school barriers may involve available school and school district budgets, workload and caseload issues of the educational staff. For instance, speech-language pathologists may be overextended in the number of students he or she has to service on a weekly basis. This may limit the number of services students receive and the amount of time allotted to attend collaborative team meetings. Within other districts and/or programs speech-language pathologists may have fewer numbers of students to service on a weekly basis. Furthermore, the knowledge base and experiences of educators may play a large role in the effectiveness of placement options.

The following questions support a collaborative problem-solving discussion regarding least-restrictive environment placement options:

- Does the district and/or school offer the needed services outlined in the student's IEP and at what level?

- How often are educational staff (e.g., resource teacher, autism consultant, hearing or vision itinerant, speech-language pathologist, occupational therapist, physical therapist, social worker, etc.) at the school?

- What is the educational collaboration process? What level of the educational team collaborative problem-solving model has been implemented?

- What is the continuum of services offered by the educational staff (e.g., resource teacher, autism consultant, hearing or vision itinerant, speech-language pathologist, occupational therapist, physical therapist, social worker, etc.)?

- How are the amount of services, where services are to take place and collaboration of services determined and implemented?

- What is the knowledge base of the educational staff in regard to the student's individual needs, disability, interventions and progress monitoring? What is the experience of the educational staff in working with students with specific needs and/or disabilities? Will training (professional development) be provided to the educational team? If so, who and how?

It would be great if we could create an educational system in which each school has adequate budget, experienced staff and adequate time to provide ongoing best practice for all students. However, that is not the reality of the current educational school system. School districts struggle to meet the financial needs of educating students at every level.

The school day and school year are fast and furious. There are many days in which students are not in school (e.g., holidays, Thanksgiving break, Christmas or Winter Break, spring break, Easter break, teacher meeting days, teacher professional development days). There are few months that have more than three five-day weeks. This causes disruptions in students' programs and impacts consistency of providing services. Educators are expected to attend many meetings at several educational levels and often need to prioritize their workload. (There are only so many hours in a school day and only so many days in a week!)

It is important that parents and educational staff understand that individual educational team members will have many levels of expertise and experiences and that budgets, schedules and workloads do have major impacts on providing services to all students. Educational teams can work to eliminate or at least reduce barriers through honest and objective collaborative discussions. By doing so, educational teams can develop programs for students that provide appropriate levels of services.

Educational Supports, Modification, Adaptations and Differentiation

The two case studies involving Tim and Sam are examples of how students can be fully included within their district's educational programs and yet not actively engaged within the learning process. Both students were assigned a one-on-one para-educator. Assigning para-educators to individual students is a common practice within inclusive education programming. A para-educator is a school employee who provides instructional or other direct support services to students under the direct supervision of certified educational team members. It is the certified educational team members who are responsible for educational programing and student progress, not the para-educator.

Para-educators are not students' teachers. However, para-educators often take on significant responsibilities for students' educational programming. This can be problematic for several reasons. Para-educators may not have the knowledge or training to do so and may not be properly supervised.

Here is a list of questions parents and educational staff can ask when a student is assigned para-educator support.

- Why does this student require para-educator support?
- What other supports will the student receive? Adaptations? Modifications?
- How will the special educational staff support the student?
- How will the regular education classroom teachers support the student?
- Where, when and how will the para-educator support the student?
- How will the educational staff collaborate with the para-educator?
- What necessary training will the para-educator receive? Who and how will this training be provided?
- Who, what, when and how will objective data be collected to ensure the success of the para-educator support?

The discussion regarding students' IEP goals, needs, adaptations and modifications should precede the educational team's discussion regarding least restrictive environment or placement options.

What do we mean when we discuss modifications, adaptations and differentiation for a student? Modifications and adaptations are individualized supports for a student to address students' needs and to facilitate active engagement within the learning process. Modifications involve changing the amount or type of information to be learned. Accommodations are adjustments made to the environment and to the way the materials are presented to meet the child's learning style so that the child is able to participate within the learning experiences. We do not remove the task demands but support the child in meeting them.

Differentiation is a broad term referring to the need to adjust teaching environments and educational programs to create appropriate learning experiences for individual students. Differentiation is adapting curricular to meet unique needs of students, making modifications in complexity, depth and pacing. Differentiation of instruction does not mean creating a separate lesson plan for the student (Brillante, 2017).

Students' complete educational profiles (including communication profile) will determine necessary adaptations, modifications and/or differentiations of instruction. The identified required modifications and/or adaptations, along with differentiation of instruction supports, help drive educational teams' decisions regarding students' educational placement. Educational teams' decisions regarding implementation of adaptations, modifications and/or differentiations should support goals that facilitate students' active engagement within the educational learning process and not simply completion of educational products. Simply adapting or modifying a test by reducing the number of choices for an answer from four to two may not reflect students' active engagement within the learning process and active learning. However, allowing students alternative ways to demonstrate comprehension and understanding of concepts will reflect true learning.

Adaptations, modifications as well as individual student supports should be implemented with consistency and fidelity across contexts (persons and environments). Students attend several different classes outside of their main class. For example, they may go to a different classroom with a different teacher for reading class and math class. They may attend library, music class, gym, art class, computer class, recess and lunch. They may attend school assemblies and a variety of in school and out of school field trips. These experiences and classes can be less structured than regular education classes, or perhaps more structured. The important concept here is that each learning environment, learning experience, can have different expectations, rules and structures from what students are experiencing within their regular education classrooms. It is crucial that students' programs remain constant in all school environments and with all communication partners. Communication and learning are dynamic processes and not simply an activity that we plan for in a particular class for a particular period of the day. Student success is dependent on consistency and fidelity in implementing adaptations, modifications and interventions within all contexts.

Educational teams should have explicit discussions regarding when, how and who will implement the needed supports, adaptations and modifications. Should the team decide a student requires para-educator support, then an explicit plan should be developed as to how educational team members will collaborate, support and train the para-educator and how the para-educator will then support the student. Inconsistencies in implementing such supports can result in increased student frustration, confusion and anxiety and ultimately increase students' overt behaviors (ineffective communications). Objective data should be collected to determine the effectiveness of any adaptations, modifications, interventions and/or supports implemented to determine whether they are successful and/or if they need to be adjusted.

Para-professionals can play vital roles in supporting students and educational teams in maintaining consistency and fidelity in integrating interventions, strategies, adaptations and modifications across school environments. Para-professionals can assist educational teams in data collection, and provide valuable feedback regarding inconsistencies. They can receive critical training in the strategies, interventions, modifications and adaptations that a student receives and support integration of these throughout the school day. They can report the amount of time a student is actively engaged within learning and social experiences and the amount of time the student is a passive observer.

An example of this would be the use of adult prompts. Adult prompts are supports that adults provide to facilitate students' success within a communication exchange, completing academic assignments, social interactions, etc. Prompts can take many forms such as full physical support; partial physical support; a direct model; visual or picture supports; verbal supports; gesture supports; and/or natural cues. It is crucial that there is consistency in the type of adult prompts used, when, why and how. It is also important that prompts are either faded or removed when the student is able to demonstrate independent communication or academic competence.

Students can become prompt dependent. Consistency and fidelity when providing adult prompts will reduce students becoming prompt dependent. There should be a balance between providing prompts and increasing students' independence. The action plan should include when and how to adjust and/or reduce prompts. We do not want to take away needed prompts nor do we want to provide prompts that are no longer required. Prompt dependency is a direct result of incomplete planning.

Adaptations and/or modifications may be made to the way instruction is delivered to students. Educational teams may implement use of visual aids, and visual supports. Educators may provide concrete examples and/ or reduce the level of abstract information. Instruction may be delivered through hands-on activities. Content may remain the same; however, changes may be made to the size or number of concepts taught. Some students may require less complex content or similar content but with functional application of the content. The pace of instruction may be altered in that some students may require a faster pace while others may require a slower pace.

Adaptations and/or modifications may be made to the way students respond to instruction or to demonstrate knowledge. For instance, students may respond verbally versus a written response or they may be allowed to express themselves through pictures or drawings. Students may use assistive technology to respond, such as a voice output system, visual supports, communication book or device, computer, iPad or iPhone. Students may be allowed to demonstrate understanding or knowledge of academic content through hands-on-materials.

Adaptations and/or modifications may be made to where instruction will take place. Adaptations and/or modifications can be made to the amount of time students are allowed to learn a skill or complete an assignment or test. Students may work in an alternative environment. Students may work in cooperative groups with peers, small groups or individually with an educational team member. Students may have individualized timelines for completing assignments, given more time or extended time to complete assignments, tests, etc.

Adaptations and/or modifications may be made to the difficulty level of academic materials or to the directions or the rules regarding how students may complete the assignments. Students can use a calculator to complete math problems. Students may be given simplified directions; directions may be broken down into smaller steps. Various rules or directions can be changed to accommodate individual students' needs. In addition, goals or outcome expectations may be adapted and/or modified while using the same materials.

Students may require assistive technology to access the environment, educational materials and/or educational activities. In addition, students may require assistive technology to communicate and interact as well as within task completion.

There are students who may require different materials and instructional procedures to meet individual goals and objectives (as outlined within their IEPs and action plans). Students may require alternative curriculum or substituted curriculum, such as functional curriculum and/or life skills programming.

Following is a list of questions parents and educational staff can ask and discuss within collaborative problem-solving discussions:

- What does "inclusion" mean for this student?

- Can the student actively participate? If yes, how? If not, why not?

- Can the student's participation be increased by changing the instructional arrangement (cooperative groups, peer partners, small groups)?

- Can the student's participation be increased by changing the lesson format (experiential lessons, hands-on, role-play)?

- Can the student's participation and understanding be increased by changing the delivery of instruction or teaching style?

- Does the student require adjusted performance standards?

- Does the student require adjusted pacing?

- Can the student engage in the same content but at a less complex level?

- Does the student require similar content with functional and direct applications?

- Does the student require an adjusted evaluation criteria or grading?

- Can we make changes in the classroom environment or the lesson location that will facilitate the student's ability to actively participate?

- Does the student require different materials to ensure participation?

    ◦ Same content but variation in size, number, format

    ◦ Additional or different mode of input

    ◦ Materials that allow a different mode of output

    ◦ Materials that reduce the level of abstraction of information

"The biggest mistake of past centuries in teaching has been to treat all children as if they were variants of the same individual and thus to feel justified in teaching them all the same subjects in the same way". Howard Gardner

Featured in Howard Gardner Quotes

Universal Design of Instruction (UDI)

Within the discussion of Inclusive Education, it is important to have a shared understanding or a shared knowledge base regarding Universal Design of Instruction. Universal Design of Instruction is crucial to creating school environments that address the needs of all learners: students with disabilities, students without impairments, students within general education classes, gifted students as well as English language learners.

Universal Design for Learning (UDL) is a set of principles for curriculum development that gives all students an equal opportunity to learn. UDL is a proactive approach that supports students' strengths. It allows educational teams the opportunity to balance the needs of all students, all learners. Educational collaborative teams work toward creating flexible instruction that meets the need of all learners as well as access to the learning environment. UDL creates learning experiences in which all students can access learning experiences (e.g., visual learners, auditory learners, tactile learners). It means that collaborative teams develop learning experiences that allow multiple means of presenting lessons and multiple means of students expressing knowledge as well as multiple ways students are actively engaged within learning experiences. UDL classroom design allows for the greatest number of children who will benefit from the academic and social curriculum without the need for adaptions and/or modifications (Brillante, 2017).

Universal Design of Instruction (UDI) creates learning environments and experiences in which all students can be actively engaged within the learning process. UDI involves designing classrooms and classroom experiences that are adaptable and can meet the needs of all students. It ensures that all students have physical access to learning environments and experiences, social emotional access as well as access to high-quality curricula. UDI is the most effective way to create inclusive classroom and school environments (Brillante, 2017).

UDI classrooms provide multiple ways educators can engage and motivate students to participate within learning experiences. UDI classrooms provide learning experiences in which teachers present lessons and information in multiple ways (e.g., auditory, visual and use of technology). UDI classrooms allow students multiple means in which they can express themselves, respond and/or demonstrate knowledge (e.g., written, orally, use of pictures, use of technology). It also provides multiple ways in which students' progress can be monitored.

The concepts of Universal Design for Learning and Universal Design of Instruction should precede discussions of specific adaptations, modifications and/or differentiations for particular students. In fact, when a collaborative team implements UDL and UDI, providing multiple means of presentation, participation and expression, it is possible that many of the needs of students with disabilities will be met. However, there will be students who have needs that are not met within UDL and UDI. These students may require additional differentiations, modifications and/or adaptations above and beyond what Universal Design of Instruction provides. The collaborative educational team would determine individual students needs above and beyond Universal Design of Instruction.

CHAPTER 10:

COMMUNICATION INTERVENTIONS AND SUPPORTS

Educational teams implement communication interventions and supports in order to increase effective communication, active participation, engagement and positive student outcomes within all school settings (e.g., strategies, prompts, communication programs and/or curricula, modifications, adaptations, visual processing supports, visual communication systems, communication devices, communication boards, language facilitating techniques, modeling, supportive means of communication and technology). Educational teams determine communication interventions and supports based on the needs of individual students. Interventions are derived from individual student's communication profiles as one component within the student's total educational profile. Interventions, modifications, adaptations, strategies, communication systems as well as technology supports are a direct result of students' Individual Education Plan (IEP) goals and objectives. Students' IEP programs, including interventions, are products of the comprehensive communication and educational assessment outcomes.

Student success is dependent on educational teams implementing effective strategies, interventions, modifications, adaptations, technology and communication systems with fidelity and consistency across all school environments and with all communication partners. Educational team collaboration supports and facilitates student success in regard to specific interventions and supports. The other domain areas (such as executive function skills, academic skills, cognitive processing skills, sensory, motor skills as well as social/emotional) are interrelated to communication skills and will have a direct impact on the success of communication interventions. Educational teams may need to prioritize interventions depending on students' current communication and educational needs; as well as, school and home contexts.

Intervention programs are not a one-size-fits-all model! What may work successfully for one student may not be effective for another. An intervention, modification and/or adaptation strategy that may be successful in one context for a student may not be successful within another context. Interventions (as well as identified goals) from various domain areas should be coordinated and supportive of students' success within academic, functional and social environments and contexts. Objective data, collected within various communication contexts, will determine the success of interventions.

Communication interventions and supports directly address identified individual student's needs in the areas of receptive language (understanding or comprehension of language), expressive language (use of language), auditory processing skills, language processing skills, five elements of language (syntax, morphology, semantics, phonology, pragmatics), speech skills, voice skills, along with executive functioning and cognitive processing skills. Effective programming depends on coordination of various interventions, strategies and supports.

Make Communication a Priority!

We must make communication a priority by supporting and facilitating students' communications throughout the entire day, within all communication contexts, academic, functional and social (total school settings). Communication interventions and supports, as well as communication systems, facilitate communication opportunities within total school settings. It is crucial that educational teams create action plans for individual students that outline the what and why behind communication interventions and supports and who and how they will be integrated within communication contexts. Collaboration allows each member of the educational team (including parents) shared knowledge of what, why, how, when and who regarding the action plan.

It is important that the action plan be implemented with fidelity and consistency across school, home and community environments with peers and adults. The action plan may need to be adjusted, based on objective data collection.

Students attend several classes and are in many school environments throughout the school day. One class or one environment is not more or less important than another when we plan for students' communication success. There are classes that are often referred to as the specials (e.g., gym class, music class, art class, library, computer class, lunch, recess, assemblies, field trips). Students' communication interventions, supports, communication systems and devices should be implemented within these contexts just as in other school environments. Unfortunately, this is not always the case. Teachers within the special classes are often not included within crucial collaborative student discussions, resulting in inconsistencies and gaps within students' communication (as well as behavior) intervention programs. This can impact students' progress and result in increased overt behaviors (ineffective communications).

Structure, Consistency and Predictability

Communication interventions that provide structure, consistency and predictability reduce levels of communication anxiety, and increase students' abilities at processing and accessing language within dynamic environments. Interventions that provide real life experiences and that provide concrete real life examples of language concepts support students' comprehension, understanding and language processing, resulting in knowledge. Providing communication interventions and supports, as well as learning experiences, that are relevant and meaningful to students will facilitate active participation within the learning process and create self-motivated learners.

The following are intervention questions that educational teams may discuss within a collaborative problem-solving discussion:

- Is there a shared understanding, knowledge base, regarding the why, what, when, where and who behind the interventions through collaboration?

- What interventions, strategies and supports would facilitate students' understanding and processing language, and in what communication contexts?

- What interventions, strategies and supports would facilitate students' abilities to use expressive language, and in what communication contexts?

- What interventions, strategies and supports would support development of speech skills, and in what contexts?

- How can interventions be implemented with consistency and fidelity across communication contexts?

- What communication interventions, strategies and supports will decrease anxiety by increasing communication competence?

Functional Communication

It is important for educational teams to assess whether a student has effective means of communication in order to express language and to create shared intents of communication within total school settings. Does the student have the functional communication skills that enable him or her to express needs, wants, feelings and emotions and to engage in effective interactions? This applies to all students, pre-verbal, verbal or highly verbal, no matter what their current communication functioning levels may be. Without functional communication skills and the ability to access them during various communication contexts (e.g., highly stressful or anxious communication situations, noisy environments, increased language load, sensory experiences, etc.), students may resort to challenging behaviors or experience communication breakdowns. What do we mean by functional communication? Functional communication skills are skills that allow us the ability to communicate a variety of communication shared intents and allow students full active engagement within all academic and social environments.

We previously discussed the various means or ways in which we communicate, speech being one way we express ourselves. There are many students who are on-verbal or who have limited verbal skills. It is crucial that we provide these students with additional means (ways) to express themselves in order to continue to expand their language and interaction skills.

The following questions may be answered within the educational team's dynamic communication assessment process:

- Does the student have the ability to communicate a variety of speech intents, speech acts? (What means or combination of means of communication does the student use to communicate?)

- Can the student effectively use verbal speech to access speech intents during highly anxious, stressful communication situations?

- Can the student effectively use verbal speech to express a variety of speech acts and share information?

- Can the student verbally say what he/she wants to say, when he/she wants to say it?

The educational team may ask the following intervention questions when determining appropriate communication interventions:

- Is the student's level of speech abilities meeting his or her communication needs in all communication environments?

- Is the student's level of speech abilities holding back language development?

- Are we talking for the child?

- Are we filling in what we think the child is communicating?

- Does the child have the opportunity to communicate a variety of intents?

- Does the child demonstrate communication frustrations, leading to overt behaviors?

Answers to the assessment and intervention questions may lead to recommendations for visual communication supports, technology and/or augmentative or alternative communication systems, (e.g., visual supports systems, visual communication boards, sign language, communication devices).

Multimodality Approach

Many students with communication deficits require visual language systems and supports as well as augmentative or alternative communication systems. These means of communication will not suppress the use of any other means of communication (such as speech). In fact, they will actually support language development and effective communication and may enhance students' abilities at using verbal speech. The use of augmentative communication systems (such as visual language systems, sign language and communication devices) can actually increase and support the development of speech (Silverman, 1996). The use of multi-modality or multiple means of communication is the preferred practice in supporting students with communication disorders (Gibbons & Szarkowski, 2019). Waiting too long to implement a combination of means of communication or alternate means of communication can have a devasting impact on students' language development and overall communication skills, leading to frustrations, anxiety and increased overt behaviors (ineffective communications).

Case study: Katie (Multimodality Approach)

Katie's (five-year-old child with limited verbal skills) educational team implemented a multimodality approach to support her receptive and expressive language by combining use of verbal speech and visual communication boards, along with sign language. Katie's receptive language as well as her ability to express herself increased. She began to access her visual communication board to communicate such responses as, "I want drink." Her teacher, speech patholo-gist, as well as her mother were amazed when Katie looked at her mother and spontaneously signed "I love you" while verbalizing "ma ma ma."

A multimodality approach to communication allows students the ability to use different means of expression, non-verbal, verbal as well as augmentative communication attempts. It encourages and enhances all means of communication and all students' communication attempts. We all use multiple means to communicate throughout the day (e.g., facial expressions, gestures, verbal speech, written language such as notes and lists as well as the use of technology). How many of us can get through our day without our iPhone, iPad, email access or without "texting"?

There are many possible language and communication systems and/or supports. One means of communication or one communication system and/or support may be effective in one situation and may not be effective in another. Honoring all of the student's communication attempts (such as verbal speech, non-verbal, communication systems and/or devices as well as sign language) will increase effective communication interactions while reducing frustration, anxiety and overt behaviors.

An assistive technology assessment may be necessary to determine the type of communication system and/or support that would be most appropriate for an individual student. The educational team may include this assessment as part of the action plan. They may recommend the consultation of an assistive technology consultant when completing this assessment. *(Note: An assistive technology assessment may have been completed as a component within the comprehensive assessment process.)*

Once a communication system and/or device has been determined, students will receive therapy (e.g., speech-language therapy, occupational therapy, physical therapy) and educational services to effectively use communication systems and/or a communication device. In addition, the educational team (including parents) may require professional development (training) as well as ongoing consultations regarding the communication system and/or device to effectively implement it with the student. Assistive technology, visual language supports, communication systems and/or devices as well as professional development (training) should be explicitly outlined within communication action plans and students' IEP.

Communication systems, supports and/or communication devices should be available to students at all times and integrated into all communication environments, both at school and at home. However, communication systems and/or supports (e.g., visual communication boards, communication devices, visual supports) are often not available to students at all times. They are often left in students' backpacks or in desks. A teacher reported that she took away a student's communication device for the day due to behavior issues. **(Red Flag!)** Would we take away a student's mouth or ears? Would we take away a student's wheelchair, hearing aids or eyeglasses? Of course not. Then why would we take away or not have consistently available to the student his or her means of communicating! We severely limit successful communication interactions and language development when we take away means of communication! **Never take a communication system, visual language system and/or communication device away from a student!**

Parents do not always see the benefit in using a communication system and/or communication device at home. Parents may be reluctant to use the communication device because they find it burdensome. They report that they are able to effectively communicate with their children at home. I previously discussed that my parents did not learn sign language to communicate with my sister (who is profoundly deaf). They did not see the need, as she could talk. However, my sister's ability to express herself verbally was significantly limited. Her abilities to process dynamic verbal language interactions and engage in dialogue were significantly impaired.

The collaborative problem-solving model would facilitate shared understanding and shared knowledge regarding communication systems, communication supports and/or communication devices. Collaboration provides educators and parents shared understanding regarding who, what, why, when and how. Furthermore, the collaborative process would problem-solve such issues as students' abilities to access the communication system and/or device as well as functional use within communication contexts (academic as well as social).

Evidence-Based Practice

The term evidence-based practice is used to determine decisions for identified communication interventions for individual students. The term evidence-based practice refers to an approach in which current, "high-quality research evidence is integrated with practitioner expertise and client preferences and values into the process of making clinical decisions" (ASHA, 2005, p. 1). Educational teams' decisions regarding communication interventions integrate information regarding evidence-based effectiveness of the interventions, the knowledge or expertise of the practitioner as well as the needs, abilities, preferences, values and interests of the students and their families.

> Our goal for all students is for them to become INDEPENDENT ADULTS! We need to balance necessary interventions and supports with increased student independence.

Winner (2005, 2008b) discusses how students' motivation is based on balancing communication supports with their abilities at independence. She further discusses the need to teach students' motivational skills by helping them understand they have the ability and skills to do things by themselves.

Successful interventions and strategies include the following:

- Are determined within the collaborative problem-solving approach
- Based on individual student's needs, challenges, interests
- Based on sound evidence

- All educational team members (including parents) have a shared understanding of why, when, who and what regarding interventions

- Data driven

- Contextually relevant

- Implemented with fidelity and consistently across all contexts

- Student understands the "why"; makes sense to the student

There are many communication interventions, strategies and curricula that support students with speech, language and communication disorders. A complete review of communication interventions is not within the scope of this text. Summaries of visual processing interventions that support language processing, expressive language, communication interactions, executive functioning skills as well as cognitive processing skills have been included and discussed in Chapter 11. Each of the visual processing interventions that are included create meaning for students and facilitate positive student outcomes through visual processing. It is recommended that the reader refer to the resources provided for each intervention for an in-depth explanation of each of the interventions discussed. Each of the interventions discussed may be adapted and applicable to

- Students with limited communication competence

- Students with communication delays or disorders (diagnosed or undiagnosed)

- Students on the autism spectrum

- Students who have intellectual disabilities

- Pre-verbal or emergent-verbal students

- Students who have good verbal skills, with significant communication deficits/challenges

- Students who have multiple disabilities

- Students with developmental delays

- Students with speech or language delays and/or disorders
- Students with hearing impairments, or who are deaf
- Students with visual impairments
- Students who have physical impairments
- Students who have cerebral palsy
- Students considered to have attention deficit disorder
- Students with emotional disturbance
- Students who are considered as having behavior challenges or disorders
- Students who have specific learning disabilities
- Student who are medically fragile
- Students for whom English is not their first language; ELL students
- Students without an identified disability
- Gifted students

CHAPTER 11:

VISUAL PROCESSING INTERVENTIONS AND SUPPORTS

The Following are Visual Processing Intervention Questions:

- How can we make language visual for those students who cannot process auditory language in a quick and efficient manner within dynamic communication environments (academic as well as social)?

- How can we facilitate students' abilities at processing, understanding, storing and retrieving language within dynamic communication environments (academic as well as social)?

There are many students who have challenges processing auditory information, language within school environments and interactions that directly impact academic and social success.

Students Diagnosed with Autism and Asperger's Syndrome

It is important to specifically address the visual processing needs of students on the autism spectrum. It can be confusing for educators and parents to understand that students on the autism spectrum, who may be extremely verbal and appear to have the ability to manipulate language concepts and engage in conversations, require any support at all, let alone visual processing supports. It is when we examine the content of the interactions or conversations (nonverbal and verbal), as well as the content of their language that we understand the significant communication deficit and the need for visual processing supports.

Visual processing supports are essential in supporting communication, academic, functional and social success (McGinnity, Hammer & Ladson, 2011)! This is true for students with a diagnosis of Asperger's syndrome as well as students with a diagnosis of autism (high, moderate or low functioning autism). Each student will present with unique, individual visual processing challenges and needs.

Students with autism process information visually. They do not process auditory information efficiently and may have difficulty processing and retaining verbal information. They have difficulty processing auditory information, especially in dynamic communication contexts (e.g., social interactions, processing classroom directions, discussions, environments with competing voices or background noise, and stressful communication contexts, etc.). They tend to be logical, concrete thinkers. Students with autism spectrum disorders are detail oriented and tend to focus on all details, even insignificant details. They get stuck in the details and can easily become overwhelmed. They have challenges identifying important or salient details as well as understanding the gestalt or the global picture. This can create confusion, frustration and anxiety. They have difficulty making connections between ideas and events. They often have difficulty seeing multiple perspectives of an idea and can perseverate on ideas or topics. They not only process visually but also store meanings of words and concepts as they first learned them or pictured them.

A collaborative comprehensive dynamic communication assessment will identify strengths, challenges and needs of individual students with autism, leading to successful communication interventions and supports.

Grandin (1995), a person with autism, stated that she thinks in pictures and that words are like a second language to her. She further stated that she translates spoken and written words into full-color movies. When she hears a word, pictures instantly come to her.

Case Study: Andrew (Visual Processing)

Introduction

Andrew was an eighth-grade student who was transitioning from junior high school to high school. He had an educational disability classification of autism. The educational team had concerns regarding Andrew's behaviors and inappropriate use of language, choice of words and tone of voice. It was reported that this student would yell and become angry and was disrespectful to adults. At Andrew's IEP meeting, the team discussed his transition from the junior high school level to high school. As the discussion progressed, Andrew's communication style became loud and inappropriate and he appeared angry.

Analysis

Andrew's inability to process dynamic and fast-paced conversations, as well as the content of the meeting created high levels of anxiety for Andrew, resulting in reactive interactions. (We forget how challenging and stressful a communication environment an IEP meeting can be for our students.) The longer the meeting went on, the more anxious this student became and his anxiety was reflected within his communication style.

Educational Team Recommendations

The educational team collaborated regarding Andrew's communication style and recommended that visual processing interventions should be initiated across communication and academic environments. The interventions (making conversations visual, mind maps, graphic organizers and thinking like a scientist) were successful in supporting Andrew.

We Learn So Much from Our Students!

After several weeks of implementing (both receptively and expressively) mind maps, explicit graphic organizers, making conversations visual and thinking like a scientist (these interventions are discussed later in this chapter), Andrew drew a picture of a face, with several video boxes in the area of the brain and two square eyes, along with two characters fighting.

*Andrew stated that when he thinks he sees a video and that he gets lots of ideas and lots of videos in his head. He stated that there are lots of different videos and the channels switch at random times. Because of this, it is hard for him to focus on the video (person, activity) that he is supposed to focus on. The channels battle over which one of them will be on the main screen. The channels switch at random times. Andrew said a lot of his ideas come from other projects he is doing or stuff from his family. This keeps switching back and forth. He explained that this is the reason it is so hard for him to think about his schoolwork. **Visual processing supported this student's ability to express his thoughts!***

When we present information verbally, the words, the information and the language are available for a brief moment. It is gone as soon as we say it. However, when information is presented visually, the information is available as long as the student needs it. The student can go back and retrieve the information at any time, facilitating the ability to process difficult and/or stressful language interactions and concepts. Supporting students' through visual language communication supports increases language understanding and processing. It further facilitates students' expressive language abilities. Visual processing can reduce anxiety levels of students and thus reduce the possible occurrences of challenging behaviors (challenging communications).

Following are Visual Processing Intervention Goals:

- To create meaning for students through visual processing
- To increase students' active engagement and participation throughout total school environment
- To facilitate students' abilities at processing, understanding, storing and retrieving language within dynamic communication environments

- To facilitate students' abilities at identification of salient information, the gestalt and making connections between experiences and concepts
- To facilitate students' abilities at use of expressive language within dynamic communication environments

There are a variety of different visual processing interventions and supports. Visual processing supports or visual communication supports are dependent on communication activities and interactions along with students' identified goal areas. One visual processing support and/or intervention may be effective in one situation and may not be effective in another. It is important that a variety of visual processing interventions and supports are developed to address students' needs in various communication contexts (academic, functional, social).

Different visual supports and interventions will facilitate and target communication, executive functioning skills, cognitive processing skills and academic skills.

Following are some examples of how visual processing, visual communication supports and interventions can facilitate students' success:

- Increase effective communication
- Process language: Language storage, organization, formulation
- Express themselves effectively
- Retrieve and initiate expressive language
- Make connections between concepts and ideas
- Increase understanding of contextual information
- Increase understanding of concrete vs. abstract vocabulary, concepts
- Clarify information to increase comprehension and understanding
- Understand what they are supposed to do, how they are supposed to do it and when and where

- Understand and follow rules
- Understand what is happening in their day and become independent in following daily schedules and routines
- Organize sequences of events so that the student can understand, anticipate and participate in the event
- Make choices about what they want to do
- Transition from one activity to another
- Understand how to complete work or play activities and tell someone when they are finished
- Increase independence and motivation

It is important to understand that not all visual supports create meaning for all students. Just because we show a student a picture, a visual, does not mean that it has meaning for that student or that the student can create a mental image with meaning. It is not a one-size-fits-all model in creating visual supports! Arwood, Kaulitz and Brown (2009, p. 4) state that, "Just because something is visual does not mean that a person can make language from the visual so as to be able to think about the visual."

Educators and parents may state that visual supports or interventions just did not work or that the student did not like them. All visual materials, activities, words and pictures have meaning. We cannot assume that when we present a visual support to a student, he or she understands what the visual language means or how to use it. The student may or may not understand the underlying language concepts or perhaps they may have a very concrete understanding of the visual support. They may not understand the structure of how the visual support was developed. Visual language supports and visual processing supports should be selected based on how they create meaning for individual students.

It is crucial that educational teams provide direct instruction to students when introducing visual supports. Educators can create meaning for students by explicitly teaching students the meaning behind visual supports, when and how to access the visual supports as well as how to use them within dynamic environments. Learning how to use visual supports is a process that can take time. The visual supports may need to be modified and adapted as objective data are gathered.

Visual processing interventions and supports (just as any intervention) are not a one-size-fits-all model. What may work in one context may not in another. Furthermore, how we design visual supports and/or interventions, can vary from student to student depending on individual students' needs (e.g., communication, cognitive processing, vision, motor, sensory), as well as contextual requirements. Unfortunately, too often a visual support is chosen because it was available and/or successful with another student.

The student's action plan should explicitly outline how the educational team will teach students the meaning behind visual supports along with how to access and use them. Para-educators can play active roles in supporting educational teams not only in development of visual supports, but also within implementation as well as data collection.

The success of visual communication and visual processing supports and interventions will depend on educators', parents' as well as students' "buy in", the level of direct teaching, as well as consistency and fidelity in implementing the supports and interventions.

It is important that visual processing, visual communication interventions and supports are implemented with consistency and fidelity across total school environments. In order for this to occur, everyone on the student's educational team must "buy in" to the importance of the visual supports and interventions within student's action plan and educational programming. In addition, visual processing, visual communication interventions and supports should consider the structures of various contexts (e.g., classrooms, activities, interactions, etc.). There should be a match between the goals of the visual supports and interventions and pragmatic use of them within dynamic contexts (environments and persons).

What do we mean when we discuss "buy in" regarding visual processing and visual communication interventions and supports? What this refers to is whether or not educators as well as parents find the interventions necessary for students' success or are annoyed by the increased workload that may be a result of the interventions. Educators may state that they find the visual supports and interventions as distractions and a burden to implement within the classroom or school environment. An administrator stated that he could not make his teachers implement the interventions. The IEP is a formal, legal document that requires implementation by all educational staff working with a student. However, in reality, this administrator's statement is true. We cannot make anyone do something they do not understand, do not find useful or that does not make sense to them.

The collaborative team model creates ongoing opportunities to create shared knowledge and understanding of the importance and significance of visual supports and interventions. It is crucial that educational teams collaborate regarding the goals for the visual supports and interventions, what skills the visual supports will target, how they should be implemented, when and where. It is important that educational teams understand what domain area or combination of domain areas the visual interventions and supports will target. Through the collaborative process, the team contextually identifies and determines visual supports based on communication needs of students as well as academic and social curricular.

Speech-language pathologists, social workers, special education teachers, occupational therapists, as well as other educators often identify visual processing supports and interventions, develop them and then present them to teachers. They may or may not provide training on how to implement them within their class. Remember best practice is situational. What can be accomplished in one context, one environment, may not be possible within another. A visual support may work within one classroom and not another. We may not have all the crucial information within each classroom (each communication context) in which to make crucial decisions regarding what visual supports would be most effective to support students.

When we involve and collaborate with teachers and parents within the process of developing visual processing supports, they have "buy in" from the beginning of the process. Within the collaborative problem-solving process, we can ask questions that are context specific (classroom specific) and that can be pragmatic in implementation.

The following should be taken into consideration in the development of visual communication, visual processing supports:

- Individualized for individual students
- Relevant and meaningful for individual students
- Contexts in which the visual supports and interventions would be implemented
- Implemented with consistency and fidelity
- Age appropriate
- Student's ability levels within all domains (communication, executive functioning, cognitive processing, sensory, motor, academic)
- Auditory as well as visual acuity levels
- Student's learning style

Following are Computer Software that Support the Development of Visual Supports for Individual Students:

Boardmaker Plus! Software supports the development of visual materials that can be individualized for specific students, or groups of students. Boardmaker Plus! is available from the Mayer-Johnson Company (www. mayer-johnson.com). It is a picture library containing over 3,500 picture communication symbols, which can be used to develop visual communication supports such as, but not limited to, executive functioning supports, communication displays, device overlays, book adaptations, classroom visual supports and visual schedules.

Inspiration (https://www.inspiration-at.com) is a visual thinking tool that supports the development of mind maps, diagrams, graphic organizers, outlines and other visual communication, executive functions and cognitive processing supports.

Kidspiration (https://learningworksforkids.com/apps/kidspiration) is a child friendly version of Inspiration, designed for children ages preschool through fifth grade.

Visualization and Active Listening are Two Effective Interventions

Visualization and active listening can be effective within our own communications with students, parents and educational professionals, as well as therapy interventions to increase students' effective interactions and communications across total school environments. When we use visualization along with active listening within our own interactions with students, parents and educational professionals, we are able to piece together important information regarding students' interactions and communications.

Visualization is the ability to see pictures in your mind, or to picture things in your head. We often refer to this as our "mind's eye". When you use visualization, you are imagining a picture in your mind. You actually imagine all of the possible senses: sounds, smells, tastes, how things feel, how you feel, colors, size, shape, etc. The more senses you include within your "mind's eye", or your mental image, the more you will remember and be able to recall quickly and efficiently. Visualization teaches students how to make mental pictures of what they hear or read (Graser, 1992). When students learn to make mental images, or to use their "mind's eye", they can then draw or write what they see and attach verbal language to the mental images. Using mental images (mind's eye) facilitates students' abilities to remember information and make connections between concepts.

A picture makes it easier for our brains to understand and to remember information. Pictures can make information (language concepts) personal, allowing students opportunities to attach prior knowledge. It also teaches comprehension checks by asking if our image or picture makes sense. If not, we can then check the meaning or our understanding.

Visualization can also assist educators in understanding students' perspectives. It can support our understanding of parents and members of the educational team's perspectives as well. We can visualize an interaction or a communication from their "mind's eye" or their perspective. When we do this, we can actually experience it from their point of view without any judgments. Can you visualize the student's perspective as to what he or she may be experiencing? This will help us understand the "why" behind students' interactions and overt behaviors and communications.

Active listening is a powerful intervention that can be implemented across age and grade levels. We can teach this strategy or intervention to our students through use of visual supports and active engagement within the process. We teach our students that communication involves taking turns between listening and talking. We listen with our eyes and ears. We pay attention to what the person is saying; we organize and hook the new information to information we already know; we then understand and remember what they are telling us so that we can respond in some way (Graser, 1992).

Visual representations (creating visual supports) facilitate students' understanding and use of the strategies within the active listening process. This single activity integrates several strategies: "hook it" to what you know, comprehension checks, paraphrasing, asking questions, responding.

Six Steps to Active Listening

Step 1: Did you hear the sound?

Step 2: Did you pay attention to the sound?

Step 3: Did you "hook it" or organize it to what you already know?

Step 4: Did you make sense of the information? Do you understand?

Step 5: Did you remember the information?

Step 6: Did you respond? Did you ask a question, say something, do something?

Case Study: Students with Hearing Impairments (Active Listening)

Students with hearing impairments, either in hearing impaired programs and/or who are included within regular education programs at times do not want to wear either their hearing aids and/or use FM systems. To counter this, educators can make use of an active listening chart, asking the students to walk up the steps. The students will stop on step one (hearing), as without their technological aids they do not hear the total messages. Educators do not need to direct the students to put on their hearing aids and/or use FM systems, as it will be implied they need to do so to move forward within the lesson and/or activity.

Active Listening is a very powerful intervention for our students. It is a very powerful tool for us! Be quiet, stop talking long enough to observe and listen with your eyes, ears, mind and heart to what the students are saying both verbally and nonverbally. Attach this information to what we already know about the student; put the pieces of the puzzle together. When we employ active listening in this manner, we can then respond with effective interventions, strategies and supports.

Case Study: Jay (Active listening)

Introduction

Jay was a fifth-grade student diagnosed with Asperger's syndrome. He was receiving private speech-language therapy. Jay had a behavior incident at his private speech therapist's office in which he ran out of the office and refused to return.

Behavior Incident

Jay ran out of his private speech therapist's office, refusing to go back in. However, prior to fleeing the room, he told his therapist he did not want to "do it." The more his therapist insisted that he return to the therapy room, the more overt and loud his communication style became. Jay's mother became very stressed and unsure of what to do, as he needed his private speech therapy and he was wasting precious time! She called me not sure what to do!

Analysis

The speech language pathologist's perceptions were that Jay was demonstrating obsessive compulsive behaviors along with defiant behavior issues. Her perceptions were that Jay was manipulative and a student with behavior issues. Our perceptions drive our actions, our interventions.

I had interactions and experiences with this young man (prior knowledge) and knew that most of the time he would comply (no child does all of the time), especially when promised a rewarding activity after. (It is okay to work in relevant and meaningful rewards for our students!) I also knew Jay was a sensitive and kind person who wanted to please adults. He was also very motivated by his after-therapy reinforcement activities. So why now? Why did he run out of the room and refuse to interact with the therapist? Why didn't he want to go back to that therapist? What was the activity from which he felt the need to flee? These are the intervention questions. This was not going to be determined at that moment with the speech-language pathologist, his mom and he himself so upset. They needed calm in the midst of turmoil. All three of them! I know what you might be thinking: by letting him go home we reinforced his behavior. Perhaps that is one way to look at the situation. Another way is that we were honoring and respecting him and his means of communications: non-verbal, verbal as well as para-linguistic.

Interventions

When Jay's mother called, I asked if he was at a point where he could have a calm conversation. The answer was no. My advice was to do nothing. Stop talking to him, ask his therapist to stop talking to him, then go home. Nothing was going to be accomplished and in fact negative communication loops were persisting for far too long within this interaction. It was obvious that Jay was extremely distraught. It was obvious his mother and the therapist were also upset. This definitely was not a positive experience for Jay, his mother or the therapist. Jay told his mother that he did not want to go back to this therapist again. She asked me if she should make him go. My advice to her was to understand why Jay was refusing to go back and to believe and respect what he told her.

When Jay was in a calm state, we had a discussion (visual conversation) with him regarding speech therapy in general and not simply that particular session.

Jay was a very bright young man, who at that time, was working on activities in which he needed to listen to some auditory stimuli (language sequences) and either repeat or respond in some way. This activity did not make any sense to him, nor did he understand why and how it was going to help him. In fact, the activity was increasing his anxiety level, to the point where he felt he had to flee. Although Jay was intelligent and highly verbal he did not have the requisite quick and efficient access to language to say at the time, "But this is really frustrating me and I do not understand the point to it. I feel really dumb." That was exactly what he told us through the visual conversation at a later calm time.

Wisdom from a MOM! I would like to share an email I received from this mother several years after this incident:

"I listened to what he said and believed him. When he didn't want to see the speech therapist, it was important to understand why and to believe him. You said what he was doing in therapy did not make sense to him and you were right. Going to therapy and doing activities that had nothing to do with what he was learning in school was meaningless to him and made him feel dumb! His therapist's perception of his behavior was an issue. She was not convinced that sensory or Asperger's could be part of the issue or that her authoritative ways were part of the issue. Giving him rewards was Okay; it was the only way to

get him to do something he doesn't want to. Preparing him ahead of time and having written schedules worked. Throwing things at him unexpectedly was like throwing water on a live wire. He began to work with a resource teacher, working on school-related activities and not on rigid activities that had no value to him. He asked that she continue to be his tutor and he continued to work with her. Having some control over who he worked with helped. He is sensitive in that he senses feelings and does not want to let anyone down. He did not want to attend difficult school activities, such as sex education in fifth grade. You told me not to force him to go or to prepare him before he goes, by making the concepts concrete as possible. I had already learned that it's OK not to push him and to listen to him. You told me to write out everything he needed to know, including slang words and what they meant. I wanted to vomit as I wrote but I am so thankful today!

He needs calm adults to guide and understand him! Instead of trying to control him, I have learned to control myself. He currently has a job at a high school fixing computers! I never thought we would get to this point!"

> Therapy and teaching are dynamic interactions which mirror the dynamic process of communication! Effective communication interactions are crucial within the therapy and teaching process! It is not what we do to our students, but what we do interactively with our students, that create positive, successful learning experiences!

Our students need to understand the why and how behind the interventions and supports we implement. This can be accomplished in different ways depending on the students' developmental levels. The interventions as well as the experiences within the therapy process should make sense to our students. We often forget that students' self-concepts can be impacted by the therapy process itself. We support speech, language and communication growth with our students. **Intervention is an interactive process!** This can be true at any developmental level. How can we make the experience useful and make sense to our students? What John Dewey said regarding all students' learning holds true through the therapy process. Dewey spoke of the importance of active student involvement within the learning process and experiences. He further emphasized the need to make learning experiences as meaningful as possible for our students, providing students with materials and experiences that are relevant and meaningful.

Visual Supports: Structure, Predictability, Consistency

Visual supports that increase structure, predictability and consistency can decrease anxiety, increase positive outcomes for students, and support students increased self-regulation. Decreased anxiety may result in increased abilities at accessing language within important academic contexts and interactions (both with adults and peers). When students understand what they are supposed to do, for how long and when they will be done, they are able to maintain focus on a task or activity. This in turn will increase students' motivation and confidence, knowing they can do it! It is important that educators and parents create safe zones, environments in which students know that they can take chances and make mistakes without being criticized or judged.

Transitions happen throughout a student's day, such as: from activity to activity, classroom to classroom, academic subjects to lunchroom, gym class, recess and school to home. Transitions can be extremely difficult for students with communication disorders, executive functioning deficits, cognitive processing deficits as well as social/emotional difficulties. Students who refuse to leave an activity, such as the computer, or a video game, are often seen as presenting with behavior challenges. Educators often state, "He/she only wants to do what he/she wants. He/she refuses to be cooperative with teachers." The activities that students are refusing to stop or leave may be activities in which they are familiar with and feel confident in completing. Leaving a comforting, familiar activity to go to unfamiliar and/or stressful activities/environments can cause anxiety and fear in students.

There are actually four components to a single transition. First, is the actual stopping of the first activity. Second, students need to be able to make a cognitive shift to the next activity. In other words, they need to be able to stop thinking about the first activity and start to think about the next activity. This requires flexibility. Third, once the student has moved to the next activity, he/she needs to be able to start, or to initiate the next activity. The final component is lack of structure and expectations during the transition. The period of time students waits for the next activity, leave one classroom and enter a new classroom, is often unstructured; there may be an increased noise level, and limited to no adult directions. Students often socialize with their peers. We can create structure for our students during these unstructured periods (Minahan & Rappaport, 2012).

It is important that educators understand the why behind students' transitioning challenges and provide explicit visual supports throughout the transition process. There is no one-size-fits-all to providing students with transition supports. What may work for one student may not work for another student, or what may work in one situation may not work in another situation. For instance, a warning may facilitate one student's ability at stopping an activity, but may not be effective with another student. Make use of natural visual supports, such as stopping at the end of a page or the end of a chapter. Additional supports that may facilitate students' abilities at stopping an activity may be providing explicit cues or warnings, visual stop pictures, analog visual clocks, one more problem or explicit task schedules.

Support students' cognitive shifts to the next activity by using photographs of students engaged in the activity and/or explicit visual directions on how to transition from one activity to another. Explicit task strips or visual directions can support this transition. Provide clear expectations and explicit visual supports that tell students where they should be, how to get there and what to do when they get there. Provide students with structured concrete activities during the unstructured transition time (e.g., cleaning off the board, collecting papers, greeting peers and/or taking attendance as students walk into the room). It is important that these activities are not only age appropriate, but also make sense and are motivating for individual students. It is important that the tasks we are asking students to transition to are within students' abilities to complete. Once they have transitioned to the next activity it is crucial that we provide explicit visual supports that allow students the ability to independently initiate the task. They know how to begin the task, how to persist at the task and how to end the task.

Intervention: Get Ready-Do-Done (Ward, 2012)

The Get Ready-Do-Done Intervention supports independent executive functioning skills and communication skills across contexts. This is a dynamic visual processing intervention that provides structure, predictability and consistency. It supports students' abilities at transitioning from one activity to another in that it explicitly visually outlines for students the final product or what "done" means, how to do it and how to get ready to do it. It further allows explicit visual information regarding what students do during the unstructured transition time. Get Ready-Do-Done is applicable for use within the academic curricular as well as social pragmatic instruction and interactions and can be adapted to students' levels of functioning. Please refer to the resource: *Executive Function Skills in Children and Adolescents [Seminar]* available at www.asha.org/shop for an explicit description and explanation of this dynamic intervention (Ward, 2012).

Get Ready-Do-Done supports the following areas of executive functioning:

- Response Inhibition: Supports students by providing structure and predictability

- Working Memory: Supports the students in making connections through visual processing

- Emotional Control: The visual structure allows the student the ability to achieve a goal and complete a task. This intervention facilitates students understanding of expectations and how to meet them, reducing confusion, anxiety and frustration.

- Sustained Attention: The visual processing and structure facilitates students' abilities at maintaining increased focus to task.

- Task Initiation - Persist at Task - End task: The student has a clear, explicit understanding of how to initiate the task, persist at completing it and what being done means.

- Planning/Prioritization: The student has a clear understanding of how to complete each step of the task and what is needed to do so.

- Time Management: Making time visual through use of an analog clock facilitates the student's ability to understand time estimation and passing of time (internal time clock/ sense).

- Flexibility – Educators can build into the plan a "what if" option, making use of change cards.

- Goal Directed Persistence: The student can visualize what the end product will be and how to get there.

One of the most important concepts within this intervention is that of declarative language. Declarative language differs from commands in that it describes what is to be accomplished. Ward (2012) discusses changing commands to declarative language, allowing students the ability to see the gestalt, the final product or the goal to be accomplished. It increases independence, teaches students self-talk and develops inner speech. Instead of telling the student that he/she needs to go get his/her reading book (giving a command), ask, "What would you have if you were ready for reading?" "What would you look like if you were ready for class?" Ward (2012) suggests teaching this concept visually by writing questions on the board or the student's planner and initially reviewing them with the class.

A second important concept within this process is making time visual and concrete. Ward (2012) discusses the importance of making time visual for students. The understanding of time and the passing of time are necessary for organizational skills. The student may be able to tell time, but not conceptualize the passing of time. The student may say, "This is taking forever!"

when actually only three minutes have passed! The use of an analog clock visually shows the passing of time.

GET READY-DO-DONE VISUAL EXAMPLE

Following is an example of a visual support that outlines the concepts within this intervention. Educators begin with what the completed task, project, group goal would look like. This can be individualized for students. Once students explicitly understand what "done" means, then move back to what they would do to complete the task, project, etc. Once students understand what done is and what they need to do, they can then decide what they need to do or get to be ready to begin. Each step (Get Ready-Do-Done) should be explicitly outlined through use of declarative language.

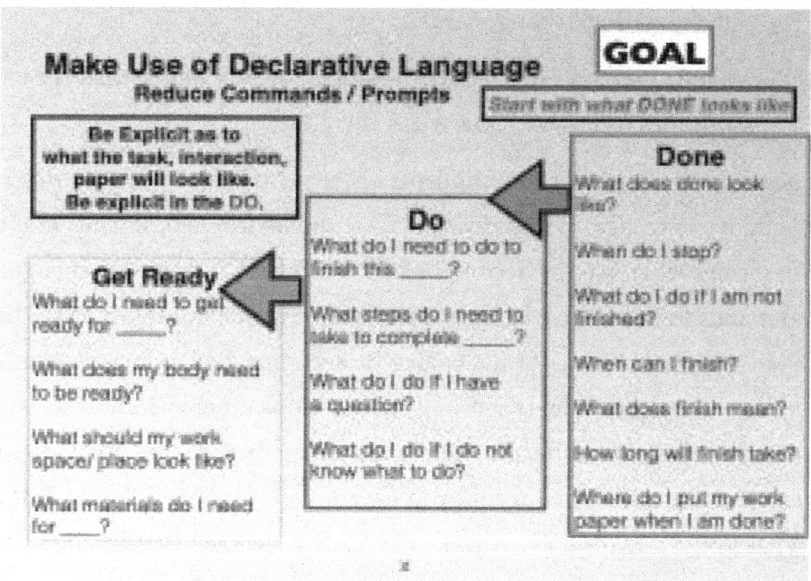

Making Conversations Visual Intervention

Educators and parents talk to students and interact with students. We explain, we tell, we inform, we describe, we discuss, and we correct students. Do students with communication deficits and/or challenges process what we say? Are they actively listening or are they tuning us out? Could our verbalizations be increasing anxiety and frustration in our students? How do we facilitate students' comprehension, their understanding, and their abilities to process difficult and often stressful information? How do we facilitate students' abilities at expressing themselves?

Making conversations visual is an extremely powerful intervention for students who do not process verbal language and conversations quickly and efficiently. Making conversations visual is an intervention that facilitates and supports receptive language or understanding of language, expressive language, social interactions, Theory of Mind, cognitive processes, executive functions, and generalization of speech skills.

Making conversations visual can be a very powerful and effective intervention when implemented with fidelity. It integrates the strategies of active listening and visualization as well as supports the concept of talk less. This allows students time to breathe and to process language. We do not need to fill every silent gap with verbal words.

Making conversations visual can be used to support students whenever and wherever language processing and expression occurs (anywhere and always). They are effective in facilitating and maintaining students' engagement, independence, and motivation.

Making conversations visual is an effective strategy in supporting students (at any age) who have deficits that impact their ability to process, store, attach meaning to prior knowledge, organize, formulate, and retrieve language in a quick and efficient manner. This intervention facilitates expressive language use within dynamic communication environments.

The goals of making conversations visual may address many different areas:

- Processing language: Language storage, organization, and formulation across environments
- Retrieving and initiation of expressive language across environments

- Problem solving: Facilitates and supports students in visually working through a problem, identifying possible solutions, and then visually compare to future problem-solving conversations and situations

- Understanding social language concepts and discourse skills

- Contextual understanding of concepts and social interactions

- Flexibility of thought

- Understanding salient details within gestalt social, academic, and vocational environments

- Understanding semantic concepts, abstract as well as concrete

- Understanding rules and facilitates increased flexibility in application of rules

- Understanding different perspectives and changes in perspective

- Assist students in identification of salient or relevant information

- Facilitates fluent speech for students with fluency disorders (stuttering, cluttering)

- Facilitates generalization of speech skills

How do we make conversations visual? How do we implement this intervention?

There are several important considerations when beginning the process of making conversations visual with a student. First is to know individual student's strengths, needs, and deficit areas as well as levels of functioning. Identify the student's goals as well as understand the specific goal for making the conversation visual. Why are you having this particular conversation and why does it need to be visual? It is important to remain positive and interactive remembering that this process, as with any conversation, is dynamic in nature. There is no right or wrong to the process. However, communication breakdowns may occur, which will need to be immediately addressed within the visual process.

Stop talking and actively listen to what the student is saying both nonverbally and verbally, without making judgement statements. Auditory conversations are fleeting; however, visual conversations are not. You can help students make connections to ideas and concepts visually. DO NOT SAY, "BUT YOU SAID!" Allow students time to make connections visually; provide them time to process the information.

General Suggestions

- Make use of a sketch pad (pages are bound in some way). A sketch pad allows conversations to be kept for future access. Students are able to reread previous conversations. This facilitates students' abilities at making connections to future situations and/or contexts. What was the same but different? Each student should have his or her own sketchpad. (You will go through lots of these.)

- Use markers (conversations can be colored coded). Color can be used to represent a speaker or a listener. Color can represent ideas, emotions, time, people, or concepts, etc.

- Make use of visual thought and speech bubbles.

- Use common icons that represent words (e.g., not, no, or stop).

- Write or draw the salient information that the student needs to understand and or process.

- It is important that the facilitator does not make verbal and/or non-verbal judgement statements or corrections.

- Model verbal words with written words and/or pictures; verbalize only the salient words.

Making conversations visual can be implemented in a one-to-one situation, small and large groups, as well as within classroom contexts. Making conversations visual can be implemented within various dynamic communication situations and environments: after a behavior incident (when the student is in a calm state), application of school rules, classroom discussions, understanding hidden rules, interactions with peers and adults, during a lesson, on the playground, lunchroom and field trips, etc.

There is no right or wrong to this process. The facilitator leads the conversation within receptive visual conversations. Expressive visual conversations are interactive between facilitator and student, as well as between students. Students can be the facilitator, leading and/or initiating the conversation. Ask the student to show you. Ask the student if he/she can write or draw their ideas. What is the picture in your head? The facilitator can draw ideas, speech or thought bubbles to begin the process. Once the student understands the process, you can take turns between receptive and expressive use of making conversations visual.

Example: Making Conversations Visual

An educational team met to problem solve placement for a student on the autism spectrum to determine possible placement within a self-contained autism program. The special education director wanted to ensure that least restrictive environment was honored for this student. The team worked diligently, meeting and collaborating every two weeks, in order to support him within his kindergarten program and then into his first grade year. Visual processing supports, communication, sensory, motor as well as executive functioning supports were implemented across his school environment. This student became successful within the regular education program and his placement was not changed to the autism program.

His speech-language pathologist, in collaboration with his educational team, implemented making conversations visual. After several months, to the amazement of both his teachers and speech-language pathologist, the student drew the above visual conversation and gave it to his speech-language pathologist (expressive use of visual conversation!).

The incident that lead to this visual conversation: His speech-language pathologist went into the classroom to take this student to speech therapy. He became very upset, yelling and crying. He went to the speech room. Once he got there, he drew this in his notebook. He was then able to verbalize to her that he was upset because he was talking to his friend and she made him go to speech! Their conversation began on the bus and they were talking!

Example: Making Conversations Visual

This student was a first grader with significant receptive, expressive as well as auditory processing deficits. He was also an English language learner (ELL) student. His speech-language pathologist along with his educational team collaborated to integrate communication supports as well as visual language supports throughout his day. They implemented making conversations visual receptively, which significantly increased both academic and social language comprehension, reducing anxiety and frustrations.

This student became attached to a female peer within his classroom and wanted to constantly interact with her to the point that she was becoming upset. His teacher changed his desk to an area in the classroom that was away from this female peer. The student became very upset and began to cry. He drew the above visual conversation and gave it to his teacher. He was then able to verbalize that this girl is his best friend and the teacher took her away. His teacher was then able to provide supports to increase his interactions with other peers in his classroom and teach him some boundaries with this female peer.

Example: Making Conversations Visual

The same student drew another visual conversation (expressive use). The class (seven students) was sitting at the board during a lesson. This student became very upset when the teacher did not allow him to talk (he did not understand the concept of turn taking, allowing other students the opportunity to talk.). He became very upset, yelling and crying. He was asked to go to his desk. He drew this visual conversation and gave it to his teacher. He was then able to tell his teacher that it was his turn to talk!

This allowed the teacher the opportunity to implement interventions to support this student's ability to take turns with his peers. They began by putting the names of each student on the board, showing visually whose turn it was. The teacher provided learning experiences in which he was able to experience the concept of turn taking!

Examples: Making Conversations Visual

The above two visual conversations were interactions with Tommy. Tommy had excellent verbal skills; however, he was not able to express himself when he was upset or when anxious. He would revert to overt behaviors, ineffective communications.

Tommy would insist that he be first in line and would become extremely upset if he was not first in line. His teacher explained that the class took turns as to who would be first in line. However, he continued to yell and cry if he was not first in line. His teacher attempted to explain to him that all the students needed to take turns, but he continued to insist that he be first.

I met with Tommy and began the first visual conversation by writing 1st, 2nd, 3rd, 4th, last with line drawings of students. "Where do you like to be?" He said, "I like to be 1st it makes me happy." I wrote that in a speech bubble.

*Then wrote "thinking?" with an empty thought bubble. He said, "Kids get too close, I don't want to talk in line." I wrote that in the thought bubble and then wrote, "Ok, for now that is a good enough reason." This honored, respected and validated his feelings, his perceptions of the situation, creating trust. At a later time, we continued the visual conversation by including the classroom rules for lining up. I visually added that if he was last in line, he would not have to talk or be close to other students, as he could move back a bit. He visually saw the connection and agreed that if it was not his turn to be first, he would be last: **The power of visual processing!***

The second visual conversation with Tommy was due to overt behaviors, ineffective communications he was having due to writing assignments. He was refusing to write or to allow his teachers to help him within the writing process. We began the visual conversation with the word writing in the middle of the page with the graphic around it. We began a mind map of his thoughts on writing, with thought bubbles. I wrote "why? Thinking?" We wrote his ideas inside the thought bubbles. After he read each one he said, "School is hard!" I wrote that at the top of the paper. I then wrote at the bottom of the paper, "Teacher's job" with visual connections to "to help make this easier", "to help you in class". In red, within a speech bubble, we wrote, "I'm stuck and I need help!". This provided him with a way to ask for help. His teacher was then able to provide visual supports for brainstorming ideas, language formulation, along with executive function supports.

Think Like a Scientist Intervention

Baker (2015) discussed, within the context of cognitive behavioral treatments, the idea of using logic and scientific reasoning to support students in lowering levels of stress and anxiety. Students with communication disorders, executive functioning deficits as well as cognitive processing deficits, may have high levels of anxiety that interfere with effective language processing, communication interactions, expressive language use, as well as the ability to engage in productive problem solving. They may fear and become anxious within various communication contexts (persons and environments).

Anxieties may present as overt behaviors such as irritability or angry outbursts; students may shut down or isolate themselves avoiding communication interactions. Fear and anxiety may interfere with students' abilities to interact, engage and participate within the educational process and/or therapy process. They may even reject interventions. Students may appear angry within the intervention process, may refuse to go to speech-language therapy and/or participate within language groups.

The concept of think like a scientist is a very powerful tool when paired with making conversations visual, visualization, active listening and use of questioning techniques. This intervention can be individualized to meet the needs of students with a variety of communication, cognitive processing and executive functioning deficits in order to facilitate or develop skills, to tolerate the intervention process and to process problem-solving discussions.

The think like a scientist intervention supports the idea that therapy and interventions are not what we do to our students, but interactively with our students. It supports the ideas that students should be involved within the therapy process and that the experiences should be as meaningful as possible for our students.

Using the concepts of logic and scientific reasoning to a variety of communication skills, theory of mind, perspective taking and problem-solving allow students the ability to have some control within the therapy process, reducing covert and/or overt anxiety. The idea of "talk less and show" facilitates student's engagement. The idea to think like a scientist facilitates students' abilities to engage in discussions and interactions regarding abstract concepts within an objective framework without judgement and/or criticism. There does not need to be a right or wrong at all times. We can visually and objectively show students how specific communication styles impact interactions. Instead of telling students how they should communicate or interact, we can ask questions visually and allow them to work within the scientific method to find answers that are personally relevant. Then students can try out the possibilities. The important concept is that in order for them to have the courage to try something new, they need to be able to do so in "safe zones", school contexts (environments and persons) in which they can take chances and not be afraid to make mistakes; not be afraid that they will be judged or embarrassed. They need contexts (environments and persons) in which they can learn from the results, whether they were positive or not. This may need to be included within the therapy process action plan.

Think like a scientist communication questions should be student specific and derived within the therapy process. Following are some questions that facilitate students' engagement within this process:

- *How do I start a conversation with kids in my class?*

- *What can I do to allow adults (teachers) to help me with my schoolwork?*

- *What communication styles would make interactions with (teachers, parents, friends) more comfortable and easier?*

- *What is logical thinking? Does logical thinking change when perspective is considered?*

- *Do my experiences change my perspective?*

- *How can I monitor and adapt my communication style in reaction to the person I am speaking to?*

- *How can I monitor my communication style, even when I am in a bad mood? What will happen if I don't?*

- *How can I consider the importance of what I am doing or what my peers and teachers are doing?*

- *How can I make friends?*

- *How can I understand the perspective of my teachers, parents or friends?*

Example: Communication Visual Chart

Examples of Communication Questions	Brainstorm Ideas (Make use of mind mapping.)	Possible Activities Possible Consequences (Make use of mind mapping.) (Contextually relevant: communication environment – communication partner)	What happened? How did you feel?
How can I change my communication style with my teachers and/or peer			
How can I allow teachers to help me with my school assignments?			
What can I say when I need help?			
How can I enter a classroom?			
How can I greet my teachers and peers?			
What can I say or do when I become frustrated?			
What can I use to begin my writing assignments?			

Mind Maps - Mind Mapping Intervention

Mind maps or mind mapping is an intervention that directly supports universal design of learning, multiple learning styles across curriculum areas (academic as well as social). Mind maps are highly visual, language organizational strategies that help students understand and make connections to and between concepts, facilitating gestalt processing. Mind maps are highly visual graphic techniques that can be adapted and used for various classroom and educational tasks. They are diagrams used to visually outline information and are created around a single word or idea, placed in the center of the page. Associated ideas, words and concepts are added to the single word or idea. The major categories radiate from a central idea, with lesser categories visually shown as sub-branches. Mind maps can be adapted to meet the needs of learners and educational experiences. Mind maps can be adapted to meet the needs of students at various levels, from early childhood to the adult learner. Mind maps can range from being simple to very complex.

T. Buzan (www.tonybuzan.com) discusses five essential characteristics of mind mapping: (1) The main idea, subject or focus in crystalized in a central image; (2) Main themes radiate from the central image as branches; (3) Branches comprise a key image or key word drawn or printed on its associated line; (4) Topics of lesser importance are represented as twigs of the relevant branch; (5) The branches form a connected structure (Tee, Azman, Mohamed, Muhammad, Mohamad, Yunos Yee, & Othman, 2014).

Following is a list of computer software programs that support the development of mind maps:

1. *Inspiration*
2. *Kidspiration*
3. *Google Chrome Mind Maps*
4. *MindMaster for Mind Maps*

(The following mind map examples were created using either Inspiration or Kidspiration Software.)

Mind map 1 was developed to facilitate students' understanding of character development in a story. Used along with visualization "mind's eye", the students were able to conceptualize the development of the character throughout each chapter.

Mind Map 1

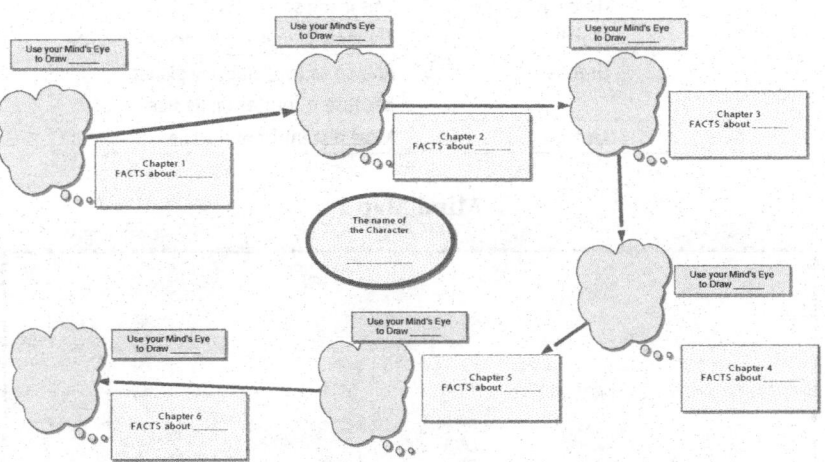

Mind Map 2 is an example of a concept mind map on the solar system. Students were given the first worksheet to study (regarding the planets). The second is a visual representation (a mind map) of the same information that was presented in the worksheet.

Directions: Cut out the words. Match the planet with the words.

Venus	This planet is closest to the sun.
Jupiter	This planet is hottest
Mars	3rd from the sun
Saturn	Scientist have explored this planet
Pluto	This is the largest planet
Mercury	This is the smallest planet
Earth	The only planet known to possess life
Uranus	Known as the "sideway planet" because it rotates on its side.
Neptune	Most distant from the sun

Mind Map 2

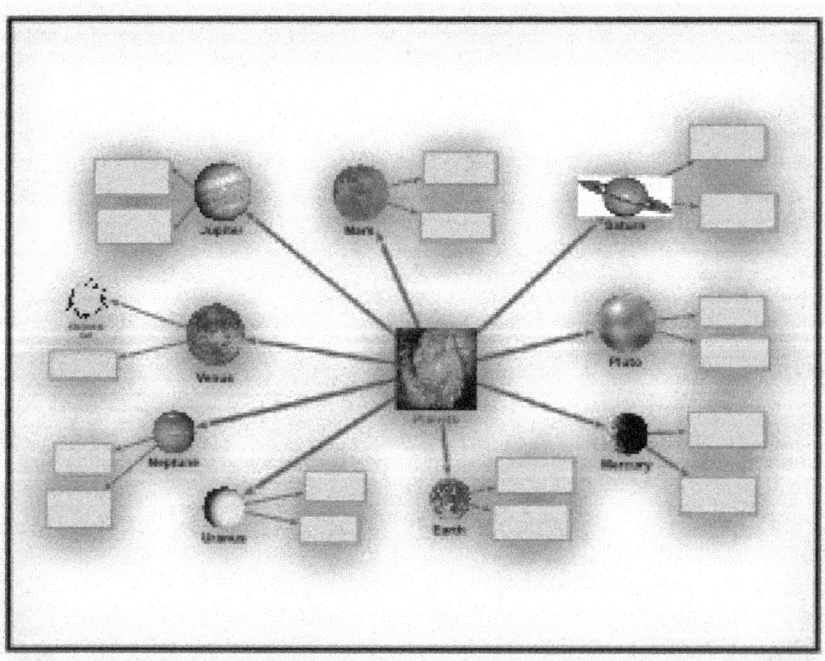

Mind Map 3 is an example of a mind map completed during a classroom discussion. The conversation was visually represented on the mind map. The students shared ideas regarding school and how the students could ask the teachers and each other for help. The students then created a classroom rule: When I am not sure I will say: "I'm STUCK and I need HELP!

Mind Map 3

Mind Map 4 is an example of how teachers can visually mind map classroom directions. As the teacher gives verbal directions, the teacher (or a para-educator or team teacher) can visually mind map what the teacher is saying.

This can be completed on the board, an overhead, smart-board and/or computer. The directions are then available to the students throughout the class. This can be adapted to ages preschool through high school (and beyond).

Visuals (such as pictures) can be used along with written words or by themselves. Consistency in use of visuals will facilitate comprehension (understanding) and students' abilities to transfer to other activities (academic and/or social).

Mind Map 4

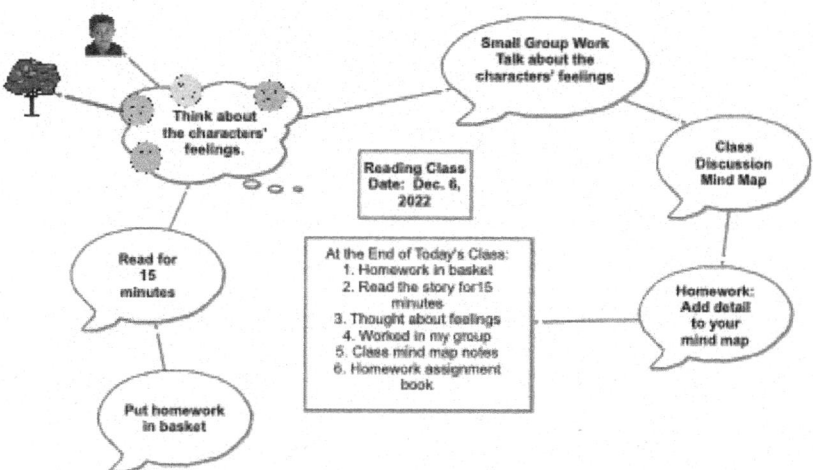

Following is an example of a high school language arts assignment.

Consider the following quote from the chapter, "Lives of the Dead": "*And yet right here, in the spell of memory and imagination, I can still see her as if through ice, as if I'm gazing into some other world...*"

Directions: We know that Tim writes and tells stories to keep his memories of people and experiences alive. He writes about Linda and Ted Lavender and Kiowa in an effort to hold onto those memories, the good and the bad, and keep them around. Consider your own life and think about someone important that you've lost. **In three written body paragraphs, complete the following:**

Paragraph 1 – Describe this person. (Who are they? Why were they important to you? What type of relationship did you have?)

Paragraph 2 – Describe your loss. (How did you lose this person? How did that feel for you? Did you grieve and how?)

Paragraph 3 – Describe at least one vivid, specific memory that you have with this person. How do you keep the memory of this person alive?

Students with communication, executive function and/or cognitive processing deficits may have the following challenges when completing this assignment.

- Literal interpretation of quote
- Difficulty understanding emotions of characters in the story
- Difficulty inferring the intentions of others as well as the characters
- Challenges differentiating fiction from fact
- Challenges understanding the social context of the story
- Difficulties following the story timeline, sequences and flashbacks
- Difficulties engaging within self-reflection. Students may have difficulty retrieving experiential memories. They may have difficulty understanding and/or expressing their own feelings.

- Difficulties describing (expressive language, both verbal and written) their loss and/or a vivid, specific memory.

- Difficulties brainstorming, formulating and expressing ideas.

- Difficulties comparing and contrasting ideas and information.

- Difficulties within planning and organization of the written assignment.

Example Mind Maps to support portions of this assignment

Mind Map 5 organizes abstract language concepts and facilitates students' abilities at making connections to the facts from the story. It supports processing and understanding abstract concepts regarding how Tim kept his memory alive for each individual character.

Mind Map 5

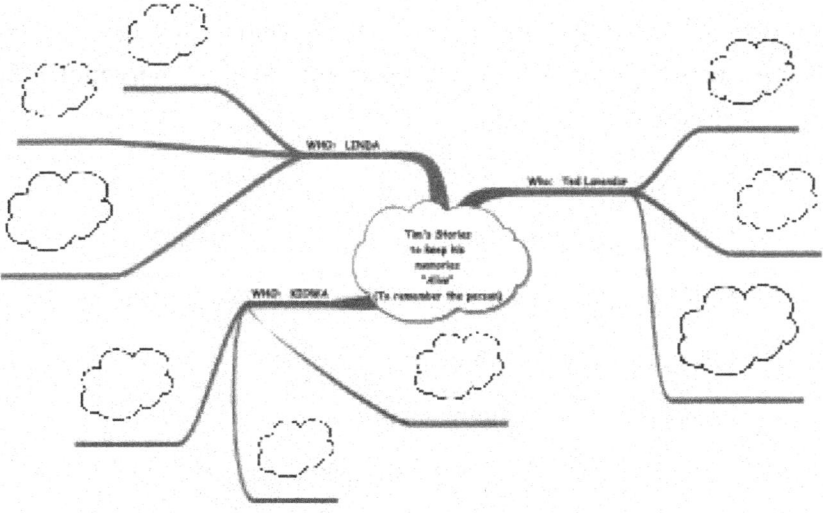

Mind Maps 6 and 7 support students' abilities at brainstorming, remembering, processing and organizing thoughts; making connections from personal life to the characters in the story.

Mind Map 6

Use your "Mind's Eye" to think about a person you lost.

Draw or write about the person in each thought bubble.

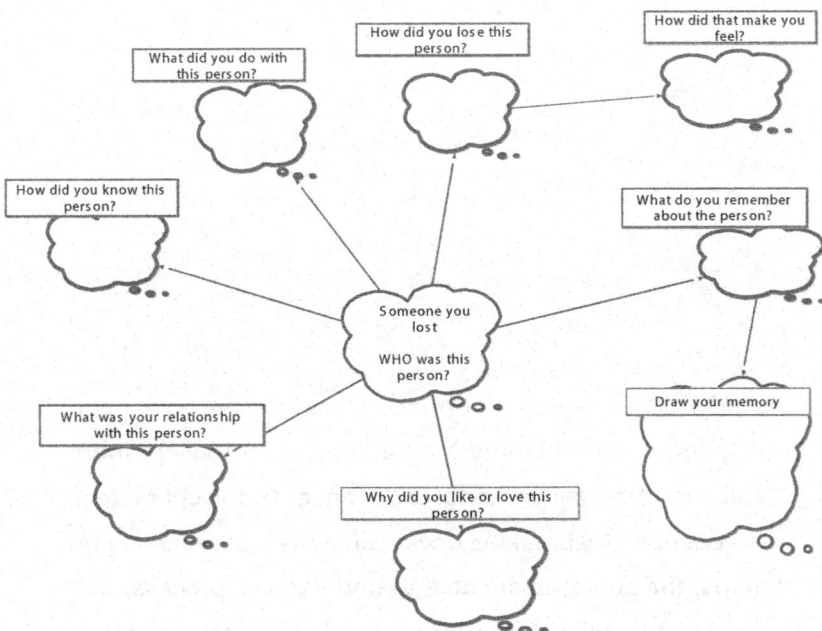

Mind Map 7

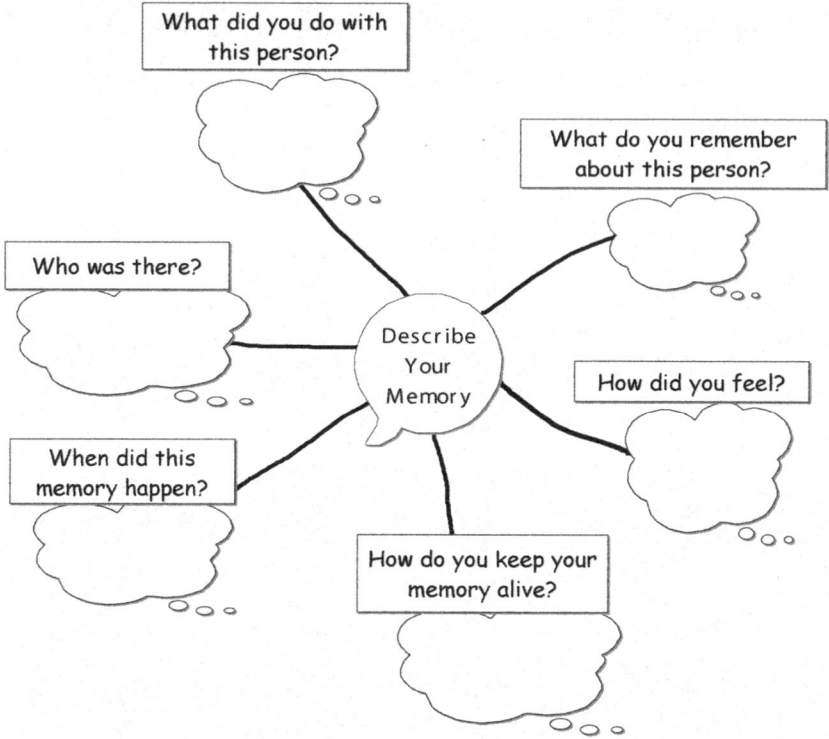

Students can use the information from the previous mind maps to complete Mind Map 8. They can now compare and contrast their personal experiences to the character's experiences. By breaking down concepts into several mind maps, the students are able to understand (process) and express some very difficult abstract language concepts.

Mind Map 8

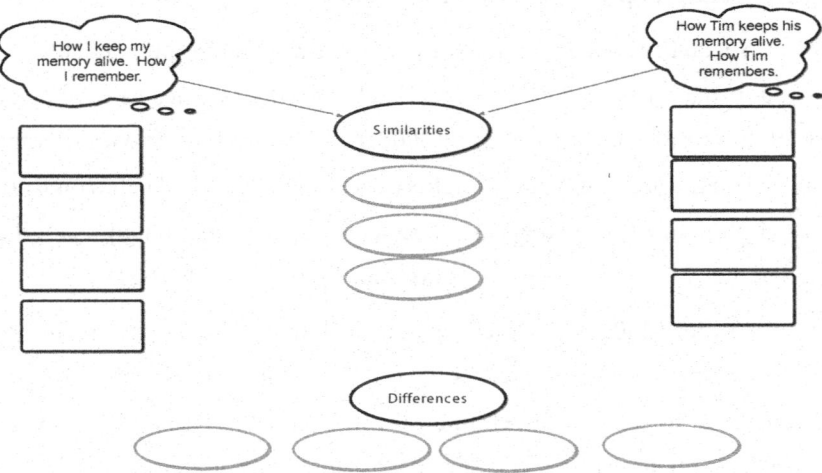

It is important to understand what we are asking our students to complete in order to create a sequence of mind maps that facilitate our students' abilities at processing, making connections, using expressive language (both verbal and written) and to organize, plan and complete their assignments. This facilitates students' active engagement and participation within the process and not simply completing a project.

Social Thinking® Curriculum
(M. G. Winner, 2000, 2007, 2008)

M. G. Winner (2008) developed *The Think Social: A Social Thinking® Curriculum for School-Age Students®* to teach social thinking and related skills to students with high functioning autism, PDD-NOS, Asperger Syndrome, nonverbal learning disability, ADHD, along with any other students who may have deficits within the area of social thinking. There are numerous resources and therapy materials to support educational teams in implementing the Social Thinking® Curriculum; they can be found at www.socialthinking.com. Social Thinking® is a teaching methodology created by Michelle Garcia Winner. This teaching methodology consists of specific social thinking vocabulary, social concepts and strategies, original characters and curricula with specific materials that are specifically developed for different age groups (preschool through adults).

"Social thinking and related social skills are a developmental, behavioral approach that utilizes cognitive behavioral strategies to teach core social thinking concepts" (Winner, 2008, p. 2). Cognitive behavior therapy is based on the idea "that our thoughts cause our feelings and behaviors, not the people, situations, and events in our environment and that by changing the way we think, we can improve our life" (Winner, 2008, p. 2).

Winner (2008) identified two areas that directly impact students' success at application of social skills. First is an inability to communicate effectively or to express oneself in both verbal and nonverbal ways and the second is the inability to effectively adapt communications and skills across different contexts.

A basic concept that is taught within this program is that students' behaviors (the way they act and talk) make people have positive or negative thoughts about them. People can have either positive or negative thoughts about us and this determines whether people want to interact with us, be friends with us or not. Winner (2000) created the *I LAUGH Model® of Social Cognition*. The *I Laugh Model® of Social Cognition* is the basis for the lessons within this Social Thinking® Curriculum. The *I Laugh Model ® of Social Cognition* outlines the relationship between social thinking and academics. It describes the social competencies that are needed for children to process and excel at academic learning (www.socialthinking.com).

The Social Thinking® Curriculum effectively integrates cognitive processing skills throughout curriculum goals and activities, such as central coherence (the ability to see the whole picture, the gestalt), joint attention, executive functioning skills, emotional processing and emotional regulation as well as sensory integration. This Social Thinking® Curriculum has application across student populations and school contexts. Implementation of The Social Thinking® Curriculum has become popular and widespread throughout educational systems. There are some schools using this curriculum to address social needs of all students as a school-wide intervention process. There are schools that implement this curriculum within social pragmatic classes.

There are many motivating and engaging materials that correspond to the Social Thinking® Curriculum available for purchase from www.social-thinking.com. However, it is crucial that the selection of materials and/or activities from this curriculum for inclusion within a specific action plan for individual students are dependent first and foremost on the student's individual needs and aligned with student's goals and objectives. The student's complete communication profile, as well as educational profile, drives the therapy process, selection of materials and activities and not the other way around. Materials, no matter how engaging they may be, do not drive or determine the therapy process. The materials as well as activities should be the last consideration when planning intervention sessions. What may seem motivating and engaging for one student may not be for another. The materials and activities should be meaningful to the students. Educators can get caught up in presenting activities and/or materials and forget that they should directly address and facilitate students' achievements toward their goals.

It is dynamic interactions between students and interventionists that create communication success, not the materials. Educational team collaboration is essential. All teachers and parents need to understand how this intervention will support students' communication success and "buy in" to the program. There needs to be a shared knowledge base, a shared understanding of why, when, who and how regarding the implementation of the Social Thinking® Curriculum for individual students. Stating that he is in our social thinking group is not enough information to create this shared knowledge base, understanding and "buy in".

The Social Thinking® Curriculum is a very powerful and effective intervention for students with social cognitive deficits when implemented with fidelity. Educators must first understand the research and concepts behind the social thinking curriculum. It is important to understand how and what to implement with whom, when and why before using any of the engaging materials or activities within specific students' action plans. Evidence based practices dictate that practitioners' expertise is required prior to implementation of specific communication interventions (ASHA, 2005). The www.socialthinking.com website provides numerous trainings, courses and professional development activities regarding the social thinking curriculum. The Social Thinking® Curriculum should be one tool within the complete therapy toolbox. It may not address all the deficit areas and needs of individual students.

Students' targeted goals and participation within this program are determined from the assessment: *Social Thinking® Dynamic Assessment Protocol* (Winner, 2008). This assessment should be one component within students' total comprehensive communication assessment profile. Students' goals and objectives are determined from the comprehensive communication assessment profile.

"The social thinking curriculum considers the whole child, rather than picking and choosing social lessons and then assume they will generalize across widely differing contexts." (Winner, 2008, p. 42). "One size does not fit all ... successful programs are those that appreciate the individual nature of each students." (Winner, 2008, p. 12), Winner further states that all good programs should take an individual student approach. Remember, not all students have the same social thinking or communication goals and do not require every activity within the social thinking curriculum. In fact, some activities and/or materials may not be appropriate for some students.

Communication, including social thinking, occurs every day, all day, not just during the 40-minute weekly social thinking group. There are many variables to consider when determining service delivery model options and identification of student social thinking groups. A once a week social group does not meet all students' needs, nor does fitting our students into groups that are currently available (e.g., Our social group meets every Friday after lunch.). Some students may require individual treatment program options; some may require group treatment program options and some may require a combination of treatment delivery options, based on individual deficit areas, needs as well as interests. Determining whether a student should be placed within a specific social thinking group, providing individual supports or a combination should be based on the individual student's need and not on the availability of groups that are in progress.

Social thinking groups may not meet students' needs in all communication, executive functioning and cognitive processing areas.

Case study: High School Social Thinking Group

A student at the high school level was refusing to attend his weekly speech therapy group session (the Social Thinking® Curriculum was being implemented within this group.) He was being asked to leave his supported study hall, in which he worked on school assignments, to go to his speech group every Friday afternoon. Academic work was a preferred activity for him. His speech group consisted of three students. This student did not understand why he needed to attend this group and saw no benefit to it. He did not have "buy in". He thought it was unfair that he was being asked to leave his study hall and was not allowed to complete his school assignments.

The speech-language pathologist was implementing the Social Thinking® Curriculum. However, the materials and activities that were presented during each group session were not always relevant or meaningful to all three students. Through several visual processing conversations, the student stated, "Does she really think I am stupid?" When asked what the data revealed regarding this student's progress towards his communication goals within the program, the speech-language pathologist stated that he benefits from this group and would interact at times. This is not objective data to support growth toward individual goals and objectives. His inclusion within this specific Social Thinking® group (of three students) was not meeting this student's individual communication needs. In fact, it was increasing his level of anxiety while negatively impacting his self-esteem!

Power Card Strategy© (Gagnon, 2001)

Power Cards are visual processing aids to assist students in making sense of social situations, daily routines, meanings of language as well as the hidden curriculum that exist in all social communication contexts. Power cards make use of children's special interests to help them make sense of daily social situations. A social situation is visually displayed that discusses the language concept being taught. The student is given a small card (the size of a business card) that has the child's special interest on it along with the communication rule that is being introduced.

The power card strategy is appropriate for students who do not understand what to do within social situations and who require language supports. Power cards are effective in supporting students in transferring or generalizing skills across communication contexts.

Gagnon (2001) provides a detailed explanation of this strategy, with explicit explanations to effectively implement Power Cards with individual students.

Social Stories© (Gray, 2010)

www.carolgraysocialstories.com

Social Story Strategy was developed by Carol Gray. It was originally developed for use with students and adults with Autism Spectrum disorders as a social learning tool to increase effective social interactions. However, it has proven to be an effective intervention for other students with communication disorders. It can be used effectively within a wide range of ages.

Social stories consist of short stories that depict a social situation that the child or adult may find difficult. They are written in response to individual student's needs. A social story is a short story that describes a situation in terms of relevant social cues and common responses. They provide the student with accurate information regarding what occurs in a situation and why. Social stories teach the social routine within a structured and visual format. Information regarding social stories (the philosophy behind social stories, what they are, how and why they are developed) is available at Carol Gray's website: www.carolgraysocialstories.com.

Structuring Classroom Groups

Cooperative groups are a significant component within academic and social curricula. Working cooperatively in a group, whether it is for academic work, socially, sports (gym) or on the playground, can be extremely difficult for students with communication disorders, executive function disorders as well as cognitive processing deficits (e.g., Theory of Mind, perspective taking). Deficits within these areas impact students' abilities to work within small, large and whole classroom groups.

In order for students to work successfully within groups, they need to integrate skills across domain areas, such as communication, executive function skills and cognitive processing skills (e.g., Theory of Mind, perspective taking). Students need to be able to process language quickly as well as access or recall ideas quickly and efficiently.

Educators cannot assume that students understand how to be a part of a group. We can provide students with supports to increase their abilities at group interactions. We can create structure within groups by explicit instruction regarding the goal of the group, the process and the end product.

The following provides students with structure when participating within group activities:

- Give each group member a specific role (e.g., note taker, time-keeper, researcher, reader, etc.). Rotate students' roles during different groups.
- Provide scripts for each group role.
- Be explicit and visual with the group goal (end product). What will the group have completed at the end of the group? How will the group proceed?

- Be explicit as to the steps and procedures the group should follow (make a checklist, a to-do list). (Consider the **Get Ready – Do – Done** intervention.)

- Be explicit and visual regarding group rules.

- Make sure the task you are asking students to complete is meaningful and within students' abilities.

- Make use of visuals to support group conversations/discussions.

Paraphrasing Strategy

Teaching students the strategy of paraphrasing during group and/or class discussions facilitates active listening, positive interactions as well as perspective taking.

Steps to Paraphrasing

- Listen to or read what someone has said or written.

- Think about what they have said or what you have read (use Mind's Eye and Active Listening).

- You do not need to agree with what you heard or read. It is their OPINION.

- RESPECT their opinion; think about their opinion.

- Say it or write it in your own words

Following are Visual Support Examples to Facilitate Active Student Participation and Engagement within Group and Classroom Discussions:

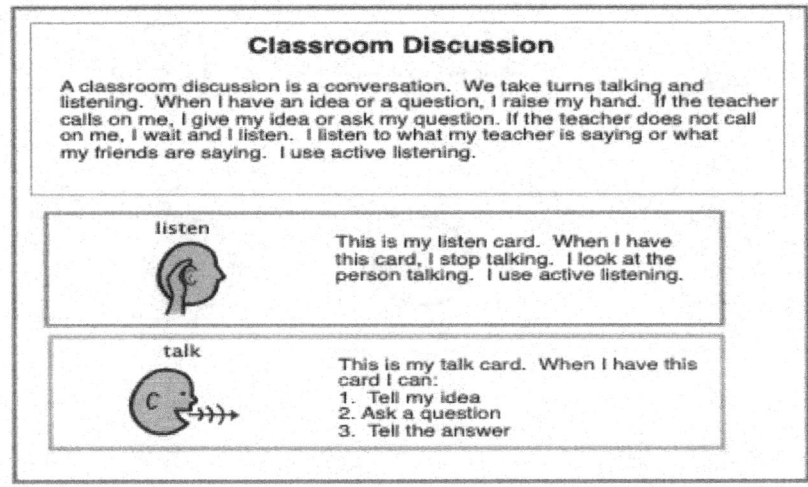

The rule is: Listen to what your friend said. Write it in your own words. You do not have to "agree". It is their opinion.

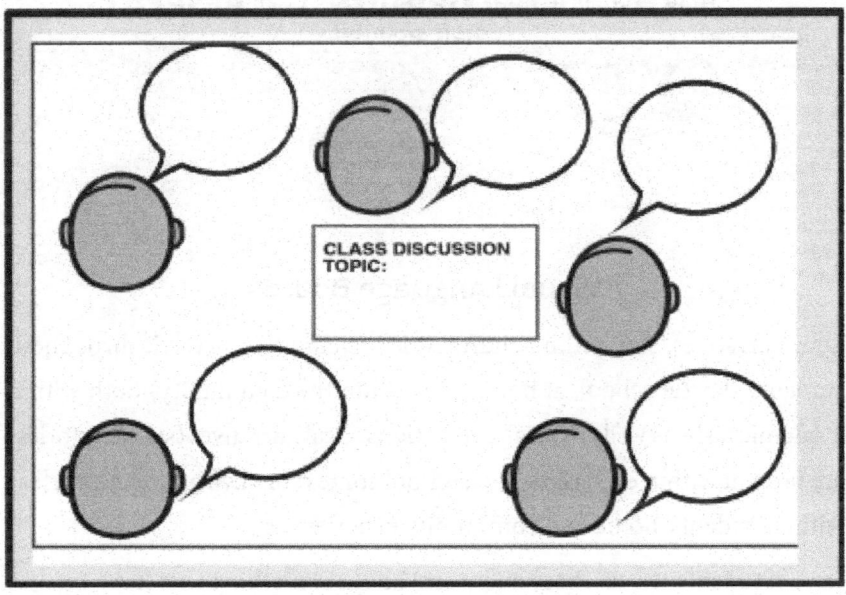

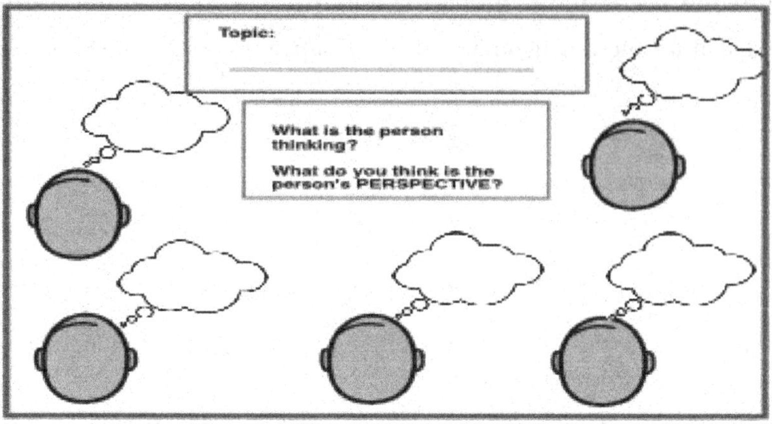

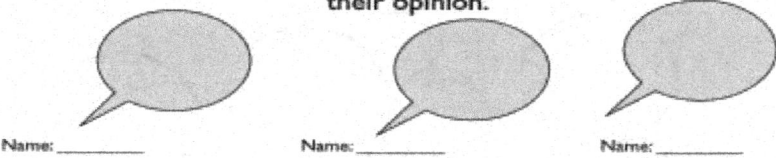

Topic:

What is the person thinking?

What do you think is the person's PERSPECTIVE?

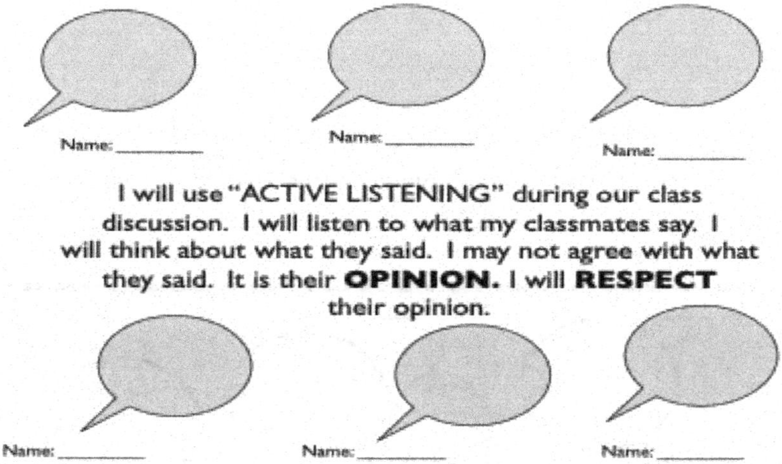

Name:_____

Name:_____

Name:_____

I will use "ACTIVE LISTENING" during our class discussion. I will listen to what my classmates say. I will think about what they said. I may not agree with what they said. It is their **OPINION.** I will **RESPECT** their opinion.

Name:_____

Name:_____

Name:_____

Visual Language Boards

Oral narratives, storytelling and/or story retelling are present throughout students' day (at school, at home and within the community) both within academic tasks as well as social interactions. Oral narratives (spoken stories) are present within each class, each school context or environment as well as within students' home and community experiences.

Students tell teachers and peers about something that happened to them at home or within the community. Student may tell parents what happened during their school day, in the classroom, on the playground, on a field trip, and with friends. Students relate experiences to peers, such as sports events, movies and activities with friends. Narratives and storytelling and/or retelling are present throughout the academic curriculum. Students are asked to tell what happened within a story, to paraphrase information from a social studies or science unit. Students may be asked to write a personal narrative regarding an experience.

The ability to tell personal oral narratives or to relate experiences (both positive experiences as well as difficult or challenging experiences) is crucial. Oral narratives parallel pragmatic, semantic, morphological and syntactic language skills. Students must be able to introduce their story, end their story, remain on topic, provide references (what, who, when they are talking about) while using appropriate sentence and morphological structures. For instance, students must be able use verb tense markers to discuss past, present and/or future information. Students need to include relevant vocabulary or semantic information in their oral narratives. Story retelling or oral narratives require active listening skills as well as use of effective dialogue interactions. The listener responds in some way by either adding additional information or asking questions. Students may need to clarify or repair communication breakdowns or confusions, while remaining on topic and maintaining sequencing of events. Students will need to access language in a quick and efficient manner to allow flow and fluency of the narrative.

Many students with communication deficits have difficulties relating personal experiences (e.g., what they did over the weekend, what they did at school, going to a party, etc.) as well as retelling academic information. How many times have you asked your child or a student in your class what they did on Saturday or what they did in school and they reply "nothing" or "I don't know". They may lack the crucial language skills, cognitive processing skills as well as executive function skills to be able to successfully relate personal experiences as well as retell information in academic textbooks. They may lack necessary organizational skills, vocabulary, concepts as well as syntax and morphology in order to tell or re-tell oral narratives effectively. Students may provide too much information or not enough information. Students who present with word finding deficits may not have quick and effective access to necessary language in order to provide listeners with relevant information (who, what, where, when). The listener may need to fill in the missing information and/or support the organization of students' oral narratives. Students may not have the ability to relate and/or use temporal (time) markers (Bliss & McCabe, 2012). Furthermore, students' oral narratives may be impacted by speech deficits such as articulation deficits, phonological deficits, apraxia of speech as well as stuttering and/or cluttering. Students with limited abilities at storytelling/retelling and oral narratives will have challenges within academic curricula as well as within social interactions (Hutson-Nechkash, 2001).

Visual language boards are interventions that support students who are non-verbal or who have limited verbal skills within the process of oral narratives, storytelling and expressive language; they integrate storytelling and narratives. Visual language boards can be used to express personal experiences, fiction and non-fiction. They can be individually adapted to language, cognitive processing and executive functioning levels of students.

Academic concepts and skills can be integrated into the content of visual language boards. They allow visual supports within reading and writing: story sequence, character development, time and place concepts within stories. Students can use visual language boards to relate present, past experiences as well as possible future happenings.

Visual language boards incorporate multi-modality or multi means of communications. They can facilitate students' abilities at processing auditory information as students store relevant language concepts. They can increase spontaneous expressive language as students transfer motivating pragmatic skills such as shared intents, establishing interactions and abilities to use language to meet needs, wants and desires. Visual language boards can be highly motivating in that they facilitate positive, successful communication interactions and can support home school connections and interactions.

Visual language boards allow educators ample opportunities at meeting individual student's needs within the five elements of language (semantics, syntax, morphology, pragmatics, phonological) as well as speech skills (articulation, apraxia, stuttering and cluttering). Visual language boards allow educators ample opportunities to teach not only the meaning (language) behind the visual (pictures) but allow students to expand receptive and expressive language through use of the visual processing procedures. Visual language boards support students' receptive and expressive language, speech fluency as well as speech production.

Boardmaker Plus! software can support development of materials that are individualized for specific students, or groups of students. (Boardmaker Plus! is available from the Mayer-Johnson Company (www.mayer-johnson. com). Visual language boards can be developed to target a variety of communication skills, goals and activities.

It is important that any picture or visual used for a specific student has meaning for that student; and if necessary, the meaning is explicitly taught to the student. Some students may respond better to real life pictures. Some students may respond better to letters and/or words.

The symbols or visual representation used within visual language boards can be generalized to other language experiences, social as well as academic. Consistency in use of the visual symbols will support generalization of both receptive and expressive language skills across curricular areas (both academic and social). Teaching students step by step understanding of visual, along with targeted language skills allows integration and generalization, expanding students' abilites at providing oral narratives.

Begin the visual language board process by teaching the visual representation for the wh-question words (ex: who, what, when, where and why) across contexts (environments and persons). The level of students' language will determine how you proceed. For instance, you may begin by using the visual for "who" in reference to people in students' environment or students can match the picture of a person to the person.

Students may need to be given choices (use of choice boards). The progression of visual language boards will be determined by students' language levels. The examples provided can be expanded or adapted depending on individual student's needs.

Examples of Visual Language Boards

The following are examples of visual language boards, created with the Boardmaker Plus! Software. Visual language boards facilitate visual processing, language comprehension and expression. Students' means of communication or combination of means of communication (e.g., communication boards, communication devices, sign language and verbal speech) are used within the visual language board process. Reading and written langauge can be incorporated into the process.

Visual Language Board Example: WH-Question Words

Visual Language Board Example: Choice Board "Where?"

Visual Language Board Example: Choice Board "When?"

Visual Language Board Example: Choice Board "How?"

Visual Language Board: Future Tense

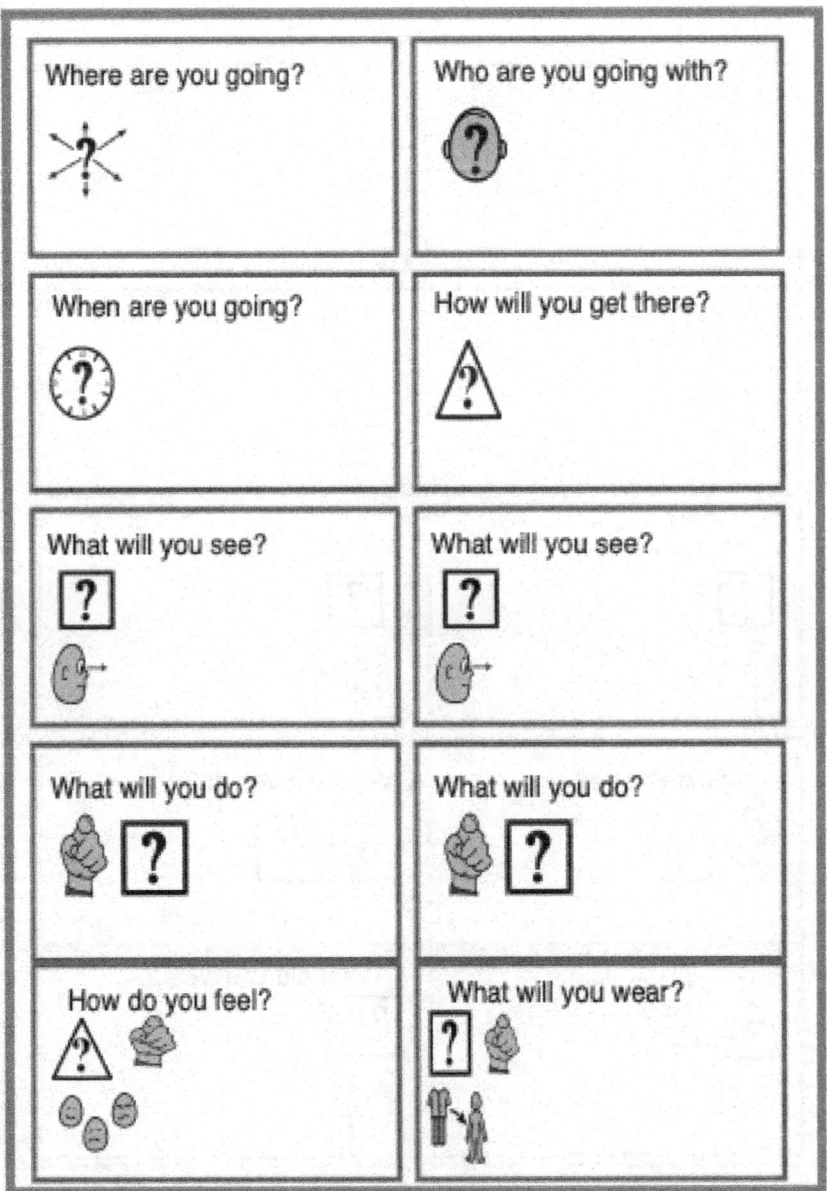

Visual Language Board Example: Past tense

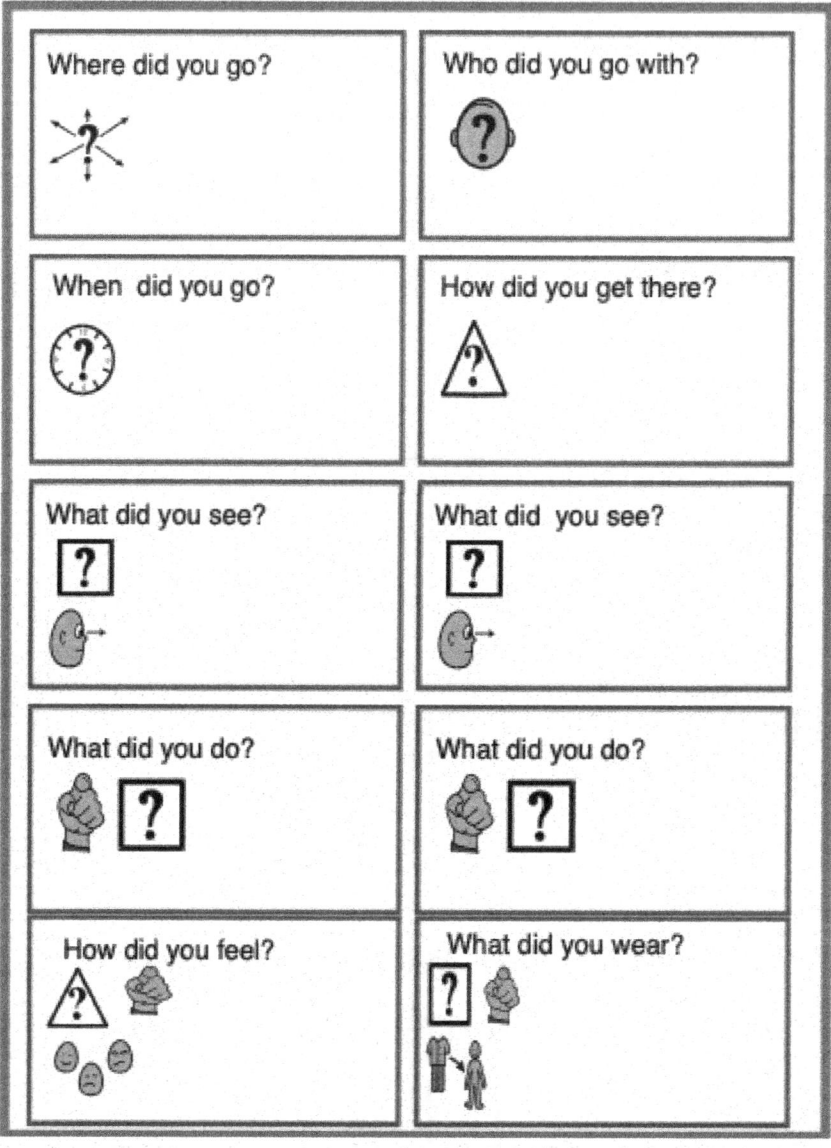

Visual Language Board Example: Brainstorming

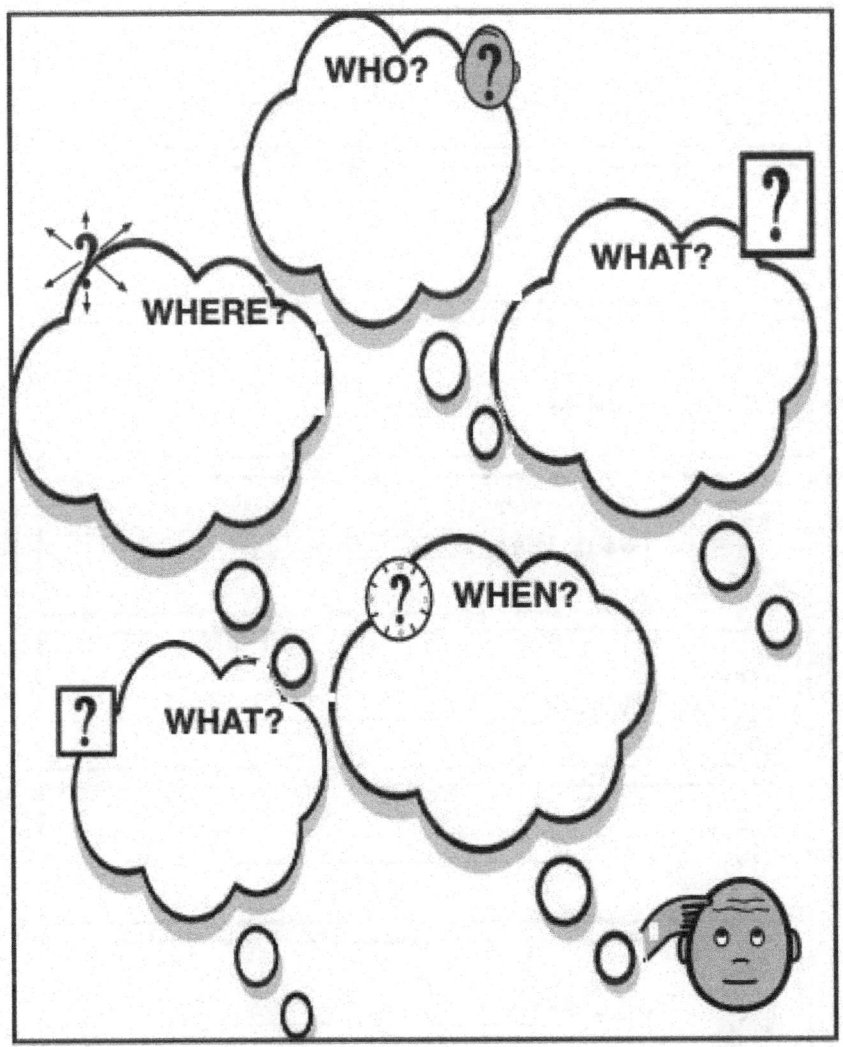

Visual Language Board Example: Integrating Reading and Writing
(Future)

what [?]	I am going to _____.
who (?)	I am going with _____.
when (?)	I will go _____
how ⚠	I will go in a _____.
see	I will see _____.
what [?]	I will _____.
wear	I will wear _____.

Visual Language Board Example: Integrating reading and writing (past tense)

what ?	I went to _____.
who ?	I went with _____.
when ?	I went _____
how ⚠	I went in a _____
see	I saw _____.
what ?	I _____.
wear	I wore _____.

Visual Language Board Example: Reading activity.

Visual Language Board Example: Retelling home experiences. It may be necessary for parents to complete visual language boards with students at home. Students can share their weekend news with the class when they return to school.

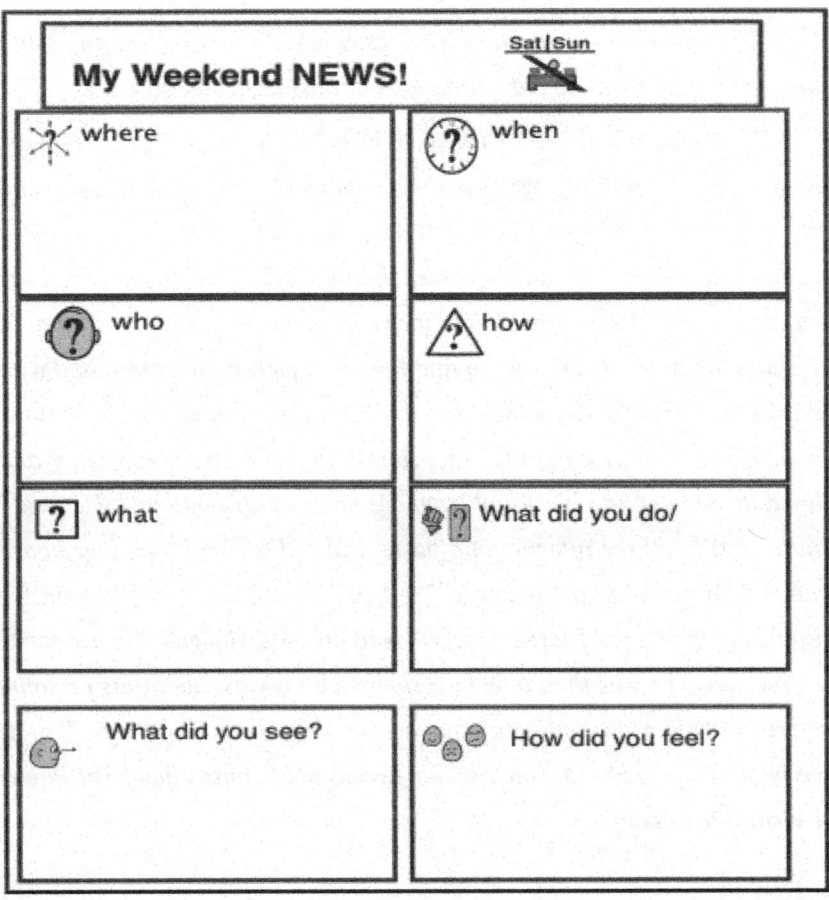

Case Study: Sixth Grade Student (Visual Language Board)

This is an example of a visual language board created with a sixth grade student who has a diagnosis of autism. This student had some verbal skills; however, he was not able to express or tell personal experiences. His family went on a vacation and he missed school for a few days.

When he returned to school his teacher asked where he was and asked him several questions. He did not respond or answer her questions.

*This student had been working on visual language boards, along with visual language processing. We sat at the computer with a visual language board structure (just the wh-question words were in each frame). When presented with the visual question word and asked the question verbally (e.g., Where did you go?) he was able to provide specific vocabulary and complete sentences. In fact, he went to the internet to find the exact pictures to correspond with his information. When he said, "Toy lab", I corrected him by saying toy store. He then found a picture of the exact store, "Toy Lab" on the computer and pasted the picture into his visual language board. This continued. He would find a picture off the internet and paste it into the visual language board frame, then verbalize the sentence. We typed the sentences together on the visual language board frames. Once he read his visual language board to me several times, he was then able to verbally tell his class about his personal experience to Florida. You notice that he was able to express feelings: That he was happy to go to Florida but also that he was sad to miss school! **The Power of Visual Processing!***

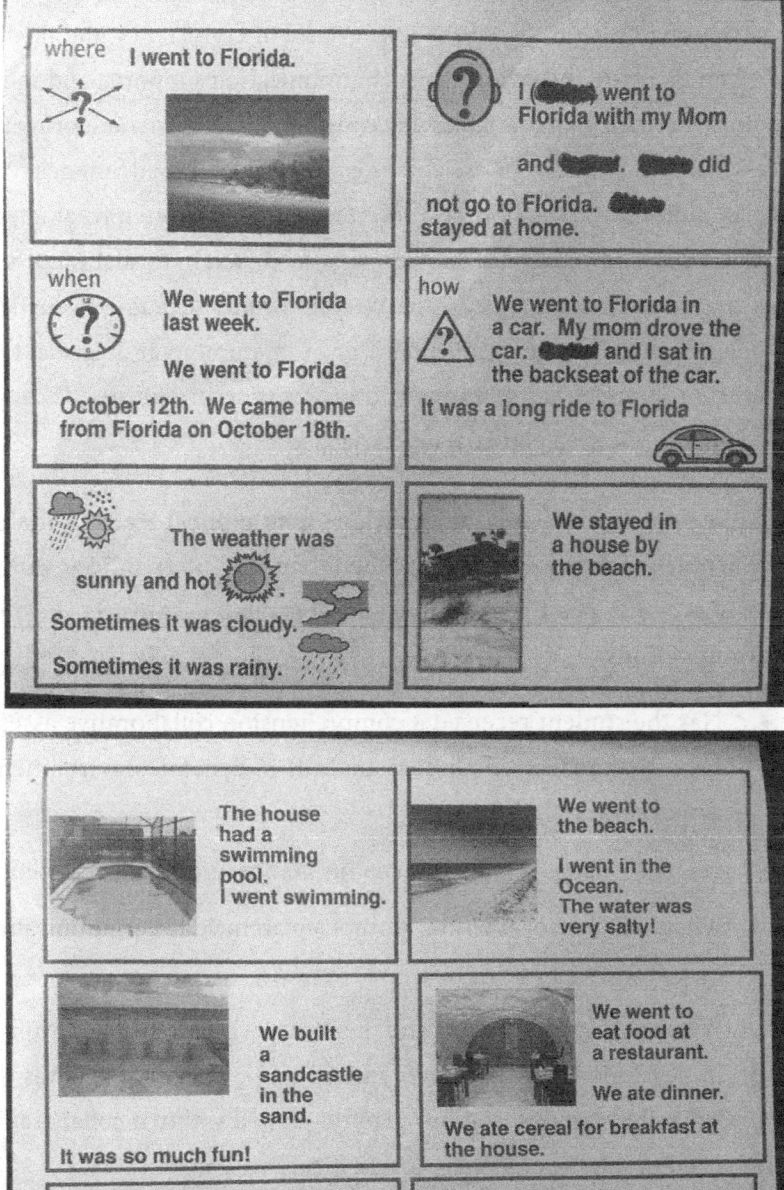

Monitoring Students' Progress

We have previously discussed the importance of consistency and fidelity when implementing behavior plans, communication supports, and interventions. There are many variables that come into play when monitoring the success of students' interventions and programs. We discussed how behavior plans, communication supports, and interventions are often fragmented with gaps and inconsistencies and how this can result in escalation of students' overt behaviors and ineffective communications leading to changes in students' educational placement and/or programming. It is crucial that students' programs, interventions and progress are monitored through relevant data collection and adapted as needed.

The following problem-solving questions may support teams' collaborative problem-solving discussions when there are interruptions within students' progress, positive outcomes and/or escalation in overt behaviors (communications).

- Has the student received a comprehension collaborative assessment that addressed all domains within dynamic environments across contexts?

- Has the student received a dynamic communication assessment?

- Did the behavior (communication) plan include communication assessments, interventions, and supports?

- Were the student's parents and the student (if appropriate) involved in development of the interventions and behavior plan? Was the behavior (communication) plan developed within a collaborative team problem-solving approach, including parents?

- Did the educational team consider all relevant information within all domain areas when developing intervention programs?

- Do the interventions and behavior plan make sense to the student (at whatever level the student may be)?

- Is the student fully aware of and does the student understand the intervention process and/or the behavior (communication) plan?

- Was the behavior plan, communication supports and interventions implemented with consistency and fidelity across school environments, communication partners with relevant data collection?

- Were there gaps: What, who, where, when and why?

  ○ Use of prompts: Were the prompts consistently implemented across communication contexts? The type and amount of prompting should be explicitly outlined within the student's intervention program with objective data to determine any needed change in adult prompts.

  ○ Visual supports: Were the visual supports consistently implemented across communication contexts?

- Did communication styles of the adults support positive outcomes?

- Are positive reinforcers implemented that have meaning to the student? Are they being implemented with consistency?

- Did the student have access to voice output or visual communication systems and/or supports across all school environments at all times?

- Was the student supported during transitions? Were the supports effective (What does the data tell us?)

- School calendar—there are so many inconsistencies within the school calendar. Were gaps within school programming considered when developing intervention programs?

- Were the interventions, behavior plan and action plan implemented long enough and consistently enough for the student to meet long-term and short-term goals?

- Were the interventions, behavior plan, and action plan adjusted, adapted and/or modified as the student either made progress or not toward long-term and short-term goals? What does the objective data tell us?

APPENDIX 1:

SPECIAL EDUCATION SCHOOL LAWS

Public Law 94-142 (PL 94-142)

PL 94-142 was passed in 1975. This law guaranteed a free appropriate public education to any child with a disability across the country. There are four purposes to PL-94-142:

1. To ensure that all children with disabilities have a free appropriate public education available to them

2. To ensure that the rights of children with disabilities and their parents are protected

3. To assist States and localities to provide for the education of all children with disabilities

4. To assess and ensure the effectiveness of efforts to educate all children with disabilities

Individuals with Disabilities Education Act (IDEA) - 2004

In 2004 PL 94-142 was reauthorized and renamed The Individuals with Disabilities Act (IDEA). Part C of IDEA pertains to infants and toddlers (birth through age 2). Children ages 3 through 21, receive services under Part B of IDEA.

IDEA is a law that makes available a free appropriate public education to eligible children with disabilities throughout the nation. It ensures special education and related services to children with disabilities. Information regarding IDEA can be found on the IDEA Website: **http://sites.ed.gov/ idea/?src=search.**

APPENDIX 2:

EDUCATIONAL DISABILITY CLASSIFICATIONS (IDEA PART B, 2006)

Disability Classification	Definitions
Autism	A developmental disability that significantly affects verbal and nonverbal communication and social interactions, generally evident before age three, that adversely affects children's educational performance. Other characteristics often associated with autism are engaging in repetitive activities and stereotyped movements, resistance to environmental change or change in daily routines, and unusual responses to sensory experiences. The term autism does not apply if the child's educational performance is adversely affected primarily because the child has an emotional disturbance.
Deaf-Blindness	Concomitant (simultaneous) hearing and visual impairments, the combination of which causes such severe communication and other developmental and educational needs that cannot be accommodated in special education programs solely for children with deafness or children with blindness.
Deafness	A hearing impairment so severe that a child is impaired in processing linguistic information through hearing, with or without amplification, that adversely affects educational performance.

Developmental Delay	Children from birth to age three (under IDEA Part C) and children from ages 3 through 9 (under IDEA Part B)—Developmental delay is a delay in one or more of the following areas: physical development; cognitive development; communication; social or emotional development; or adaptive [behavioral] development.
Emotional Disturbance	A condition exhibiting one or more of the following characteristics over a long period of time and to a marked degree that adversely affects educational performance: (a) inability to learn that cannot be explained by intellectual, sensory or health factors; (b) inability to build or maintain satisfactory interpersonal relationships with peers/teachers; (c) inappropriate types of behavior or feelings under normal circumstances; (d) a general pervasive mood of unhappiness or depression; (e) tendency to develop physical symptoms or fears associated with personal or school problems. This includes schizophrenia.
Hearing Impairment	Impairment in hearing, whether permanent or fluctuating, that adversely affects educational performance, but is not included under the definition of "deafness".
Intellectual Disability	Significantly sub-average general intellectual functioning, existing concurrently with deficits in adaptive behavior and manifested during the developmental period, that adversely affects educational performance.
Multiple Disabilities	Concomitant impairments (such as intellectual disability-blindness, intellectual disability-orthopedic impairment, etc.) the combination of which causes such severe educational needs that they cannot be accommodated in a special education program solely for one of the impairments.
Orthopedic Impairment	A severe orthopedic impairment that adversely affects educational performance.
Other Health Impairment	Having limited strength, vitality or alertness, including a heightened alertness to environmental stimuli, that results in limited alertness with respect to the educational environment, that is due to chronic or acute health problems such as *asthma, attention deficit disorder or attention deficit hyperactivity disorder, diabetes, epilepsy, heart condition, hemophilia, lead poisoning, leukemia, nephritis, rheumatic fever, sickle cell anemia and Tourette syndrome.* It has an adverse effect on educational performance.

Specific Learning Disability	A disorder in one or more of the basic psychological processes involved in understanding or in using language, spoken or written, that may manifest itself in the imperfect ability to listen, think, speak, read, write, spell or to do mathematical calculations. The term includes such conditions as perceptual disabilities, brain injury, minimal brain dysfunction, dyslexia and developmental aphasia. The term does not include learning problems that are primarily the result of visual, hearing or motor disabilities; of intellectual disability; of emotional disturbance; or of environmental, cultural or economic disadvantage.
Speech or Language Impairment	A communication disorder such as stuttering, impaired articulation, a language impairment or a voice impairment that adversely affects educational performance.
Traumatic Brain Injury	An acquired injury to the brain caused by an external physical force, resulting in total or partial functional disability or psychosocial impairment, or both, that adversely affects educational performance. The term applies to open or closed head injuries resulting in impairments in one or more areas, such as cognition; language; memory; attention; reasoning; abstract thinking; judgement; problem solving; sensory, perceptual and motor abilities; psychosocial behavior; physical functions; information processing; and speech. The term does not apply to brain injuries that are congenital or degenerative, or to brain injuries induced by birth trauma.
Visual Impairment Including Blindness	An impairment in vision that, even with correction, adversely affects educational performance. The term includes both partial sight and blindness.

REFERENCES

American Speech-Language-Hearing Association (n.d). "Culturally and linguistically diverse students (IDEA Issue Brief)." Retrieved from: https://www.asha.org/advocacy/federal/idea/idea-part-b-issue-brief-culturally- and-linguistically-diverse-students/

American Speech-Language-Hearing Association (1993). "Definitions of communication disorder and variations" [Relevant Paper]. Retrieved from: www.asha.org/policy.

American Speech-Language-Hearing Association (2005). "Evidence-based practice in communication disorders" (position paper). Retrieved from: https://www.asha.org/policy/PS2005-00221

Arwood, E. L, Kaulitz, C. & Brown, M. (2009). *Visual thinking strategies for individuals with autism spectrum disorders: The language of pictures.* Shawnee Mission, Kansas: Autism Asperger Publishing Co.

Ash, A. C., Christopulos, T. T. & Redmond, S. M. (2020). "'Tell me about your child': A grounded theory study of mothers' understanding of language disorder." *American Journal of Speech-Language Pathology,* Vol. 29, 819–840. American Speech-Language-Hearing Association.

Ashley, S. (2007). *The Asperger's answer book: Professional answers to 275 of the top questions parents ask.* Naperville, IL: Sourcebooks, Inc.

Baker, J. (2008). *No more meltdowns: Positive strategies for managing and preventing out-of-control behavior.* Arlington, TX: Future Horizons.

Baker, J. (2015). *Overcoming anxiety in children & teens*. Arlington, TX: Future Horizons.

Bliss, L. W. & McCabe, A. (2012). "Personal Narratives: Assessment and Intervention." *Perspectives on Language Learning & Education*, 19(4), 130–138.

Brillante, P. (2017). *The essentials: Supporting young children with disabilities in the Classroom*. Washington, DC: National Association for the Education of Young Children.

Brown, R. (1973). *A first language: The early stages*. Harvard University Press.

Cannon, L., Kenworthy, L., Alexander, K. C., Werner, M. A. & Anthony, L. (2011). *Unstuck & On target: An executive function curriculum to improve flexibility for children with autism spectrum disorders*. Baltimore, Maryland: Brookes Publishing.

Daly, D. A. (1996). *The source for stuttering and cluttering*. East Moline, IL: LinguiSystems, Inc.

Dawson, P. & Guare, R. (2010). *Executive skills in children and adolescents: A practical guide to assessment and intervention*. New York, NY: The Guilford Press.

Dewey, J. (1938). *Experience and Education*. New York: The Macmillan Company.

Division for Early Childhood. (2015). *DEC recommended practices: Enhancing services for young children with disabilities and their families* (DEC Recommended Practices Monograph Series No, 1). Los Angeles, CA: Author.

Ehren, B. J. & Jackson, J. M. (2003). *The pragmatics of teaming*. Rockville, MD: The American Speech-Language-Hearing Association.

Estomin, E., Flynn, P., Mele-McCarthy, J., Rudebusch, J. & Witmire, K. (2007a). *Implementing IDEA 2004 Part I: Conducting educationally relevant evaluations: Technical assistance for speech-language pathologists*. Washington, D.C.: ASHA.

Estomin, E., Flynn, P., Mele-McCarthy, J., Rudebusch, J. & Witmire, K. (2007b). *Implementing IDEA 2004 Part II: Developing Educationally Relevant IEPs: Technical assistance for speech-language pathologists.* Washington, D.C.: ASHA.

Friend, M. & Cook, L. (2007). *Interactions: Collaboration skills for school professionals (5th ed).* Upper Saddle River, NJ: Pearson/Merrill.

Gagnon, E. (2001). *Power cards: Using special interests to motivate children and youth with Asperger syndrome and autism.* Shawnee Mission, Kansas: Autism Asperger Publishing Co.

Gardner, H. (1999). *Intelligence reframed: Multiple intelligences for the 21st century.* New York, NY: Basic Books.

Gardner, H. (n.d.). *Howard Gardner Quotes.* Retrieved from: https://www.inspiringquotes.us/author/2444-howard-gardner

Gibbons, S. M & Szarkowski, A. (2019). *One Tool in the Toolkit Is Not Enough: Making the Case for Using Multisensory Approaches in Aural Habilitation of Children with Reduced Hearing.* Perspective of the ASHA Special Interest Groups: Vol. 4(2), pp. 345–355.

Grandin, T. (1995). *Thinking in pictures: And other reports from my life with autism.* New York: Doubleday.

Graser, N. S. (1992). *125 Ways to be a better listener: A program for listening success.* East Moline, IL: LinguiSysems, Inc.

Gray, C. (1994). *Comic strip conversations: Illustrated interactions that teach conversation skills to students with autism and related disorders.* Arlington, TX: Future Horizons Incorporated.

Gray, C. (2010). *The new social story book.* Arlington, TX: Future Horizons Incorporated.

Hickman, L. A. (1997). *The apraxia profile: A descriptive assessment tool for children.* San Antonio, Texas: Communication Skill Builders.

Hodson, B. W. & Paden, E. P. (1983). *A phonological approach to remediation: Targeting intelligible speech.* San Diego, CA: College-Hill Press, Inc.

Hutson-Nechkash, P. (2001). *Narrative toolbox: Blueprints for storybuilding.* Eau Claire, WI: Thinking Publications.

Illinois State Board of Education (ISBE) (2002). *Serving English language learners with disabilities: A resource manual for Illinois educators.* Springfield, IL: ISBE

Illinois State Board of Education (ISBE) (2009). *Educational rights and Responsibilities: Understanding Special Education in Illinois.* Illinois State Board of Special Education and Support Services.

Kanner, L. (1943). "Autistic disturbances of affective contact." *NERV Child* 2: 217–50.

King-Sears, M. E., Janney, R. & Snell M. E. (2015). *Collaborative teaming: Teachers' guides to inclusive practices, 3rd edition.* Baltimore, Maryland: Paul H. Brookes Publishing Co.

Kowalski, T. P. (2010). *Social-Pragmatic success for Asperger syndrome and other related disorders.* Orlando, FL: Professional Communication Services, Inc.

Kuder, S. Jay (2013). *Teaching students with language and communication disabilities,* 4th Ed. U.S.A.: Pearson Publishing.

McGinnity, K, Hammer, S. & Ladson, L. (2011). *Lights! Camera! Autism! Using video Technology to enhance lives.* Cambridge, Wisconsin: Cambridge Book Review Press.

Minahan, J. & Rappaport, N. (2012). *The behavior code: A practical guide to understanding and teaching the most challenging students.* Cambridge, Massachusetts: Harvard Education Press.

Moore, S. T. (2002). *Asperger syndrome and the elementary school experience. Practical solutions for academic & social difficulties.* Shawnee Mission, Kansas: Autism Asperger Publishing Co.

Moyes, R. (2011). *Visual techniques for developing social skills.* Arlington, Texas: Future Horizons, Inc.

Nicolosi, L., Harryman, E. & Kresheck, J. (1996). *Terminology of communication disorders: Speech-language-hearing*, 4th ed. Baltimore, Maryland: Lippincott Williams & Wilkins.

Prizant, Barry M. (2015). *Uniquely human: A different way of seeing autism.* New York, NY: Simon & Schuster Paperbacks.

Prutting, C.A. & Kittchner, D. M, (1987). A *clinical appraisal of the pragmatic aspects of Language.* Journal of Speech and Hearing Disorders, Volume 52 (May), 105–119.

Sapienza, C. & Ruddy, B. H (2018). *Voice Disorders,* 3rd ed. San Diego, CA: Plural Publishing.

Silverman, F. (1996) *Communication for the Speechless*, 3rd ed. Boston, MA: Ally & Bacon.

Tee, T.K., Azman, M.N.A., Mohamed, S., Muhammad, M., Mohamad, M. M., Yunos, M., Yee, M. H. & Othman, W. Buzan. (2014). "Mind Mapping: An Efficient Technique for Note-taking." *International Journal of Social, Human Science and Engineering,* Vol. 8(1). Retrieved from: http://www.researchgate.net/publication/260244896

Vermeulen, P. (2012). *Autism as context blindness.* Shawnee Mission, Kansas: AAPC Publishing.

Ward, S. (2012). *Executive function skills in children and adolescents: Assessment and treatment.* [Seminar]. Retrieved from: www.asha.org/shop.

Weatherby, Amy. (1995). *Checklist of communication functions and needs.* Retrieved from: http://jenaparsons.weebly.com/uploads/6/6/7/2/6672522/checklist_of_communicative_functions.pdf

Winner, M. G. (2000). *Inside out: What makes a person with social cognitive deficits tick?* San Jose, CA: Think Social Publishing, Inc.

Winner, M. G. (2005). *Strategies for organization: Preparing for homework and the real world.* Zeeland, MI: The Gray Center for Social Learning and Understanding.

Winner, M. G. (2007). *Thinking about you thinking about me: Teaching perspective taking and social thinking to persons with social cognitive learning challenges*, 2nd ed. San Jose, CA: Think Social Publishing, Inc.

Winner, M. G. (2008a). *A politically incorrect look at evidence-based practices and teaching social skills: A literature review and discussion*. San Jose, CA: Think Social Publishing, Inc.

Winner, M.G. (2008b). *Think social: A social thinking curriculum for school-age students*. San Jose, CA: Think Social Publishing, Inc.